Foreword

This is a report of the countryside management experiments carried out in two areas of London's urban fringe: in Hertfordshire/Barnet and in Havering, each representing a different range of complex urban fringe problems. The aim of the experiments was to encourage farming, create recreation opportunities and prevent the continuing deterioration of the landscape.

The Countryside Commission's interest in the urban fringe arises from the following:

i.   Urban fringe agriculture and its proper use as an economic resource is important in national as well as local terms. Alternative sources of food can be achieved only by reclaiming land for production in the marginal uplands or by intensifying production in the lowlands, both of which have significant environmental consequences.

ii.   The positive management of land is an essential complement to strict planning control in maintaining the environmental function and in realising the recreation potential of the Green Belt.

While there were differences in emphasis between the two areas, it is clear that the countryside management approach was successful in bringing about a change for the better in both areas, while also pointing to opportunities for action in other directions. It is now possible to identify the essential ingredients which ensured success:

i.   The support of the local authorities, at both county and district or borough level, in providing the planning background for the work and in giving it political backing.

ii.   Strong links with, and the co-operation of, the farming community—agriculture is a main user of land and manager of the landscape and encouragement of viable farming is therefore an important underlying factor; as most of the practical work takes place on farmland, their support can result in improvements to the landscape and in better opportunities for public access.

iii.   An enthusiastic, knowledgeable and tactful project officer, who is fully conversant with the problems and opportunities of the local area and its inhabitants.

iv.   Delegated financial and administrative responsibility, allowing the project officer flexibility giving the ability to respond to problems quickly, and providing independence from any particular authority.

v.   A positive response to advice and suggestions arising from the local communities regarding local problems.

vi.   A capacity to undertake a wide range of small-scale practical work which has the objectives of alleviating farming problems, improving facilities for recreation and conserving the landscape.

vii.   An ability to identify opportunities and to provide information to local authorities which helps them to respond more sensitively and effectively to the particular needs of areas.

The Countryside Commission believe that the benefits of introducing countryside management schemes in the urban fringe can be very great. The characteristics of such schemes—positive action on the ground, a simple and flexible method of working and the consequent better liaison and understanding between the many land management interests—all contribute to relieving a wide range of farming and landscape problems while, at the same time, developing opportunities for increased access to the countryside.

Both experiments also demonstrated that many small-scale conflicts or points of stress between farming, landscape and recreation can be resolved effectively and economically as the project officer can respond quickly to things which are both of a smaller scale and changing on a much shorter time-scale than those in which the machinery of public authorities can normally operate. However, it must be stressed that, to be fully effective, countryside management must be part of a comprehensive approach to resource management in the urban fringe as a whole and, in areas like parts of Havering, a much greater input of resources will be required to complement and to provide a context for the countryside management service.

In publishing this report, the Countryside Commission hope that other schemes will be established on a permanent basis by local authorities in the urban fringes around our towns and cities. Co-operation between organisations, even across local authority boundaries, is seen to have particular advantages. The techniques have now been tried and tested; the circumstances necessary for success are known; the need for such work is indisputable; and the Countryside Commission's grant-aid resources are available towards the cost of its implementation.

Derek Barber
Chairman, Countryside Commission
February 1981

Countryside Management in the Urban Fringe

A report on experiments sponsored jointly by the Countryside Commission, the Greater London Council, Hertfordshire County Council, the London Borough of Barnet and the London Borough of Havering

Published by:
Countryside Commission, John Dower House, Crescent Place, Cheltenham, Glos GL50

£10.30

CCP

© Crown copyright 1981

ISBN 0 86170 022 8

Acknowledgements

The Countryside Commission wish to acknowledge the help received from the Steering Groups and all members of the project staff whose contributions—both written and verbal—were used in the compilation of this report by Helen Williams, Senior Research Officer with the Countryside Commission.

The Figures were produced in the Drawing Office of the Countryside Commission. The maps are based on Ordnance Survey maps and are reproduced by permission of the Director General. The information for Figure 10 is from the Land Utilisation Survey of Britain, 1933 and is used with the permission of Geographical Publications Ltd.; the information for Figure 11 is from the Second Land Utilisation Survey of Britain, 1970 and is used with the permission of Alice Coleman.

The photographs were taken by the project officers, with the exception of the bottom photograph on page 96, which is reproduced by permission of the Sand and Gravel Association, the photograph on page 99 and on the back cover, which are reproduced by permission of the Aerial Photography Unit of the Ministry of Agriculture, Fisheries and Food, and the photograph on the front cover which is reproduced by permission of Hunting Surveys and Hertfordshire County Council.

Contents

PART THREE: HAVERING URBAN FRINGE MANAGEMENT EXPERIMENT

FIGURES

ILLUSTRATIONS

About this Report

Countryside management is the process by which the objectives of conservation, recreation and access are secured for public benefit in the management of both public and privately-owned land. At its present state of development, countryside management involves three main inter-related techniques:

i.   the practical resolution of small-scale conflicts within a stretch of countryside (area management);

ii.   the production of management plans, which may be broad statements of policy intent or site-specific;

iii.   the implementation of site-specific agreements on a simple and informal, or a legal, basis.

(It should be noted that countryside management is sometimes used as an alternative to area management.)

This report is divided into three parts which may be read independently. These are preceded by a summary of the conclusions drawn from the report.

Part One gives a general evaluation of countryside management in the urban fringe based on the evidence from the Hertfordshire/Barnet and Havering experiments. It outlines the historical development of countryside management and the problems and opportunities of the urban fringe. It then describes the countryside management approach and evaluates its usefulness in solving the problems of these two areas, giving guidelines on its application to other urban fringe areas.

Parts Two and Three give detailed accounts of the Hertfordshire/Barnet and Havering experiments respectively. They include an outline of how the experiments were organised, descriptions of the project areas, an analysis of the problems, how these problems were tackled and an evaluation of the results. Detailed case studies are given in the Appendices.

In the Commission's other countryside management experiments, the project officer has evaluated the work on an intuitive and subjective basis and success has been measured by local acclaim and support from local authorities. However, for these two experiments, a project evaluator was appointed to assess the effectiveness of the methods developed, their usefulness in solving the problems of the urban fringe and their applicability to other urban fringe areas. The conclusions of the evaluation exercise form an integral part of this report.

The report refers to what happened during the first phase of the experiments, which ended in March 1979. Additional information has since become available; where relevant this has been incorporated.

Summary of Conclusions

1. The countryside management approach, through close co-operation with many different interest groups, attempted to resolve conflicts in the area and, in so doing, to change attitudes. This resulted in visible effects on the ground, while the liaison work, the monitoring and feeding back of information to the various planning agencies attempted to provide the key element to a unity of administration in the countryside.

2. The experiments showed that small-scale practical work can have considerable success in improving the urban fringe environment, alleviating irritating conflicts and mobilising the resources of volunteers effectively. There is scope for much more of this type of work in the urban fringe.

3. The role of the project team is to make voluntary efforts effective by matching the needs of the farmer, the resident and the visitor with the resources of the local authorities and the voluntary organisations. The small scale of the work involved warrants a different organisation from the normal local authority approach.

4. The future development of countryside management in the urban fringe, where the public authorities are closely involved with planning and management and where much of the land is publicly-owned, is inextricably linked with the local authority framework, which can provide the context in which the methods are able to work. However, the project officer can respond quickly to things which are both of a smaller scale and changing on a much shorter timescale than those in which the machinery of public authorities can normally operate.

5. The countryside management approach achieves value for money through simplified administration by delegation of an agreed financial authority to the project officer and through the mobilisation of voluntary labour. This approach attempts to secure public benefits for the many different interests in the countryside; in measuring its effectiveness account must be taken of non-monetary benefits to the many different groups in the community.

6. The essential features of a successful countryside management service are:

    i.   the support of the local authorities, at both county and district or borough level, in providing the planning background for the work and in giving it political backing;

    ii. strong links with, and the co-operation of, the farming community—agriculture is a main user of land and manager of the landscape and encouragement of viable farming is therefore an important underlying factor; as most of the practical work takes place on farmland, the support of farmers can result in improvements to the landscape and in better opportunities for public access;

    iii. an enthusiastic, knowledgeable and tactful project officer, who is fully conversant with the problems and opportunities of the local area and its inhabitants;

    iv. delegated financial and administrative responsibility, allowing the project officer flexibility, giving the ability to respond to problems quickly and providing independence from any particular authority;

    v.   a positive response to advice and suggestions arising from the local communities regarding local problems;

    vi. a capacity to undertake a wide range of small-scale practical work which has the objectives of alleviating farming problems, improving facilities for recreation and conserving the landscape;

    vii. an ability to identify opportunities and to provide information to local authorities which helps them to respond more sensitively and effectively to the particular needs of areas.

7. The social and educational benefits of using voluntary labour must be considered as well as the practical results. Involving local people in the management of their own environment is of great value and, in general, people are more likely to have continued respect for something in which they have been involved and to understand the reasoning and have sympathy for the objectives behind the work.

8. The long-term educational benefits of involving school children cannot be over-estimated, both at the practical and at the project level. Local education authorities should be more closely involved with a long-term countryside management service.

9. Surveys have shown that the experiments were not very well known in the local area; public awareness needs to be increased by greater involvement of local people in the practical work and by local promotion and publicity of the objectives.

10. In areas where there are underlying strategic land use and land management problems and where the overall climate is one of uncertainty and speculation, the potential of countryside management is limited and, in areas like parts of Havering, there is even a danger that the resulting improvements, by obscuring the real nature of the problems, might be counter-productive, unless they are put in the context of a much more comprehensive planning and management framework. Countryside management can identify and point the way to the solution of large-scale problems outside its own remit, but implementation then depends on political will and the allocation of financial resources.

11. There is evidence that publicly-owned land is not being positively managed. Existing resources held in public ownership should set an example of how agricultural, conservation, recreation and education objectives can be reconciled.

12. The urban fringe is typically an area at the edge of administrative boundaries, where policies for town and country are often in conflict. The existence of a countryside management service focuses the attention of all public bodies with responsibilities in the area on the need to work together in the review and implementation of these policies, even across local authority boundaries. Co-operation developed between local authorities and between departments within those authorities where little or no contact had existed previously, except at a very formal level. This could be seen as the beginning of a recognition of the need for a comprehensive approach to the planning and management of the countryside around towns, with the project officer acting as the catalyst.

PART ONE

COUNTRYSIDE MANAGEMENT EXPERIMENTS IN THE METROPOLITAN GREEN BELT

Pressures on the urban fringe

▲ *What people expect to see and visit in the countryside — high quality landscape in south Hertfordshire*

First class agriculture in the foreground with the threat of gravel works in the background, Havering ▶

◀ *Badly-managed land after gravel extraction, used for poor-quality horse-grazing, Havering*

Chapter 1: Introduction

The development of the concept of countryside management

1.1   The Countryside Commission are concerned with landscape conservation and the provision of informal recreation in the countryside. The major land use in the countryside is agriculture and the landscape has largely been moulded by this, with the management of countryside features an almost unconscious by-product of agriculture. With the rapidly-changing fortunes and methods of farming, some features are now maintained to a lower standard, while still others are neglected or even removed because they no longer have an agricultural function.

1.2   The Countryside Commission recognised the need for positive management of the countryside, both to maintain and enhance the landscape and to cope with increasing informal access. They had felt for some time that the interests of farmers, visitors, local authorities and other public and private organisations in areas of conflict, like the national parks, would be best served by some means of ensuring that farming was encouraged while at the same time recreation opportunities were created and measures taken to prevent the deterioration of the landscape. A new approach was needed requiring positive measures to be taken to help solve the problems and to reconcile the conflicts between different interests. This approach involved bringing together the different interest groups, obtaining their agreement to joint working, making use of goodwill and voluntary labour, and co-ordinating the use of public and private funds.

1.3   The nature and extent of conflict between different interests in rural areas had been considered in several planning studies, e.g. the East Hampshire Area of Outstanding Natural Beauty[1] and the Sherwood Forest[2] studies had brought together local and central government and its agencies in an attempt to define common objectives, exchange information, identify areas where conflicts of policy existed and suggest how they might be solved. This had helped to clarify the extent of common and diverging interests of those concerned with town and country planning, agriculture, forestry, conservation and recreation. It also showed that there was far more small-scale conflict between the interests, generally not open to planning solutions, than had been appreciated. The Countryside Commission's countryside management schemes were designed to look at these small-scale problems.

1.4   The first countryside management experiments started in 1969 in the Lake District and in Snowdonia and came to be known as the Upland Management Experiments (UMEX).[3,4] These showed that positive management measures helped to reconcile the conflicts between farmers and visitors, while they both benefited from small-scale improvements to the landscape. More important was the dialogue that started between all the people and agencies involved in agriculture, recreation and conservation. This worked through the appointment of a project officer who acted as a catalyst for action and for bringing people together.

1.5   The work in the Lake District, after a six-year experimental stage, is now an established service of the Lake District Special Planning Board and the other national parks have set up similar schemes of their own. This success in the uplands led to the idea of applying the same method to the heritage coasts[5-7] and to the urban fringe.[8] They all had similar aims—the resolution of conflicts between various user interests, the promotion of better resource management, landscape and wildlife conservation and the improvement of recreation provision.

Countryside management in the urban fringe

1.6   In the urban fringe, the countryside management approach was first tested in an experiment set up in 1972 in the Bollin Valley[8], in the southern urban fringe of Manchester. Here attempts were made to develop the work within a statutory planning context, with positive action complementing negative development control; this marked a substantial change from the more limited objectives of UMEX on which the original approach had been based. A management plan was produced to define the objectives of the different interest groups in the area, to agree the common objectives, and to suggest methods of achieving them, through consultation, negotiation—often requiring changes in attitudes— and finally implementation. It was thus not just concerned with methods of solving practical problems, but also of reconciling the objectives of different user groups,

---

[1]Numbers relate to References listed on pages 134–5.

through a process of participation. In many respects, this is almost exactly the opposite of the approach used in statutory planning for development, where the plan is made by an expert planner and then subjected to a process of consultation.

1.7 The Bollin Valley was, in a sense, a relatively simple example of the urban fringe, where all those with an interest in the area had a highly developed awareness of the problem and a commitment to finding a solution. The landscape was of a high inherent quality, with agriculture still the dominant land use, and there were few major land use problems. The Countryside Commission therefore recognised the need to test the approach in more complex areas, exhibiting the full range of urban fringe problems. It was decided to develop and promote management methods designed to assist in the realisation of the aims of the Metropolitan Green Belt, which is subject to a range of pressures particularly along its inner edge, where it is at its most vulnerable. These pressures include the market forces inherent in an expanding urban area, the pressure from persistent visitor use, the need for mineral resources, and the introduction of new techniques of agricultural production. Speculation and the hope of development can result in an unstable situation, with fragmentation of large estates and land not being farmed properly. Physical evidence of this, in the form of a deteriorating landscape, is seen in the wasteland, the run-down and fragmented agricultural holdings and the concentration of urban uses such as sewage works. The area thus presented challenging problems requiring effective overall management if the interests of the farmers, the visitors and other groups were to be harmonised in such a way that farming was protected, recreation opportunities created and the landscape maintained and improved.

1.8 The two project areas chosen were in Hertfordshire/Barnet and in Havering, both of which make up part of the inner zone of the Metropolitan Green Belt (Figure 1). A brief history of the development of the Metropolitan Green Belt[9] helps to explain the background to that choice.

The Metropolitan Green Belt

1.9 The concept of the Green Belt evolved towards the end of the nineteenth century, with the early ideas of the garden city movement led by Ebenezer Howard[10], although the Green Belt approach to land acquisition and planning had begun as early as 1878, when the City of London obtained parliamentary powers to acquire land within a 40 km. radius of the City boundary as open spaces for the recreation and enjoyment of the public and to preserve the natural features. Howard saw his rural belt as a means of separating and containing towns, ensuring food production and providing opportunities for recreation in an attractive landscape. In 1933, Unwin's Plan[11] for a 'Green Girdle' advised local authorities to acquire land around London to reserve it for recreation purposes.

1.10 The London County Council Green Belt scheme of 1935 was intended "to provide a reserve supply of public open spaces and of recreational areas and to establish a green belt or girdle of open space lands, not necessarily continuous, but as readily accessible from the completely urbanised area of London as practicable".[12] To achieve this, grants were offered to local authorities in the home counties for the purchase of open space and farmland in order to prevent their development. This became embodied in the Green Belt (London and Home Counties) Act, 1938.

1.11 Abercrombie's Greater London Plan in 1944[13] also proposed a green belt, the aims of which were to restrict urban growth, while actively encouraging agriculture, developing recreation opportunities and enhancing the landscape. Since then, the Green Belt has increasingly been recognised as a tool for restricting urban growth rather than for promoting countryside activities. The Town and Country Planning Act, 1947, brought in adequate powers to control development and, with the approval of the last of the Home Counties' Development Plans in 1959, the Metropolitan Green Belt became a reality.

1.12 The Green Belt is not in itself a land use, but an area of land within which particular sets of policies are applied to maintain its open character. The main instrument of these policies has been the strict prevention by the local authorities, through development control, of uses not appropriate to a rural area, in order to prevent the further growth of the built-up area except in approved locations. However, planning authorities have only negative control over building development and, except by ownership, have no powers to enforce the positive management of land in the Green Belt, where the principal countryside activities are agriculture and recreation and where pressures for landscape change are great, e.g. accelerating changes in farming and forestry remain largely outside the process of town and country planning, which was not designed to generate the positive responses necessary to accommodate the increasing number of townspeople in search of countryside recreation.

1.13 The new development planning system resulting from the Town and Country Planning Act, 1968 presented an opportunity for framing relevant policies and positive action. In this system, the Structure Plans prepared by the county councils contain overall policies for economic development, housing, shopping, environment and transport, with the emphasis on particular topics varying from county to county. The Structure Plan thus gives the strategic context and indicates in general terms where Green Belt policies should be applied. The Local Plans, usually prepared by the district or borough councils, provide the detailed interpretation and analysis of local matters and define the precise boundaries of the Green Belt, specifying policies for it.

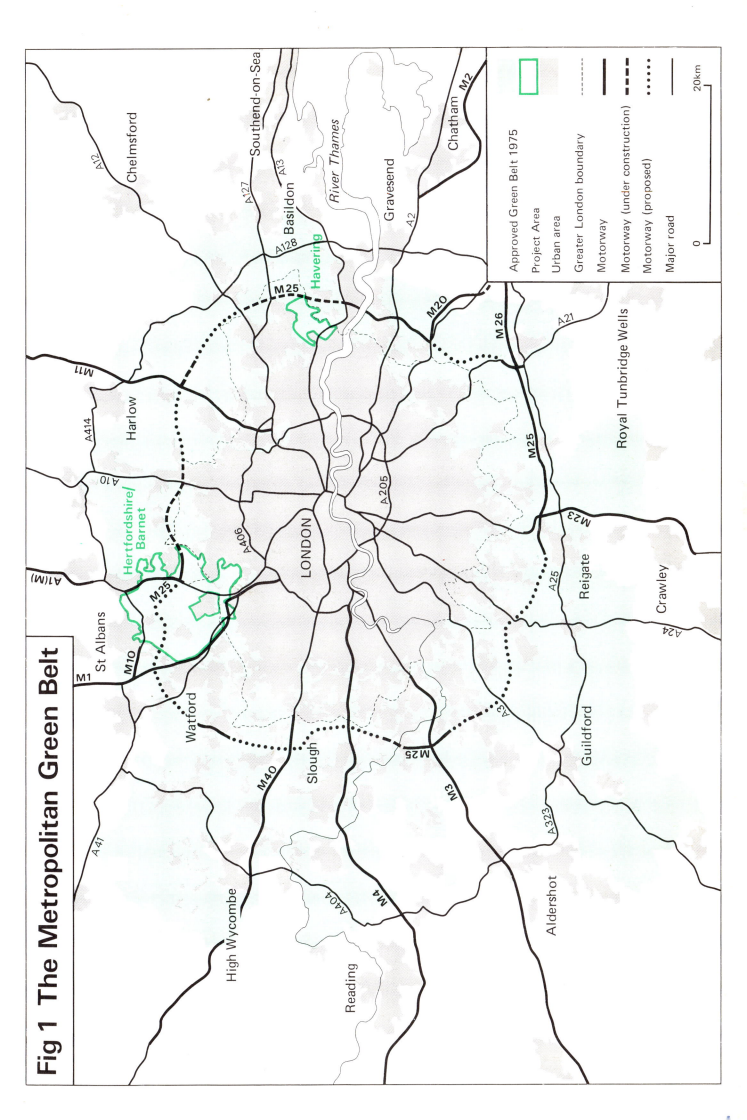

Fig 1 The Metropolitan Green Belt

Legend:
- Approved Green Belt 1975
- Project Area
- Urban area
- Greater London boundary
- Motorway
- Motorway (under construction)
- Motorway (proposed)
- Major road

20km scale: 0 — 20km

Map labels:
Chelmsford, Southend-on-Sea, River Thames, Gravesend, Chatham, Basildon, Havering, Harlow, Hertfordshire/Barnet, St Albans, Watford, LONDON, Reading, High Wycombe, Slough, Aldershot, Guildford, Crawley, Reigate, Royal Tunbridge Wells

Roads: A12, A127, A13, A128, A2, M2, M20, M26, A21, M25, M11, A414, A10, A205, A406, A23, A25, A24, M10, M1, A41, M40, A404, M4, M3, A323, A3, A1(M)

Implementation of these plans involves the powers and resources of various bodies with a wide range of interests. In the urban fringe, where there are complex and fragmented local government patterns, there is no unity of administration and a co-ordinated approach is difficult, although Hertfordshire's submitted Structure Plan attempted to apply such an approach for its area and this was an important factor in choosing the Hertfordshire/Barnet project area.

1.14 While it is generally agreed that planning policies in the Metropolitan Green Belt have been effective in protecting land from building development, the Countryside Commission recognised the need for a new approach, involving positive management measures to help solve the problems and to reconcile the conflicts between the different interests: those who live and work in the Green Belt and those who use it for recreation or who enjoy its natural beauty.

1.15 This was being echoed by the Standing Conference on London and South East Regional Planning. Their report[14], published in 1976, took as its theme the urgent need for measures to support agriculture and other preferred uses in the Green Belt, to safeguard "threatened" landscapes and to improve "deteriorated" landscapes, particularly along the urban edge. It put forward a variety of ideas to support and encourage desired uses, particularly recreation, and to safeguard and improve landscapes. Their subsequent unpublished reports have made specific proposals for a programme of action for the improvement of the Green Belt.

Choosing the project areas

1.16 When the Commission approached the Greater London Council and other local authorities in the Metropolitan Green Belt for their support in setting up a countryside management experiment, the strategic planning context had already been set in the Strategic Plan for the South East[15] and in the approved Greater London Development Plan[16] which supported the continuation of the Green Belt and recognised the need for policies to reconcile the increasing demand for recreation with the needs of the agricultural industry and with conservation. In addition, Hertfordshire County Council's submitted Structure Plan included a policy for positive management schemes to reconcile these conflicts.

1.17 The Metropolitan Green Belt is by no means an entity. In selecting the two project areas along its urban fringe, the following criteria were used:

  i.   a relatively high proportion of disused and derelict land, which had an inherently high potential for agricultural and recreational after-use;

  ii. a number of agricultural holdings owned by the local authorities;

  iii. examples of rural, non-productive land uses, such as horse-grazing.

1.18 The aim was to test a method of management designed to:

  i.   secure the positive use of land which was under-used, disused or derelict;

  ii. safeguard areas in primary productive use and ensure that they make a positive contribution to the landscape;

  iii. assess and realise opportunities for informal recreation, compatible with other land uses.

1.19 The two areas selected—Hertfordshire/Barnet and Havering—were chosen not only because they demonstrated the problems of landscape decline and of conflict arising from informal recreation but because the local authorities were anxious to solve these problems and to take part in the experiment. In the final analysis, the Countryside Commission can carry out experiments only with the support and co-operation of the local authorities so that this became an essential factor in the final choice.

1.20 The two areas presented very different problems and opportunities and allowed the methods and techniques to be tested in different ways. The experiments were set up, in co-operation with the local authorities concerned, in October 1975 in Hertfordshire/Barnet and in February 1976 in Havering, with a project officer being appointed in each case.

The Hertfordshire/Barnet project area

1.21 The Hertfordshire/Barnet project area covered 130 sq. km. in South Hertfordshire and the northern part of the London Borough of Barnet, straddling the boundary between the Greater London Council and Hertfordshire County Council (Figure 2). Its agricultural land was classified by the Ministry of Agriculture, Fisheries and Food (MAFF)[17] as being of good quality and it had a relatively high landscape value. Thus it was a natural development of the approach in the Bollin Valley[8] towards reconciliation between farmers and other users but on a larger scale, with more complex problems, more numerous and sophisticated amenity societies, more in the public eye, being close to London, and a more complicated local government involvement with a greater range of departments taking an active part. In addition, a significant amount of land in the area was in public ownership. Crossed by several major roads, it was a particularly complex area, under heavy pressure for

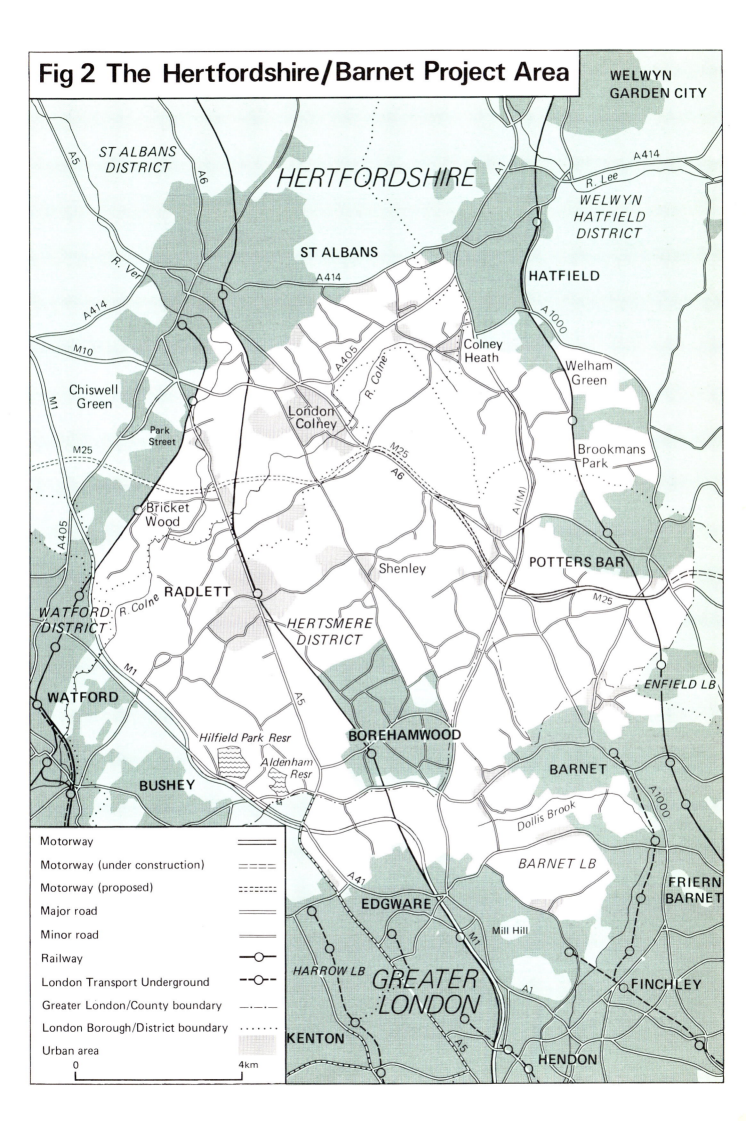

Fig 2 The Hertfordshire/Barnet Project Area

development and persistent pressure for recreation and there were many conflicts, particularly between farmers and other users. Horse-riding presented a particular problem because of the increasing number of riders on an inadequate bridleway network and the large amount of pony grazing. Other significant problems identified were trespass and vandalism, fly-tipping of household waste and garden rubbish, a large population of gypsies* with inadequate site provision, gravel extraction, and a decline in the number of trees through Dutch elm disease and the removal of hedgerows. Hertfordshire County Council's submitted Structure Plan, which recognised the need for countryside management, provided the planning context for that part of the area, while the London Borough of Barnet were embarking on the production of a Borough Plan, and the district councils in Hertfordshire were preparing Local Plans, to include the Green Belt area.

The Havering project area

1.22 Nineteen sq. km. of the Green Belt in the southern part of the London Borough of Havering (Figure 3) were chosen because the area met all the stated criteria (paragraph 1.17). It was classified by MAFF as an area of first class agricultural land, where farming was made difficult by existing gravel workings, uncertainty over future gravel extraction and by trespass from the surrounding housing estates. It was therefore dominated by large areas of semi-derelict landscape, waste and vacant land retained for possible development (with the aim of realising their 'hope' value), or unusable or badly-managed land because of poor-quality restoration after gravel extraction was finished. Although attractive pockets remained, further deterioration in the landscape had been caused by Dutch elm disease, rubbish dumping and poorly-managed horse-grazing. At the same time, the area offered considerable opportunity for the provision of recreation facilities, of which there were few in existence, and a derelict airfield site which was to come into local authority ownership was of particular significance here. The planning context was to be provided by the Local Plan being prepared by the London Borough of Havering. This area presented the greatest challenge yet for the techniques of countryside management—the need to reconstruct rather than to conserve the landscape and to make the remaining flat, intensive vegetable-growing land attractive and accessible to visitors without undue conflict. Although it was clear right from the beginning that only some of the problems would respond to countryside management methods, the Havering project area provided an excellent opportunity for testing the technique to its limits.

---

*See paragraph 2.31 for definition of the term 'gypsy'.

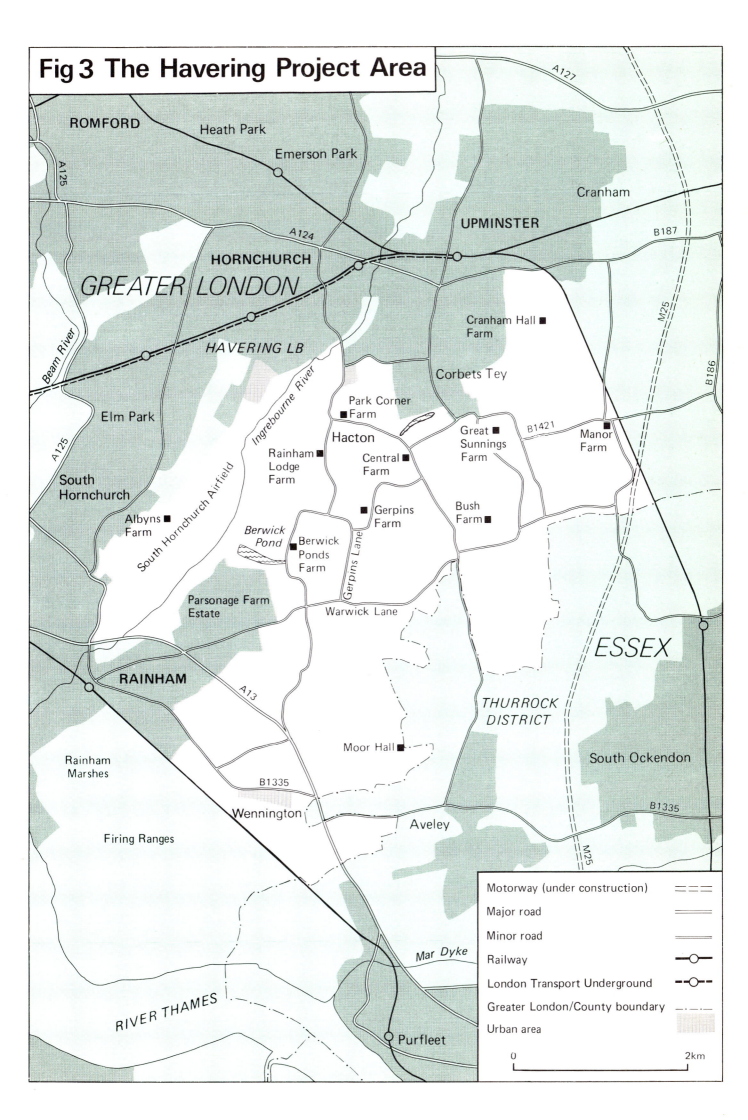

Fig 3 The Havering Project Area

ROMFORD

Heath Park

Emerson Park

A127

Cranham

A125

A124

UPMINSTER

B187

HORNCHURCH

GREATER LONDON

M25

B186

HAVERING LB

Cranham Hall
Farm ■

Corbets Tey

Beam River

Elm Park

Ingrebourne River

Park Corner
Farm ■

A125

Hacton

Great
Sunnings
Farm ■

B1421

Manor
Farm ■

South
Hornchurch

Rainham
Lodge
Farm ■

Central
Farm ■

Albyns ■
Farm

South Hornchurch Airfield

*Berwick
Pond*

Berwick
Ponds
Farm

Gerpins
Farm ■

Bush
Farm ■

ESSEX

Parsonage Farm
Estate

Gerpins Lane

Warwick Lane

RAINHAM

A13

*THURROCK
DISTRICT*

South Ockendon

Rainham
Marshes

Moor Hall ■

B1335

B1335

Wennington

Aveley

M25

Firing Ranges

Mar Dyke

RIVER THAMES

Purfleet

Motorway (under construction)	= = =
Major road	
Minor road	
Railway	—○—
London Transport Underground	--○--
Greater London/County boundary	-·-·-
Urban area	

0   2km

Chapter 2: Problems and Opportunities in the Urban Fringe

Introduction

2.1   In choosing the two project areas, the Countryside Commission focused its attention on the inner zone of the Green Belt, where it is at its most vulnerable. The 'urban fringe', as it is generally called, is difficult to define precisely as it is neither town nor country: an area of uncertainty, a zone of transition between urban and rural land uses, dominated by urban activity, where the pace of change contrasts sharply with that in the more traditional rural areas and where conflicts of interest are many and varied.

2.2   The urban fringe means different things to different users. To the farmer it is a place of work; to the city dweller it is often the nearest 'real countryside'; to the developer, it offers potential for housing, industry, mineral extraction and leisure facilities. To central and local government it may be a 'green belt', but also a place to locate the urban services which cannot be located elsewhere—sewage works, rubbish dumps, airfields, motorways, hospitals (2.5 per cent of the Hertfordshire/Barnet project area is taken up by mental hospitals), prisons and other institutions—and to develop recreation activities. The most complex mixture of these is found along the immediate urban edge.

2.3   In the urban fringe there is such a bewildering number of interests that safeguarding or restoring environmental values is made very difficult. It illustrates the "problems of resource management in a situation of conflict"[18] and there is evidence of wasted opportunities and of inefficiency in the ways in which resources are used and activities practised. There is no unity of administration, with complex and fragmented local government patterns, thus making a co-ordinated approach more difficult.

2.4   It can be seen, therefore, both as a problem and as an area of opportunity. Green Belt policies, the most recognisable planning policies effectively applied to these areas, are of necessity largely negative in their application (Chapter 1). The urban fringe brings together, often in an extreme form, all the problems and opportunities found elsewhere but, where fringe problems have been identified at all, they have been seen "in isolation, neither linked outwards to the activities and resources of the countryside, nor inwards to the demands and needs of the town"[18]. Conservation planning measures, the only other recognisable planning policies, have not alone been sufficient to achieve the efficient management of resources.

Concern for the urban fringe

2.5   There is evidence from various sources of a developing interest in the urban fringe, its problems and its opportunities. The run-down quality of much urban fringe landscape has been the subject of a report of the Standing Conference on London and South East Regional Planning (SCLSERP)[14] and of later unpublished SCLSERP reports and was recognised in the "Area of Opportunity" policies in the approved Greater London Development Plan (GLDP)[16].

2.6   The opportunities for recreation in the urban fringe have been widely discussed in the Layfield Report of the Panel of Inquiry into the GLDP[19], the SCLSERP reports and at the 1975 Countryside Recreation Research Advisory Group Conference[20]. The White Paper on Sport and Recreation[21] and the Issues Report of the Greater London and South East Regional Council for Sport and Recreation[22] recognised the urban fringe as a specific location for recreation facilities. The Advisory Council for Agriculture and Horticulture (the Strutt Committee)[23] and the Countryside Review Committee[24,25] have also recognised the need for the better management of a wasted resource.

2.7   The Countryside Commission, in addition to setting up countryside management projects, give the urban fringe priority for other landscape and recreation projects when allocating grant aid. Their interest arises from the following:

    i.   Urban fringe agriculture and its proper use as an economic resource is important in national as well as local terms. Alternative sources of food can be achieved only by reclaiming land for production in the marginal uplands or by intensifying production in the lowlands, both of which have significant environmental consequences.

    ii.   The positive management of land is an essential complement to strict planning control in maintaining the environmental function and in realising the recreation potential of the Green Belt.

2.8   In spite of this developing interest from various sources, there is still a need to examine the interactions between different activities and policies in the urban fringe on a comprehensive basis.

Underlying factors

2.9   The conflicts in the urban fringe are the results of underlying factors which need to be taken into account if the scale of the issues involved is to be assessed and the application of countryside management techniques is to be put in context.

2.10   Economic pressures associated with continuing urban growth mean that the main entrepreneurs in the urban fringe, e.g. the farmers and the gravel companies in Havering, take a highly commercial attitude, as close proximity to the market, the high price of land and the need for large capital investment are the dominating factors. This can lead to short-term speculation at the expense of long-term environmental considerations. The high level of uncertainty disrupts long-term investment and management decisions, to the detriment of the landscape, and of food production in the case of gravel extraction in Havering where there are few incentives to carry out high-quality restoration. Property speculation can result in the fragmentation of farm holdings and in the retention of land in an unused condition in the hope of planning permission for development.

2.11   Political pressures for development and a strong roads lobby come into conflict with the smaller, but growing conservation lobby. The impact of the road construction programme is felt particularly in the urban fringe which provides the routes for the circular motorways around most of our major cities, e.g. the M25.

2.12   Problems of administration include the division of responsibilities between the two tiers of local government, made worse where the urban fringe tends to straddle urban and rural authority boundaries. In addition, the division of responsibility in central government and its agencies has meant that at national and regional levels there is a large number of unco-ordinated policies being applied to the urban fringe.

2.13   No two areas in the urban fringe are exactly similar, but the differences are largely of scale and emphasis. Only a brief description of the activities typical of the urban fringe, and of the problems and opportunities associated with them follows, as these have been generally well documented elsewhere[18,26-29] and more specifically in Part Two (Hertfordshire/Barnet) and Part Three (Havering) of this report.

Agriculture

2.14   The problems associated with agriculture in the urban fringe fall into two main categories:
   i.   those which make farming impossible, e.g. competing demands for agricultural land for development, such as for roads, housing, gravel working, etc.;
   ii.   those which disrupt farming operations, e.g. trespass, vandalism, livestock-worrying, etc.

2.15   Agriculture is the major overall land use, but can be very different from the traditional idea of farming often seen in the deeper countryside. Farming on the urban fringe, except where land is in public ownership, is dominated by uncertainty as, in spite of Green Belt legislation, the threat of non-rural development is always present and this is reflected in the high land prices. 'Hope value' has been one of the main causes of change in estate management and farming practice, as long-term capital investment in the farm becomes less worthwhile for land-owner, tenant and grant-aiding body alike. The case studies of Bury Farm and Cranham (Appendices 1 and 6) illustrate this problem well, the latter also providing evidence of fragmentation, when a viable holding is sold off in separate lots in the hope of attracting buyers who want a higher return on capital invested.

2.16   Land is also lost to roads, radiating out from and circulating around London, often causing severance of a farm holding and leaving parts of it economically non-viable. Other uses allowed in the Green Belt, such as mineral extraction, cause particular problems, even though they are in theory only of short-term duration. This is well-illustrated in Havering (Chapter 12), where there is an obvious conflict with agriculture, both in direct land loss and the uncertainty this engenders and in poorly-restored land never being brought back to anything like its original Grade 1 quality, with the land remaining vacant in the hope of planning permission for development. In addition, there is often the problem of the decline and loss of the specialist agricultural workforce in areas subjected to prolonged mineral extraction.

2.17   The steady encroachment of urban development brings with it a demand for informal recreation in the countryside; bridleway provision in particular is seldom sufficient to meet this demand. Rights of way have been eroded or have disappeared altogether as new roads and mineral workings disrupt the networks and routes have not been recognised on the Definitive Maps. Paths that no longer appear to lead anywhere fall into disrepair and become overgrown, thus putting an additional burden on the remaining paths, which become badly worn and, in winter, impassable. This also puts pressure on adjacent farmland, often resulting in trespass, vandalism, litter problems and damage to hedges, trees, footpaths, gates, crops and machinery. This gives cause for concern as its 'nuisance value' to the farmer is as important as its economic disbenefit. These factors can combine to make the farmer change his farming system in order to reduce these pressures (paragraph 2.26), particularly if the economy of the farm is affected. At worst, the farmer will leave the farm and move elsewhere, although only one example of this was found in the project areas, where trespass and vandalism was a contributory factor in one farmer leaving Havering (paragraph 13.21). Generally speaking, the farmers in Havering have a higher tolerance of urban intrusion than those in Hertfordshire/Barnet, even though they are virtually surrounded by urban development, and trespass and vandalism occur frequently. Possible explanations for this are described in paragraph 4.32.

2.18   Many farmers in the Hertfordshire/Barnet project area said that they suffered from problems with horse-riders. The current pressures are the result of a number of factors: the concentration of people seeking recreation, inadequate rights of way networks (bridleways, Roads used as Public Paths (RUPPs) and 'green lanes'), the distribution of open land and the availability of stabling and/or grazing to support horses. In the latter part of the nineteenth and the early twentieth centuries, these pressures were felt most acutely in the formal parklands and the Metropolitan Commons of inner London. Growth in interest, provision and participation continued until brought to a halt by the war years, when many riding establishments were closed to make way for alternative uses. In the post-war years, urban renewal led to the removal of horses, riders and establishments to outer London areas, where the horse and rider population was already increasing. At the same time, bridleway provision in the Green Belt was being steadily eroded by a rapidly-changing road network which either completely obliterated bridleways or severed them, making them inaccessible or dangerous to horse and rider. Existing bridleways are the fragmented remnants of an outmoded system which was never intended to fulfil the recreational needs of present-day riders. This transference of activity to the Green Belt also brought riding into conflict with agriculture.

2.19   Modern agricultural practices, particularly in arable farming, have meant the removal of old hedgerows and the enlargement of fields, with the result that many old routes now cross fields rather than following their boundaries. Rights of way that go through farmyards are particularly irritating to the farmer. However, the original networks are vigorously defended by enthusiastic amenity societies, even though the rationale behind many of these routes no longer exists, and this brings them into regular conflict with the farmers. Little Munden Farm in Hertfordshire provides an interesting case study (Appendix 3).

2.20   There are also advantages to farming in the urban fringe, although in a farmers' survey[30], 61 per cent of respondents could think of none. Proximity to markets and available temporary labour are important contributing factors in the economic buoyancy of the horticultural industry in Havering. However, the apparent benefits of working good land are often outweighed by the competition from building and mineral working which wants to use the same land. Urban-related activities, such as farm shops, integration with the London markets, part-time jobs and horse-keeping, are used to supplement the farmer's income and can eventually dominate the farm business when other farming activities are abandoned as no longer economically viable, e.g. horse-grazing in Hertfordshire/Barnet (paragraph 6.15).

Recreation

2.21   It has become widely accepted[20,21,29,31] that the urban fringe should provide informal recreation opportunities for its adjacent urban population, as access should be relatively easy in terms of distance from the main centres. Large areas of the Green Belt as a whole have already been given over to sports grounds, often institutional, and Public Open Space in the form of country parks, commons and woodland: Ferguson and Munton's study[32] revealed that 9 per cent of the approved Metropolitan Green Belt is used for informal recreation. However, the two project areas are not particularly well-provided in the sense of general public access, nor are those facilities that exist particularly well-used, according to recreation site surveys[33] carried out by the Countryside Commission, in association with the local authorities (Figures 4 and 5).

2.22   The overall level of recreational use in the project areas was somewhat lower than expected and the overall pattern appeared to be one of dispersal rather than of concentration on specific sites. It was found that existing recreation sites were used predominantly by local people and the general impression gained was that virtually all the sites had the potential to absorb more visitors. The majority walked to the sites, even where they had access to a car and this seems to confirm that informal outdoor recreation in the urban fringe is not necessarily a substitute for countryside recreation. Given the environmental quality of much of the urban fringe, its assumed attractiveness as a recreation resource has obviously been over-estimated. However, the opportunity is there for attracting more people from the urban areas of London, given improvements in environmental quality, in accessibility and in the promotion of existing facilities.

2.23   As well as the sites which are exclusively set aside for recreation, e.g. country parks, it is clear that large numbers of people also enjoy rights of access (in some cases 'permissive') to other areas, e.g. gravel pits and farmland, and this is where conflicts of interest often arise. The rights of way networks (Figures 5 and 9) do little to provide for the recreation needs of the walker or rider, both of whom require circular routes that link with the

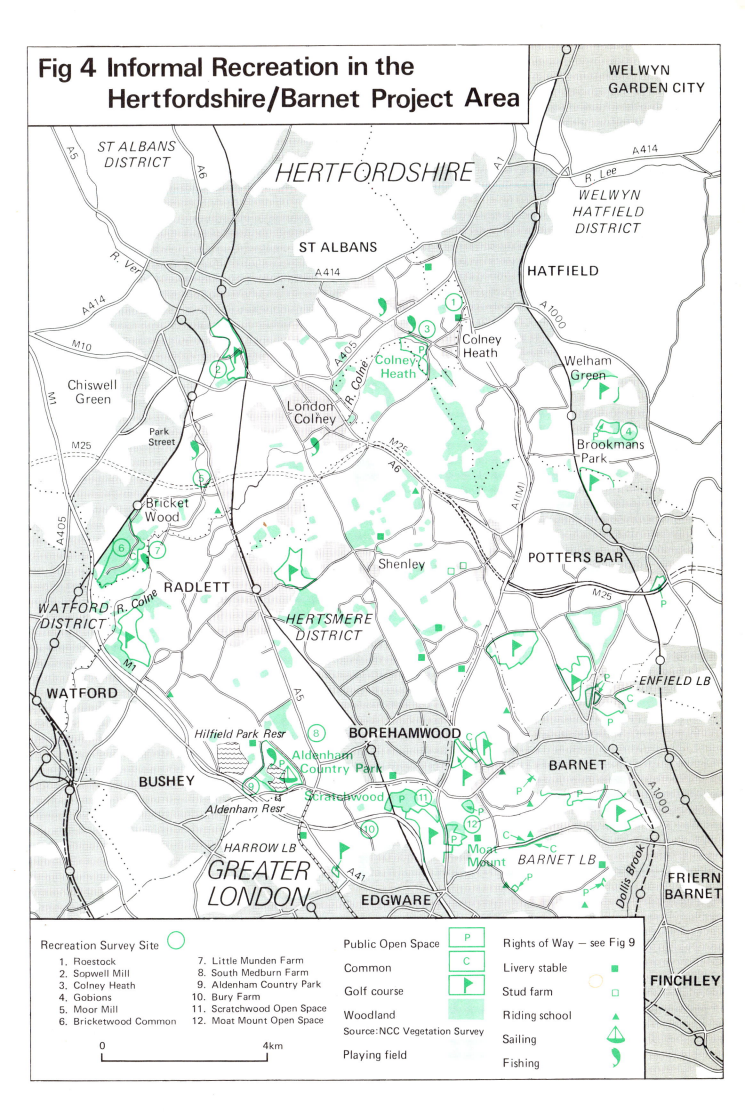

Fig 4 Informal Recreation in the Hertfordshire/Barnet Project Area

Recreation Survey Site ◯

1. Roestock
2. Sopwell Mill
3. Colney Heath
4. Gobions
5. Moor Mill
6. Bricketwood Common
7. Little Munden Farm
8. South Medburn Farm
9. Aldenham Country Park
10. Bury Farm
11. Scratchwood Open Space
12. Moat Mount Open Space

0 ——————— 4km

Public Open Space ▢P

Common

Golf course ▷

Woodland
Source: NCC Vegetation Survey

Playing field

Rights of Way – see Fig 9

Livery stable ◼

Stud farm ▢

Riding school ▲

Sailing △

Fishing ⌒

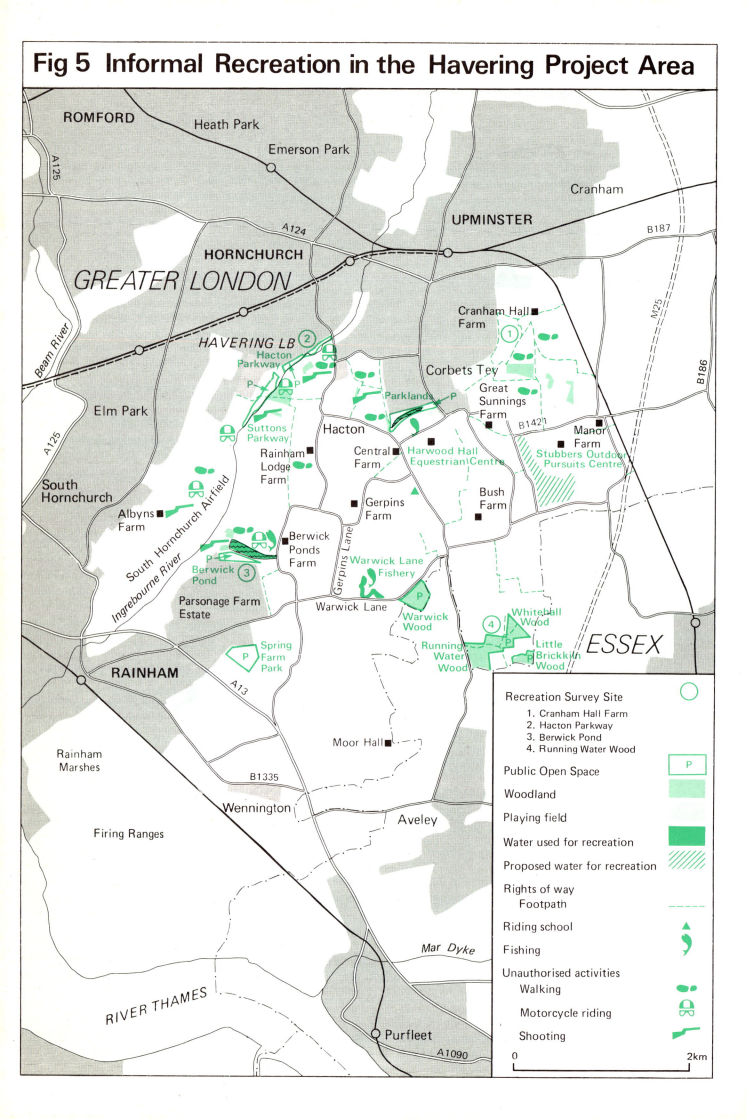

Fig 5 Informal Recreation in the Havering Project Area

transport system. Work carried out by farmers on field enlargement consistent with modern farming methods, particularly on arable land, can cause problems, as the removal of traditional landscape trees and hedgerows to facilitate the use of heavy mechanical equipment has left many rights of way following non-existent field boundaries, with old stiles and signposts disappearing through lack of maintenance. The farmers argue for the rationalisation of an outdated system, while the Rights of Way Societies argue for its preservation. There is also much *de facto* use of private land, where no clear boundary exists between public and private land—the design and layout of the urban edge encourages this—and where existing rights of way are poorly maintained and waymarked.

2.24   In addition to the conflicts which exist between recreation-seekers and landowners, there are conflicts between different types of recreation, e.g. walking and motorcycling. In some areas, vacant sites provide an opportunity to accommodate noisy activities, but landowners seem reluctant to let their land, even on a temporary basis. In the Hertfordshire/Barnet project area there were particular conflicts between horse-riders and landowners and horse-riders and walkers, outlined in paragraph 7.15.

Landscape

2.25   The effect of the conflicts in the urban fringe is seen in the deteriorating landscape, where under-capitalised and uneconomic farm units are common and fragmentation of holdings is often found. In some cases, where planning permission for development has been refused, it may even be advantageous to create an unattractive landscape in the hope that such land might then be developed in order to remove an eyesore. Many farmers, particularly owner-occupiers and tenants with certainty of tenure, have a deep concern for the long-term health and appearance of the countryside, but lack the financial incentive to retain trees and hedges which might help to lessen the intrusive effect of buildings and other developments like mineral workings.

2.26   In some parts of the Hertfordshire/Barnet project area, modern farming practices have resulted in the removal of up to 80 per cent of the old hedgerows to allow the maximum use of heavy machinery, thus denuding the landscape and destroying wildlife habitats. Boundary hedges are only really necessary as shelter or wind-break areas for livestock which, except for horses, are becoming increasingly rare in the urban fringe because of the dangers of worrying by dogs and disturbance by people. In a farmers' survey[30], 39 per cent of the farmers said that they had altered their pattern of husbandry because of disturbance from the urban population. This mainly involved dispensing with livestock, especially sheep, because of the risks from dogs, open gates or damaged fences.

2.27   In Havering, in those areas where agriculture is still the main activity, traditional landscape features remain, although intensive horticultural practices have had their effect. However, gravel extraction has transformed the landscape by the removal of field boundaries, hedges and trees, leaving a flat, open landscape,

Gravel workings still have an effect even after the gravel has gone: poorly-restored land in Havering

dominated by poorly-restored land, gravel tips, silt ponds and rubbish dumps. The effects of over-grazing on land given over exclusively to horses is also an important element (see illustration on page 6), compared with Hertfordshire/Barnet, where horse-grazing areas were generally better integrated with the farming system.

2.28   Many of the woodlands in the two project areas have been neglected or poorly-managed. The result is that the trees are over-mature and all the same age and they lack any diversity of wildlife. There is little tree regeneration and the woodlands are becoming overgrown. Dutch elm disease and the drought of 1976 have intensified the loss of trees in the landscape.

2.29   There are enough existing landscape features in an area such as Hertfordshire/Barnet to present opportunities for conservation and enhancement. However, most of the Havering project area will require the reconstruction of the landscape on a much larger scale.

Rubbish dumping

2.30   Fly-tipping of household waste and garden rubbish, and of construction rubble by contractors, is fairly typical of the urban fringe. Unauthorised tipping tends to take place at night, usually builders' rubble, although

Gypsy encampments and fly-tipping of household waste, on the A41 in the London Borough of Barnet, are an ugly eye-sore

the amount of household rubbish increased substantially during the local authority strike in 1979, when there were no urban refuse collections in London. Larger items of household rubbish tend to be dumped indiscriminately in woodlands or in fields and lanes near housing areas.

Gypsies

2.31   The 1968 Caravan Sites Act defines gypsies as "persons of nomadic habit of life whatever their race or origin", referring to a way of life rather than to an ethnic group and this definition, which includes romanies, didicois, mumpers, tinkers, hawkers etc., is used in this report. The Act requires local authorities to provide adequate accommodation for gypsies residing in or resorting to their areas. However, it is clear that even the statutory provision of gypsy caravan sites is inadequate to meet the needs of the gypsy population in and around London. Gypsies earn their living from dealing in scrap, from small contract work and from seasonal farm work and therefore need to live in a place where both rural and urban environments are accessible. Official sites which do not make provision for their activities, e.g. sorting scrap, often result in trespass on adjacent land or the use of other unofficial sites.

Land ownership

2.32   The attitudes of the landowners, both in the short and the long term, will have a direct effect on the future of the urban fringe. The problems associated with speculation and deliberate fragmentation have already been outlined, but the large amount of publicly-owned land, more than 25 per cent in the Hertfordshire/Barnet project area, provides an excellent opportunity to demonstrate how the objectives of the Green Belt can be achieved. A Working Party was set up in the Hertfordshire/Barnet Experiment to see how this might be done in practice.[34] Its conclusions are given in paragraph 4.51.

Summary

2.33   The urban fringe is an area where complex systems of inter-relationships exist. Conflicts of interest and competition for land create problems. The problems are seen differently by the various interests and can be defined as conflicts of land use or of land management, but often one can be the symptom or the cause of the other. The source of all the conflicts is the competing demand for a limited and therefore valuable resource. The rest of this report describes how the two countryside management experiments have used informal methods to solve small-scale conflicts and points to opportunities for action in other directions, given the political will and the allocation of resources.

Chapter 3: The Countryside Management Approach

Introduction

3.1   As has been described in Chapter 1, small-scale conflicts between recreation, conservation and agriculture in the countryside are widespread, particularly in the urban fringe which has been shown in Chapter 2 to be suffering from the stresses imposed by rapid landscape change, persistent visitor use and uncertainty over future patterns of development. The experiments in Hertfordshire/Barnet and Havering were designed to test a new approach to resolving the small-scale conflicts, involving close co-operation between local authorities, farmers and landowners, and the local community. They were set up in conjunction with the local authorities to develop a method of managing areas of the countryside to benefit, as far as possible, all interested parties. The problems were studied and solutions tested on a scale requiring only a relatively small input of financial and staff resources. It was hoped that the lessons learned could then be extended to similar situations elsewhere.

Objectives

3.2   The aim of the experiments has been outlined in paragraph 1.18. The objectives of both experiments were:

  i.   to identify and analyse the land management problems in a defined area of the Metropolitan Green Belt;

  ii.   to explore how far and by what means management arrangements can be introduced to help solve these problems and to implement solutions in a manner which will allow the results to be effectively monitored;

  iii.   to communicate the results of the study, through the Countryside Commission, to interested parties, particularly other local authorities, by means of reports, other publications, lectures and seminars.

3.3   The experiments were designed to resolve conflicts of interest, particularly between those who live and work in the countryside and those who use it, in order to protect agriculture, to conserve and enhance the landscape and to increase informal recreation and public access.

The approach

3.4   In essence, countryside management is getting things done to resolve or reduce the conflicts between the interests in rural land and actions by the public which affect those interests. To make countryside management work it is necessary to gain the confidence of all those concerned with the particular stretch of countryside in which the work is being undertaken: farmers, landowners, villagers, recreationalists, conservationists and public authorities. To gain that confidence it is necessary to establish direct contact with the people immediately affected: in the main the landowners. Their co-operation is gained by offering them a service. It may be to give them advice. It may be to obtain their agreement to do something from which the public will benefit, either by using direct labour, or volunteers, or by paying the owner to do the work. It may be no more than to provide the owner or land manager with an opportunity to voice his complaints, the importance of which must not be discounted, as it is by listening to complaints that the roots of conflict can often be identified.

The project officer

3.5   Experience has shown that the key factor in the approach is the project officer. He is concerned with getting things done. Success depends very much on the personality and abilities of the project officer. He needs to understand the countryside and farming. He must be reliable and absolutely trustworthy, because of his delegated responsibility to spend sums of money. He needs to be able to respond to the ideas of others, and have a high level of commitment to achieve practical results. Ability to listen is more important than a readiness to prescribe solutions. He must be able to communicate his specialist knowledge, including information on grants and application procedures, to local people, in order to develop and implement management solutions in close association with farmers and other landowners. Finally, he should be able to organise and inspire voluntary effort and the variety of other sources of labour available in the community, e.g. the Community Service Order scheme, operated by the probation service, where young offenders have to take part in community service as an alternative to prison sentences or fines.

3.6   The project officer is essential in fostering goodwill, ironing out conflicts, especially between visitors and farmers, and harnessing local initiatives to improve the landscape and accessibility. The fact that he is available in the locality to lend a sympathetic ear and is able to respond quickly to complaints and ideas is fundamental. Moreover, this method tends to avoid local authority systems which are designed to execute works on a much larger scale than is required in countryside management, which uses the goodwill and practical efforts of interest groups co-operating with each other to solve problems rather than unwieldy legal powers. The project officer thus becomes identified with the local area and the local community and not solely with the authority by whom he is employed and this apparent neutrality is important in contacts with owners and land managers. He acts as a builder of bridges between them and the government system, which is often remote and has cumbersome administrative machinery.

3.7   The essence of the management approach, then, is its simplicity and its use of persuasion, reinforced by modest inducements, to secure the achievement of objectives by others. It thus complements, and may sometimes obviate the need to use controls exercisable under planning legislation. It is concerned with the identification and resolution of conflicts of interest through direct practical works and personal contact with the parties involved. While individual tasks are small, their incremental effect should in time make a significant contribution to landscape and nature conservation, to the creation of opportunities for informal recreation and to the reduction of conflicts between different interests.

Relationship between the project officer and the local authorities

3.8   The practical work and the guidance from the local authorities are both complementary features of the approach as they link officials and public, strategy and tactics, policy and implementation, with the project officer acting in a liaison role. Both project officers found that access to expertise was absolutely vital on many occasions. The professional skills of a landscape architect or highway engineer etc are usually available at county council level and other departments can supply policy advice on forestry or agriculture. At the local level, district or borough council staff are essential with their advice and services and a different field of knowledge is available through local societies with their long-term, intimate connections with the area.

3.9   A complex relationship was developed with all the local authorities, the project staff providing a useful feedback and monitoring service for the Structure Plans and making a valuable input into the Subject and Local Plans being prepared. In Hertfordshire, countryside management services were developing in two other areas of the county and useful comparisons were able to be made between the methods used in these and in the experiment. However, contacts were also made with many other departments in the local authorities. This resulted in the development of co-operation between local authorities and between departments within those authorities where little or no contact had existed previously, except at a very formal level. This might then be seen as the beginning of a recognition of the need for a comprehensive approach to the planning and management of the countryside around towns, with the project officer acting as the catalyst.

3.10   The local planning authorities found the 'man on the ground' invaluable for feeding back information. He also acted as a vehicle for public participation, not at first on broad policy issues but on the detailed solution of schemes which together would lead to policy formulation. He helped to stimulate a debate on agricultural and Green Belt issues which was particularly valuable in the urban-oriented London boroughs, and he succeeded in involving the public in policy issues at an earlier stage than would otherwise have occurred (Appendices 1 and 6).

The management plan

3.11   The Countryside Commission saw the preparation of a management plan for the area as a responsibility that the project officer, in association with his Steering Group (paragraph 3.18), should be capable of undertaking. He would not only quickly develop a good knowledge of the area but he could tap the vision of those who were even more knowledgeable about it. He would also be able to relate his understanding of the possibilities and constraints in the area to the ideas the local government planners might have. The management plan for the area would come, in consequence, from a process of participation and would be submitted by the project officer to the local authorities for their adoption on an informal basis. In many respects, this is almost exactly the opposite of the approach used in statutory planning, where the plan is made by an expert planner and then subjected to a process of consultation.

3.12   The management plan was thus seen as an important bridge between the action taken on the ground and the broader policy objectives, setting priorities and providing a framework for co-ordinated management in the area on private and, particularly, on publicly-owned land. In this way it would guide the use of the manpower and financial resources of local authority departments and other agencies working in the area and would provide a link with the implementation of the statutory planning process. It should not be a complicated document; an outline of what a management plan might contain is given in the Countryside Commission's Advisory Series booklet No. 10[35].

3.13   In neither of the areas was the project officer able to complete a management plan in the three year period and this has implications for the length of time for which employment contracts should be made (paragraph 4.18). It was inevitable that there would be difficulties in working out priorities between action on the ground and the production of a plan and it was right that the balance should have been firmly in favour of the former in the early years of an experiment.

3.14 In the Hertfordshire/Barnet area, a management brief had been prepared by Hertfordshire County Council at the beginning of the experiment. This document included the strategic issues which would form the context for a management plan. However, given the size of the area and the project officer's role as Countryside Management Adviser to the Countryside Commission (see paragraph 5.4), action on the ground and the wider promotion of the countryside management approach were given priority and work on a management plan had only just begun when the officer left. A management plan for the area is being prepared during Phase Two of the experiment (paragraph 3.30).

3.15 In Havering, a large proportion of the project officer's time was taken up in providing an information base and in articulating the broader problems of the area, and again work on a management plan had only just begun when the project officer's contract ended. A permanent local authority countryside management service is being set up to cover the whole of the Green Belt in the London Borough of Havering and one of its objectives will be the production of a management plan.

Finance and administration

3.16 The Countryside Commission provided 75 per cent of an agreed budget, details of which are given in Parts Two (Table 1) and Three (Table 8), while the other sponsoring local authorities shared the remainder of the costs between them. This covered staff salaries and expenses, the cost of tools and materials, administrative and publicity costs. In each case, the local authority planning departments, Hertfordshire County Council and the London Borough of Havering, provided office accommodation and services but, in practice, the project officers worked mainly from home, giving their home as well as their office addresses on experiment-headed notepaper. This was an important psychological point in maintaining neutrality (paragraph 3.6), especially as viewed by their 'clients', the individual farmers and residents.

3.17 In each experiment, policy matters and approval of the annual budget were referred to Annual Review Committees, which consisted of elected members nominated by the sponsoring authorities and which were chaired by the Chairman of the Countryside Commission.

3.18 Direction of the work of each experiment was provided by a Steering Group to which the project officer was directly responsible, although for administrative purposes he was employed by one of the local authorities. The Steering Group was made up of officers from the sponsoring authorities and met on a quarterly basis. Its purpose was to receive the project officer's monthly reports, to approve the forward work programme, to co-ordinate the involvement of the government agencies and of the different departments within the local authorities so that their activities mutually supported the overall objectives of the experiment and the work programme, to approve the management brief and management plan, and to suggest action on schemes outside the project officer's resources.

3.19 The Steering Group delegated a certain amount of financial and administrative responsibility to the project officer. He was allowed to spend up to £300 on any one task without reference to them, thus increasing his flexibility and speed of action by allowing him to purchase equipment and materials, finance labour and the hire of additional plant or equipment, make payments to individual landowners to undertake approved works, support the involvement of voluntary labour in the project, promote the work of the experiment and undertake public relations exercises. This often led to a simple and informal method of management agreement with the landowner who was prepared to make concessions on a *quid pro quo* basis, e.g. the free use of tools and machinery and the donation of materials or a strip of land to solve problems such as trespass by horses (Appendix 3). It provided an alternative to grant aid which can be a costly procedure involving application, inspection and committee decision (Appendix 5). Value for money was gained through simplified administration, by delegation of authority to the project officers, and by use of voluntary and other labour. On larger schemes, outside their remit, the project officers could also act as catalysts in mobilising the wide range of statutory and special grants available, e.g. from the Countryside Commission and Forestry Commission, and advice and expertise from other agencies, such as the Ministry of Agriculture, Fisheries and Food, the Nature Conservancy Council, the Sports Council and the National Farmers Union.

Method of working

3.20 The two experiments developed different approaches to problem-solving because of the difference in size of the areas, the manpower available, the nature of the problems encountered and, to some extent, the personalities and previous experience of the project officers.

3.21 During the initial stages of both experiments, the emphasis of the work was on identifying and analysing the land management problems. The project officers assessed their areas—they got to know the locality and the people, the public officials, the private owners and the local voluntary leaders at an individual level. At this level it was found to be an advantage to be prepared to work outside normal office hours and often from home.

Relatively few individuals representing farming or amenity interests can conveniently attend the local authority office during the day and often prefer more informal surroundings. The initial contacts took up a lot of time, but were essential in identifying the conflicts and learning about the pressures.

3.22   The primary objective for the project officers was to identify the problems and to make a careful appraisal of them in order to establish feasible programmes of action within a scale of priorities. They then established a number of areas where immediate action on the ground, using low-key methods typical of the Countryside Commission's other experiments, was possible. These are described in Chapters 8 and 13 and in the Appendices. In Hertfordshire/Barnet the work was carried out by the project officer and two full-time assistants, but in Havering the project officer initially worked alone. Getting things done required the use of compromise, resolving local conflicts, providing leadership to stimulate the imagination and interest of local land managers and the local community, organising voluntary action and deploying other labour. It was desirable that a high standard of work was achieved, as this commanded the respect of landowner and visitor and generated support for the work. Reactions to the work were monitored both by the project officers and the project evaluator. These stages of assessment, appraisal and action were continuous and simultaneous rather than sequential.

3.23   In Hertfordshire/Barnet, extensive survey work had been carried out by Hertfordshire County Council before the experiment started, and by London Borough of Barnet immediately afterwards (paragraph 7.1) whereas the information base in Havering was very limited. In Hertfordshire/Barnet, therefore, the project officer was more quickly able to carry out a programme of practical work. In Havering, he became involved in survey work which, in conjunction with the study carried out by University College London[28], immediately identified the large-scale land use problems which were the major cause of the devastation in that part of the borough. In the absence of a Local Plan for the area, he became more involved in the analysis of these problems than he would otherwise have done and found it difficult to assess his work priorities. As a result, fewer practical schemes were initiated, and those that were carried out were also used to gain a deeper insight into the complex land use/land management problems of the area (Appendices 3–6).

3.24   It soon became obvious that the fairly broad objectives identified at the beginning (paragraph 3.2) needed clearer definition to enable the project officers to respond to the increasingly complex situations in which they found themselves. The more specific objectives for each area reflected the different nature of the problems encountered. They are outlined in paragraphs 5.2 and 14.22.

Assessing priorities
3.25   Given the complexity of the problems in both areas, assessing priorities was particularly difficult because so many interests were in conflict with each other, all competing for scarce resources, and because the three-year time scale of the experiments made the particular choice of work undertaken somewhat different from that which would be carried out by a long-term countryside management service. Within a relatively short time the project officers were expected to produce examples of practical solutions, which were seen as the major part of the work. Important early factors included accessibility to the work site for coaches and lightly-shod visitors, and visually-dramatic situations which lent themselves to putting across the message photographically. Slide shows, talks and tours of the area became essential parts of achieving the objective of communicating the results of the experiments to a wider audience.

3.26   The essential priority in early work was to establish the credibility of the experiment. Solving a variety of problems was the obvious course although, inevitably, a number of issues arose which, for financial or political reasons, would not lend themselves to a solution in the short term. Maintaining a balance between the various competing interests was difficult and those solutions which provided benefits to all parties concerned were obviously the most desirable. The idea of *quid pro quo,* give and take, had to be established from the outset, although works which were primarily in the interests of the private land occupier were often carried out in order to create a climate in which long-term solutions, including amenity improvements on his land, could be more favourably considered.

3.27   Later, the balance changed and other factors became more important. In Hertfordshire/Barnet, the sponsoring authorities expected to see a reasonable proportion of work in each of their own areas. Planning authorities were anxious to see the implementation of their policies and to monitor the results; the sponsors expected written reports; administrative work increased. However, for most observers it was the visible results on the ground that mattered. The balance between immediate solutions and long-term educational objectives was a delicate one and this is where the role of the Steering Groups was very important, particularly in assessing priorities for effecting a balance of achievement between the three objectives.

Experimental solutions
3.28   Many small-scale problems were capable of fairly rapid solution by various physical works. Simple, small-scale tasks achieved many of the objectives of the local people, e.g. erecting stiles, footbridges, fences,

The countryside management approach: simple, small-scale tasks solved many problems

A new stile on the footpath to Berwick Pond, Havering

Improvements to a path, including erecting a kissing gate, in Havering

Improvement of a footbridge and stile in Hertfordshire

gates, signposts; clearing or draining paths; felling dangerous trees and replanting; tree planting by school-children and arranging farm visits for them. In other cases, a number of interest groups agreed to try compromise solutions for an interim period. Legally-binding agreements could seldom be obtained in the short term and to use extra resources in trying to achieve these was difficult to justify in three-year experiments. Informal management agreements achieved results by being interim and 'permissive', allowing all parties time to reconsider their often entrenched views, e.g. the creation of a permissive path rather than a public right of way (Appendix 3) allowed the occupier future flexibility in management, should the use become inappropriate, and allowed recreation interests to consider the possible long-term consequences of altering an existing right of way. Often small areas of work were undertaken to demonstrate what could be achieved by similar work on a larger scale should resources permit, e.g. the clearance of a small length of bridleway.

Major schemes

3.29 Inevitably, problems and opportunities occurred which, although achieving the objectives, were beyond the resources of the experimental budget or would have commanded a very high proportion of it. Three main methods were employed to show what could be achieved, given adequate resources:

   i.   the work was undertaken as far as experimental resources would permit;

   ii.   a programme of action was prepared, costed (taking into account grant aid sources) and submitted to the local authority or other organisation concerned for approval and implementation;

   iii.   a programme of joint action was undertaken, employing the resources of the experiment and those of other interested parties, both local authority departments and private interests.

The limits of the budget, staff time etc. all had to be assessed in deciding which aspect of the work was to take priority, but the three-year limit of the experiment imposed its own particular discipline.

3.30 In addition, issues which were outside the remit of the experiments were revealed and the project officer played an important role in analysing these problems. In Hertfordshire/Barnet, the Steering Group set up working parties to look at the specific issues of bridleways and the management of publicly-owned land (Chapter 8). Their reports[34,36] provided the basis for a continuation of the experiment for another three years. Phase Two is currently developing and implementing a programme of major schemes based on the problems identified in the area. In addition, it is consolidating, developing and expanding the work as opportunities arise and confidence in countryside management grows. The work is being related to the policy and implementation process to determine more comprehensive solutions to the problems and is looking particularly at the role of countryside management on publicly-owned land, the future maintenance commitment and a suitable administrative framework for a long-term countryside management service. A management plan will be produced.

3.31 In Havering, where there was a complete spectrum of urban fringe problems, it was clear from the beginning that only some of these would respond to countryside management methods. The dereliction and waste of resources close to the urban areas presented problems on such a scale that small jobs organised or undertaken by the project officer could have no more than a cosmetic effect. Major decisions about land use and methods of land management over extensive tracts of land needed to be taken by the local authorities in conjunction with government departments and in negotiation with landowners. The project officer played an important part in articulating the problems as seen by those who owned or managed land or lived there. The Local Plan and the experiment had been seen as complementary parts of a total programme of action, the project officer influencing the content of the plan and using it as an information base. Unfortunately, the preparation of the Plan, which was to have been the vehicle in which the major issues would have been explored and in which the options for political decision would have been outlined and which would have provided essential background to the activities on the ground, was not able to be given priority by the local authority.

3.32 Given these fundamental land use and management problems, the potential for small-scale management solutions in the Havering project area was limited and a wider set of objectives was defined during the final year of the experiment with a view to setting up a second five year-phase on a much larger scale and with a substantial resource input, bringing in both the Ministry of Agriculture, Fisheries and Food and the Department of the Environment. The aim was to test solutions to the problems identified in the context of an overall approach, linking planning and management. Its objectives are outlined in paragraph 14.22. Unfortunately, the economic climate resulted in the Countryside Commission having to withdraw its funds and a unique opportunity was lost.

Chapter 4: Evaluation of the Countryside Management Approach in London's Urban Fringe

Introduction

4.1   In discussing what the Hertfordshire/Barnet and Havering experiments have achieved, two things must be taken into account. Firstly, in an experimental situation artificial goals are set up and the criteria used for determining work priorities necessarily differ from those in a long-term service: the need for quick, effective results which have immediate impact and the short three-year period meant that long-term solutions could not be tested. Secondly, in a countryside management service maintenance will become a long-term commitment, whereas in an experiment maintenance does not form a major part of the work so that more time is available for new projects, which are meant to show by example. Each one should be measured as a model of what can be achieved rather than for its direct impact over a total area.

4.2   The achievements in the two areas were necessarily different. In Hertfordshire/Barnet, where the project area covered 130 sq. km., small-scale management tasks were spread over the whole area (Figure 6), in order to make an impact on the landowners and tenants and to establish credibility. In Havering, fewer tasks were concentrated in one small area (Figure 7), in order to establish a presence and to obtain information on the fundamental problems, particularly on the conflict between agriculture and gravel extraction.

4.3   The evaluation of the countryside management approach in London's urban fringe is in three parts:

i.   an appraisal of the way the experiments were organised, so that local authorities considering the introduction of countryside management in their areas can benefit from the lessons learned;

ii.   conclusions on the concept of countryside management as an approach to the resolution of the problems in the urban fringe;

iii.   the future of countryside management and its development within the wider planning context.

Appraisal of the organisation of the experiments

Size of the area chosen

4.4   There can be no prescription for the size of area chosen for management purposes. Each will differ—the Hertfordshire/Barnet project area covered 130 sq. km., while the Havering project area covered only 19 sq. km. The deciding factors involved were:

i.   the character of the area and its unity of identification, which often crosses administrative boundaries, as in the Green Belt of Hertfordshire/Barnet;

ii.   matching the resources available to the problems identified, e.g. in a small area like Havering one assistant was sufficient as long as two pairs of hands were available for certain practical work, particularly where the work contained a safety element such as using a chainsaw;

iii.   the limitations of a three year experiment period.

Other factors which should be taken into account include:

iv.   the ability of the staff to live in the area and the corresponding amount of travelling time required;

v.   the availability of a convenient administrative centre and facilities for storage;

vi.   ensuring where possible that complete farm units are included within the boundary;

vii.   the existence or preparation of statutory plans.

The budget

4.5   The initial budget of £20,000 per annum in Hertfordshire/Barnet and £8,000 per annum in Havering, over a three-year period, was based on experience in the Uplands[3,4] and the Bollin Valley[8]. In Hertfordshire/Barnet, apart from allowances for inflation, to accommodate which the budget was increased to £23,000 per annum after the first full financial year, it proved to be the minimum sum that would support the most efficient staffing level in carrying out the experiment's objectives, where a project officer with two assistants made an effective operational team. In Havering, it was insufficient to support the employment of an assistant project officer and the purchase of a vehicle and it was increased to £10,000 in the second financial year to allow for the appointment

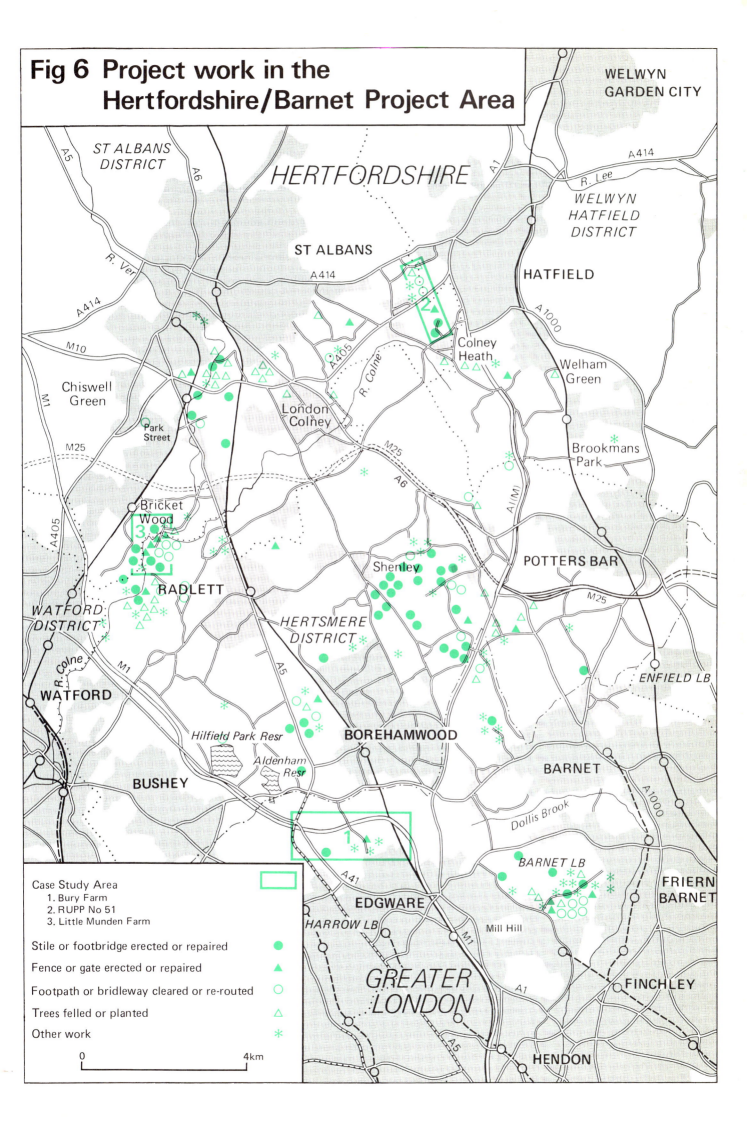

Fig 6 Project work in the Hertfordshire/Barnet Project Area

Case Study Area

1. Bury Farm
2. RUPP No 51
3. Little Munden Farm

● Stile or footbridge erected or repaired

▲ Fence or gate erected or repaired

○ Footpath or bridleway cleared or re-routed

△ Trees felled or planted

✳ Other work

0 _____ 4km

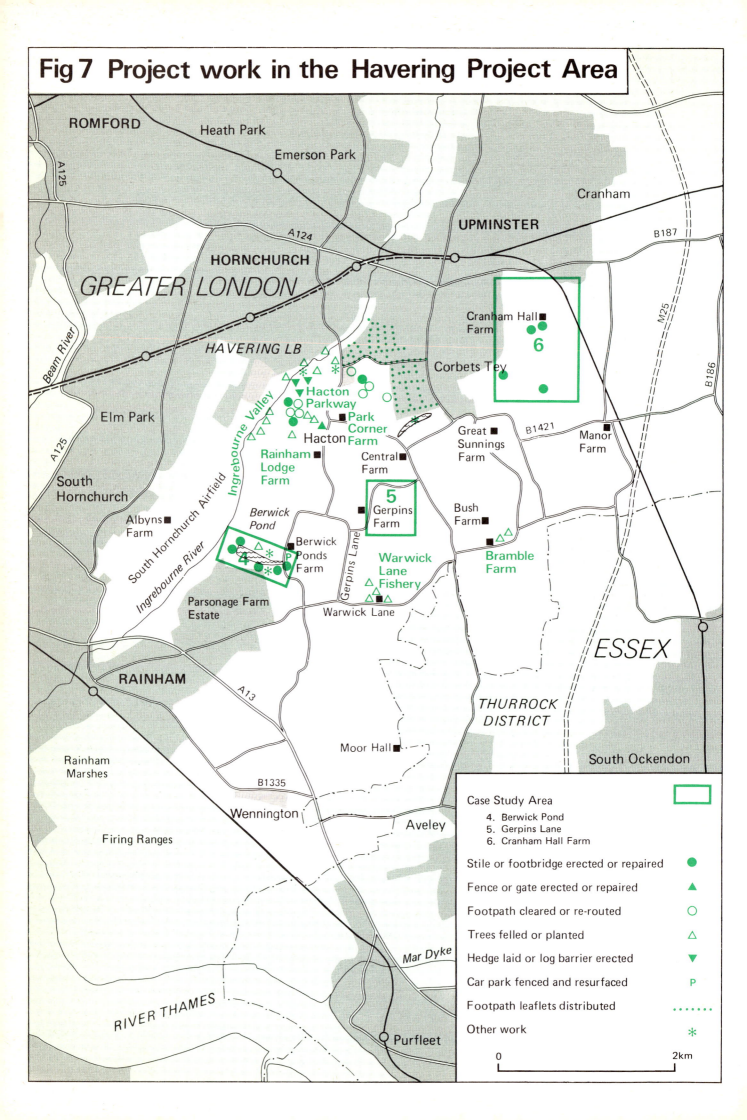

Fig 7 Project work in the Havering Project Area

ROMFORD
Heath Park
Emerson Park
Cranham
UPMINSTER
HORNCHURCH
GREATER LONDON
A124
B187
M25
B186
Cranham Hall Farm
6
Corbets Tey
HAVERING LB
Elm Park
Hacton Parkway
Park Corner Farm
Hacton
Great Sunnings Farm
B1421
Manor Farm
Central Farm
Ingrebourne Valley
Rainham Lodge Farm
South Hornchurch
Albyns Farm
5 Gerpins Farm
Bush Farm
Berwick Pond
South Hornchurch Airfield
Ingrebourne River
Berwick Ponds Farm
4
P
Gerpins Lane
Warwick Lane Fishery
Bramble Farm
ESSEX
Parsonage Farm Estate
Warwick Lane
RAINHAM
A13
THURROCK DISTRICT
South Ockendon
Rainham Marshes
Moor Hall
Firing Ranges
B1335
Wennington
Aveley
Mar Dyke
RIVER THAMES
Purfleet

Case Study Area ☐

4. Berwick Pond
5. Gerpins Lane
6. Cranham Hall Farm

Stile or footbridge erected or repaired ●

Fence or gate erected or repaired ▲

Footpath cleared or re-routed ○

Trees felled or planted △

Hedge laid or log barrier erected ▼

Car park fenced and resurfaced P

Footpath leaflets distributed ⋯⋯

Other work ✳

0   2km

of an assistant. The most important items of expenditure in both experiments (Tables 1 and 8) were staff salaries (including superannuation and national insurance contributions) and travelling and running expenses, particularly in the larger Hertfordshire/Barnet area.

4.6   In practice, it proved extremely difficult to co-ordinate the committee cycles of the various sponsoring authorities in order to grant additional funds and, although the total budget had been agreed by all the authorities at the beginning of the experiment, the Greater London Council could give no guarantee of increasing financial support until their annual budget had been approved each year. This uncertainty did not make the work of the experiment any easier, particularly for the project staff.

4.7   It was essential to have a great deal of flexibility in allocating funds as many of the project tasks were seasonal, e.g. tree planting and bridleway and footpath work: the costs of a 'permissive' bridlepath, for example, can affect project spending significantly, although as much as possible was done when the weather permitted. In addition, before the larger schemes were carried out, there were often protracted negotiations, the length of which was difficult to predict. As a result, the project staff found that towards the end of the first financial year more than £1,000 was left in each budget, because unsuccessful negotiation or adverse weather conditions had resulted in allocated funds being unspent. Annual budgeting, although essential in the forward planning of the work, imposes a constraint on a service which is responding to problems as they arise. The ability to carry over project funds from one financial year to another would have allowed for more flexibility. However, the money was spent on tools and materials, the storage of which proved a problem (paragraph 4.22).

4.8   The original intention of having project funds was as a pump-priming exercise. Many farmers and amenity societies made contributions in kind to the project work, e.g. the provision of manpower, tools, tractors and materials, but rarely, if ever, were direct financial contributions made.

4.9   Project funds were not intended to be used for work which was already the statutory duty of a local authority or government department, nor where grant aid was available from an official source. In practice, the cut-off point was difficult to define, especially in relation to rights of way. This did not give rise to any particular problems in a short-term experiment but there are long-term maintenance implications which, in a permanent countryside management service, will need to be clarified at the outset in the form of guidelines.

4.10   Large-scale projects became an integral part of the work. Although local authorities made financial contributions over and above the running costs of the experiment, e.g. in the provision of new bridlepaths in Barnet, or in the acquisition of land in Havering, the design of plans and delays in processing sometimes detracted from the image of the work of the experiment. Where other funds were not available, the project officer often went ahead, where practicable, using project funds instead, to demonstrate what could be achieved. The project officers also acted as catalysts in mobilising the wide range of statutory and special grants available, e.g. from the Countryside Commission and the Forestry Commission. In a long-term countryside management service, this role could be exploited further and should also involve private funds, both on an individual and an institutional basis.

Steering arrangements

4.11   In both the Hertfordshire/Barnet and the Havering experiments, major policy decisions and budgetary reviews were carried out at elected member level. Nominated members from each sponsoring authority met under the chairmanship of the Chairman of the Countryside Commission. Annual meetings were found to be sufficient. These Review Committees spent the morning touring the project area before discussing the development of the work in the afternoon. Member involvement, particularly in seeing practical results on the ground, was seen to be extremely important in continuing the support and priority given to countryside management by the sponsoring authorities and in ensuring that this was taken into account in the determination of related local authority policies and the allocation of resources.

4.12   The technical steering of both experiments was carried out at officer level and the full range of departments involved was represented (paragraphs 5.6 and 10.6), although the lack of involvement of the Hertfordshire Engineer in setting up this experiment was seen to be a disadvantage in the use of local authority equipment. The planning and land management staff were seen as essential representatives at both local authority levels. Co-option of other members is always possible and each area will have different arrangements. A representative of the National Farmers Union joined the Hertfordshire/Barnet Steering Group, but not the Havering Group, as the latter felt that there was a danger that other sectional interests would wish to be represented, thus making the Group too large although, so far, no pressure of this kind has arisen in Hertfordshire/Barnet. The importance of the project officer's liaison role with all the sectional interests who might otherwise have a claim to representation cannot be stressed too vigorously. It is essential that the Steering Group is kept to a manageable size so that it can perform its functions efficiently. Quarterly meetings were generally found to be adequate, although while a project is being set up, they will need to meet more frequently.

4.13   Although the project officers in each case were employed by one of the local authorities for administrative purposes, they were directly responsible to the Steering Groups, from whom they received their delegated financial and administrative powers. This served two purposes: it gave them flexibility and the ability to respond to problems quickly, and an independence from any particular authority, an essential element of countryside management. The role of the Steering Group is to voice the opinions of the local authorities and of the private interests and thus to reinforce at a policy level the independence of the project officer. The way in which the financial arrangements are made will be that most suitable to the employing local authority, but flexibility and the capability for instant purchase and an agreement to retrospective authorisation of expenditure must be guaranteed.

4.14   The project staff should identify themselves with the local area and the local community, acting as a bridge between them and the local authority. In the Hertfordshire/Barnet and Havering experiments, this was achieved by:

    i.   working directly to the Steering Groups, made up of many different departments and authorities, from whom they had delegated financial and administrative authority;

    ii.   living in the area and working from home, using experiment-headed notepaper with both their home and office addresses and telephone numbers, so that evening and weekend contact with local people was made easier—the normal administrative services provided by Hertfordshire County Council and the London Borough of Havering were used once or twice a week.

The Havering Project Officer moved right out of the area half way through the experiment and this made efficient working more difficult, thus demonstrating the importance of 4.14 ii.

4.15   In order to achieve the right blend of independence and responsibility, it is essential that the project officer should be absolutely reliable and that the sponsoring authorities should give him their trust—choosing the right man for the job is crucial. In order that the project officer can identify with the local community, it is essential that he lives in or near the project area. It is sometimes difficult to find suitable accommodation in the urban fringe and the sponsoring authorities should be prepared to give this aspect priority when initiating a countryside management service.

The project staff

4.16   The role of the project team is to make voluntary effort effective by matching the needs of the farmer, the resident and the visitor with the resources of the local authorities and the voluntary organisations. The small scale of the work involved warrants a different organisation from the normal local authority approach. Two levels of skills are required:

    i.   **The project officer** is involved in setting up the project work, negotiating with local authorities, amenity groups, landholders etc., the administrative work, giving lectures, and also has a role in the practical work, instructing staff and volunteers. He therefore needs administrative and negotiating skills; he must be able to put across his ideas both orally and in writing and generally get on with people; but he must not be averse to lending a hand with the practical work when he is needed.

    ii.   **The assistant project officers** organise the implementation of practical work, most of which takes place on farmland and involves day-to-day contact with farmers. Wardening and the supervision of volunteers and their training are also part of their job. Practical and communication skills are therefore essential, plus the ability to channel people's enthusiasms in useful directions. In both these experiments, sandwich students from Seale-Hayne College, where they were studying for an HND in Natural Resources and Rural Economy, were employed and made a very useful contribution, both in the practical work and in producing project work—Appendices 2 and 3 are examples of their work.

4.17   The number of staff employed will vary with the size of the area and the problems encountered. In Hertfordshire/Barnet, the large area and the complexity of the problems necessitated a team of three. Two assistant project officers were appointed to organise the implementation of the practical work, as two pairs of hands were required for many of the tasks, and this left the project officer to get on with the other aspects of the work. In Havering, one assistant was sufficient as long as two pairs of hands were available where the work contained a safety element, e.g. chain saw work.

4.18   The project staff in these experiments were on three year contracts which were under review for possible extension, but the lateness of the review led to uncertainty and loss of staff. Although for experimental purposes three years was a reasonable length of time, local authorities will be at a disadvantage unless they make full-time appointments for a long-term countryside management service, as they will find it difficult to attract the right calibre of staff who will have a long-term commitment to the job. Continuity will be lost and the commitment of the local community will be difficult to retain. It is now Countryside Commission policy to grant aid long-term local authority countryside management services[37]. If full-time appointments cannot be made, the staff contract should be for five years as a minimum, with renegotiation at the end of the third year. This will involve a long-term financial commitment from all concerned.

4.19   There is a need for an adequate career structure, with in-service training and links with colleges and universities. In these experiments, the link with Seale-Hayne College proved mutually beneficial and provided a source of suitable training material for the project officers of the future. The Countryside Commission and the Ministry of Agriculture, Fisheries and Food have important advisory roles in the establishment of suitable skills on a country-wide basis.

Equipment

4.20   One suitable vehicle, such as a Land Rover or a Ford Transit van, needs to be provided from the outset, although in an area as large as Hertfordshire/Barnet two vehicles may be justified. In Havering, the project staff provided their own vehicles. This was impractical, as the wear and tear involved in the transport of heavy tools and materials and in travelling over rough ground was generally unacceptable and the consequent service bills large. Tools and materials should be built up as and when necessary, although a full range of equipment would be impractical and uneconomic for a small operation. This dictates much hand rather than machine work, with a consequential lowering of productivity and, in routine tasks, of morale. In Hertfordshire, the county council has set up long-term countryside management services in two other areas of the county and in Phase Two of the Hertfordshire/Barnet experiment the sharing of jointly-purchased equipment is being tested.

4.21   In Hertfordshire/Barnet, the level of expenditure on tools and materials was sufficient to keep the two assistant project officers almost wholly engaged in practical work throughout the year. In the first 18 months, the majority of practical tasks was carried out in response to requests for assistance, so that very little of this work could be planned in advance and the costs of materials were usually very small, e.g. a stile would cost about £10 in materials at 1979 prices. As the experiment took on more development work, e.g. creating new bridlepaths, the costs escalated, e.g. the surfacing and ditching of one bridlepath cost more than £1,000 in 1978, and more sophisticated equipment was needed.

4.22   The supply of materials was determined by the available storage space. This supply was important to allow the staff to respond quickly to problem situations. The storage problem was never properly resolved in either of the experiments. Adequate storage facilities should be available at the outset, as this can dictate the amount of equipment held and the amount of materials that can be stockpiled, thus affecting flexibility of working. They need to be as central to the project area as possible in order to minimise staff travelling time and expenses. Storage of materials for particular jobs can be conveniently arranged near the site if relationships with the land occupiers are good.

4.23   Although it was understood that local authority departments would make their tools and machinery available for use by the project staff, the nature of the work made it difficult to plan ahead and they were seldom available when most needed, i.e. at weekends or in the evenings. In addition, they did not always have the appropriate equipment, e.g. ditching machinery. The equipment needed was usually hired as, even if the budget had been sufficient to allow acquisition, the great variety needed would have made purchase an uneconomic proposition, although additional funds would have been useful for the purchase of higher-quality materials. The output of practical work would have been considerably lower without the hire of contractors; some major works, e.g. bridleway clearance, would not have been possible in the time given. There is also some evidence to suggest that the farmers approved of the higher standards of work achieved by contractors compared with that of untrained volunteers and this was important in establishing the credibility of the experiments.

Maintenance

4.24   Maintenance became an increasing element in the work as the experiments proceeded. Many of the problems associated with footpaths, bridleways and small woodlands had arisen from lack of maintenance in the past and this had resulted in the need for major practical tasks, which themselves carry a future maintenance commitment which must be recognised at the outset. In the experiments, it was difficult to negotiate mainten-ance agreements with landowners as so many of the solutions were untested. Until the solutions had been proved successful, it was generally felt that their upkeep should be the responsibility of the project staff.

4.25   The maintenance of footpaths and bridleways is the responsibility of the local authorities but is very low on their list of priorities, e.g. one district council allocated only £3,000 in their 1979/80 budget for this purpose, but this did not even cover the cost of employing staff to do the work. They offered the money to the Hertfordshire/Barnet project officer to carry out the work but he turned it down on the grounds that the continuing commitment was a legal responsibility of the local authority and therefore outside the remit of the experiment. It was for the project staff to demonstrate by example how things could be done rather than to take on the local authority's ongoing work. If the project staff had committed themselves to extensive maintenance, they would not have had time to carry out any new works.

4.26 The work of the project staff has led to local expectations of high standards; in future countryside management work, adequate attention will have to be paid to the maintenance implications before the work is started. Responsibility for maintenance will have to be clearly set out and a commitment from the landowner, where appropriate, or from the local authority will need to be obtained beforehand, e.g. Hertfordshire County Council have made contractual arrangements for the maintenance of trees planted under their tree planting scheme, which has been running for two years and is working successfully. Where it is the responsibility of the local authority, a re-ordering of priorities for expenditure will have to be made in order to make finance and staff available.

4.27 Various solutions to maintenance problems are being tested and evaluated in Phase Two of the Hertfordshire/Barnet experiment. This will include the use of volunteers, e.g. where tree planting has been carried out by amenity groups it is expected that they will carry on a programme of management as part of a broader educational programme. In addition, various techniques for bridleway surfacing and different methods of tree maintenance are being tested to cut down on the amount of maintenance required.

Conclusions on the concept of countryside management in the urban fringe

4.28 The original aim of the experiments was to test the concept of countryside management in areas where severe urban fringe problems prevailed. Parts Two and Three of this report give a description of how this was carried out, indicating the problems encountered in each area and the strengths and weaknesses of the original approach. General conclusions will be given here, including those drawn from the evaluation research carried out during the experiments. As the work is still continuing, some of these conclusions will necessarily be interim ones.

The impact on the agricultural community[30]

4.29 The objective of both experiments in relation to agriculture was to help reduce the conflicts and irritants associated with farming in the urban fringe, particularly the problems of trespass and vandalism. The Havering area was much smaller and more compact than the Hertfordshire/Barnet area. There were only 18 holdings (including a vegetable packing station) in the Havering area, compared with 85 in Hertfordshire/Barnet. The small size of the Havering area made it more 'manageable' in one sense: it was much easier for the project officer to maintain contact with all the farmers. Not surprisingly, therefore, all the farmers in Havering were familiar with the experiment, if not by name, then at least in the person of the project officer. In Hertfordshire/Barnet, however, this proportion dropped to 78 per cent.

4.30 The average size of holding was larger in Havering than in Hertfordshire/Barnet and there was a larger proportion of holdings over 120 hectares. In Hertfordshire/Barnet the farmers gave the impression of being constrained by a whole range of problems—commercial, tenurial, the threat of development and recreation pressure—which restricted their freedom of action. In Havering, however, more farmers have turned the major benefit of urban fringe farming—proximity to the market—to much greater advantage, and a high proportion of them were commercially integrated with the nearby urban market by growing vegetables for sale in London. The nearest equivalent in Hertfordshire/Barnet would be horse-grazing, a much more passive and arguably less integrative activity than the daily contact with the urban world which vegetable production in Havering frequently demands. These differences are, of course, connected with the quality of the land but the farmers in Havering tended to be more market-oriented than their counterparts in Hertfordshire/Barnet.

4.31 The farmers in the two areas also had different attitudes towards their urban neighbours. The Havering project area was hemmed in on three sides by urban development and the very visible presence of large housing estates should have made problems relating to trespass and vandalism much more of a potential threat to the Havering farmers. However, they were much more sanguine about them than the farmers in Hertfordshire/Barnet. Only one of the Havering farmers thought that these problems were becoming worse, while the increasing pessimism of the Hertfordshire/Barnet farmers was quite noticeable, although there was no independent assessment of the actual incidence of disturbance.

4.32 Possible interpretations of this difference, none of which may be mutually exclusive, include the following:
  i. The pessimism of the Hertfordshire/Barnet farmers may reflect their greater economic marginality, with the urban population providing an easy scapegoat, while the production of high-value crops in the Havering project area means that crop loss or damage must be very severe before the economic viability of the farm is affected.
  ii. The smaller scale of enterprise in Hertfordshire/Barnet may make each act of trespass or vandalism appear more threatening and more economically damaging, so that isolated acts of vandalism are vividly recalled years after their occurrence, even though they may be atypical. The high proportion of livestock farming also makes the area more vulnerable to acts of vandalism than the predominantly arable farms of Havering.

iii. Havering farmers have become better integrated with the urban world and are therefore more tolerant of urban ways, regarding the problems as no more than the inevitable hazards of modern life, and have successfully accommodated themselves to them. The actual incidents of trespass and vandalism may be greater in number, but their symbolic significance to the farmer is reduced and resignation rather than outrage is the typical response.

iv. Farmers in Havering were concerned by the major problem of gravel extraction (paragraph 12.8) which was mostly absent from Hertfordshire/Barnet. Its visible impact loomed across the whole area and far outweighed the relatively minor damage caused by individual acts of vandalism. The activities of the gravel companies presented more of a direct threat to the commercial viability and economic livelihood of the local farmers, who felt helpless at the apparent failure of the planning system to control them or to enforce adequate restoration. Concern over these problems might also have had the effect of masking the farmers' other worries relating to the urban population, accounting for their less vehement condemnation of them.

4.33 The overall impression of the farmers' assessment of the effects of modern farming on the environment was that while in both areas they retained a certain amount of sympathy with conservation in principle, they were forced to override environmental arguments because of the demands of modern agricultural economics. There is some evidence that the experiments have shifted attitudes amongst those who have experience of project work, although the farmers themselves deny that the experiments have had much influence on them. Perhaps it would be unrealistic to expect such changes. A modestly-financed, small-scale and short-term experiment of this kind could not be expected to transform the outlook of long-established farmers with, apparently, intractable problems. Nevertheless, a majority of farmers were "favourable" or at least "accommodative" towards the local urban population, and a majority were also favourable towards the principle of conservation. This suggests a greater potential for success in the long term.

4.34 The experiments were viewed in very specific and pragmatic terms. Most farmers found the project staff helpful in dealing with specific irritants: footpaths, bridleways and stiles predominate. They were generally happy in accepting such a programme of "minor works" providing that someone else would do the work and foot the bill, although an encouraging proportion of them were prepared to consider management agreements over their land.

4.35 Pragmatic solutions to particular problems do not solve the broader issues but were nevertheless welcome to the farmers. The work carried out so far has removed the more obvious irritants and provided some marginal relief to some of the farmers. The project officers have already contributed to the feeling among many of them that at least someone cares about their problems, but probably more will need to be achieved in this area in the future than by a continuing programme of minor works. Given the farmers' sense of having been "taken over" by an urban population, this function should not be underestimated or neglected. In itself it may contribute towards some mutual accommodation in the two areas. In this wider sense, the potential of countryside management has hardly begun to be explored.

Recreation and access
4.36 The objectives of both experiments in relation to recreation and access were to increase facilities for informal recreation and to indicate solutions to the problem of illegal access onto private land. Work on increased provision concentrated on creating bridleways, particularly on publicly-owned land, in Hertfordshire/Barnet and on the use of derelict land in Havering. Priorities for future provision should be concerned with maximising the potential of existing sites, providing adequate circular routes for walkers and horse-riders and developing small-scale informal recreation facilities when and where opportunities arise, particularly along the immediate urban edge, thus helping to improve the overall environment.

4.37 It is clear that a number of conflicts arise in those areas where housing estates adjoin farmland (Appendix 1). Where rights of way provide easy access from housing areas onto farmland, the attitude of many of the residents using these sites is that the farmland is merely an extension of the estate from which they come and provides an attractive and convenient playground. There is evidence that considerable thought needs to be given to the design and layout of housing estates on the urban edge, particularly in relation to the provision of children's playspace and access points. An understanding of the needs of both the residents and the farmer is of paramount importance. The feasibility or desirability of 'buffer zones' might be considered in particular instances in the fringe areas where the demand for local open space is high and the problems of the farmer acute.

4.38 Involvement of schools in education programmes, including practical work, relating to the problems of unrestricted recreation access, and to the more positive aspects of appreciating the countryside could also be beneficial. This was borne out by a study that was made of the problems of trespass onto farmland in Havering. Where trespass did occur, it was usually due to ignorance rather than by design. Poor maintenance of signposts, fences, hedges and footpaths have meant that people are unaware that farmland is private property and has a productive rather than an open space function. In addition, what the farmer experiences as trespass and vandalism may mean adventure play to children, who have no alternative facilities and in many cases do not realise the significance of the damage they are causing.

More thought needs to be given to the design and layout of housing estates on the urban edge

This housing estate in Hertfordshire, built on compulsorily - purchased farmland, immediately adjoins remaining farmland with no 'buffer zone'

An acceptable 'buffer zone'? A closely-fenced public footpath in Hertfordshire is all that separates farmland and housing

4.39　Attempts have been made to increase understanding between the farmer and the urban community by means of project work on the ground but, unless the community is physically involved in these practical schemes, there will be little alteration in awareness or in their patterns of behaviour. Regular maintenance of clear boundaries between agricultural land and access land, so that urban children understand that there is a difference between the two, are important factors. Suitable alternative facilities e.g. for motorcyclists, must be provided. Long-term education should be through community involvement as well as through the normal structured channels.

4.40　Wardening has become an important aspect of countryside management work, particularly in areas like the Lake District, where visitor pressure is acute and where it is the only means of making contact with the public, who are mainly tourists from outside the area. However, in Hertfordshire/Barnet and Havering, the majority of the visitors live locally and the farms suffering from the greatest incidence of trespass are those adjacent to housing estates. There is a constant low level of use rather than a large number of visitors at any one time although the majority use the area in the evenings and at the weekends, a very different pattern from the seasonal peaking in a national park, for instance.

4.41　The surveillance role of wardening by project staff and volunteers in the project areas was carried out on farmland known to be under pressure, mainly on Sunday afternoons and occasionally on Bank Holiday weekends. While it proved a useful means of making contact with the public, it has not been possible to determine whether it has been successful in reducing incidences of trespass or vandalism. In the past, many farmers carried out their own supervision and were aware of when damage had been done and by whom. While wardening may, to a certain extent, relieve the farmer of the necessity for this task and thereby reduce his anxiety, the lack of manpower made a comprehensive coverage of the project area impossible—damage was as likely to occur in the evenings as at weekends. However, it provided an opportunity for project staff and trained volunteer rangers to familiarise themselves with the area and to note and respond to any changes. It also provided a useful contact with the public, but it is arguable that the project staff's involvement in environmental education and in training volunteers was equally if not more effective. A true evaluation is impossible on such minimal experience but, in a long-term countryside management service, early consideration should be given to wardening becoming an integral part of the service.

4.42   Many local authorities have set up ranger services. The ranger has functions additional to surveillance, including information and interpretive duties and site management. If a ranger service already exists in an area where a countryside management service is to be set up, relationships between the two need to be carefully established. Rangers, in their conventional role, are primarily concerned with visitors, but the interests of the two services overlap. To avoid unnecessary duplication and misunderstanding, especially with local people, ranger services and countryside management staff must be co-ordinated. A management plan would help to clarify their roles[38].

Landscape

4.43   Although much importance was attached to implementing new tree planting schemes in both project areas, particularly along the urban edge, little was actually achieved. The main attempts at landscape improvements in the initial stages were largely remedial—removing and replacing dead or dying elms and rehabilitating existing woodland. This was largely because, in responding to immediate problems, little time was left in a three-year period for any large-scale planting. The project staff showed by example what could be done with limited resources over a short period of time. However, the incremental effect must not be underestimated and, over a longer period of time and with the political commitment of the local authorities, much can be achieved.

4.44   The general attitude of the farmers towards landscape improvements varied from indifference to active support, although hedgeline plantings were not usually favoured. Owner-occupiers were usually easier to convince than tenants on privately-owned land. Local authorities, while not being opposed to landscape objectives, had done little to incorporate them in their management planning, so that totally inadequate resources were being committed to their implementation. A much greater impetus by the local authorities is required, particularly on land in their ownership, and the implementation of major tree planting schemes is of the utmost priority.

4.45   Horse-keeping may have an adverse effect on the landscape of an area through bad management and over-grazing of fields and a general lack of care for the land. The erection of stables, jumps and loose boxes can also have a considerable impact on the landscape. With the increase in standard of living and increased leisure time, more people can afford to keep horses. Horse-keeping has therefore become an increasingly profitable alternative to agriculture, particularly on land which is severed from the rest of a holding or is vulnerable to trespass and other urban fringe pressures. There is concern about the conversion of agricultural land to horse-keeping, particularly as this takes place outside the control of the planning system and entails a loss of agricultural production as well as creating problems for adjoining farmers. It is obvious that a more complex economic relationship exists between agriculture and horse-keeping than had been realised and more information is required. From the study carried out in the Hertfordshire/Barnet project area[39] it is clear that there are management problems which need to be overcome. The implementation of voluntary guidelines in Hertfordshire will be watched with interest.

4.46   In Havering, the scale of physical deterioration over large parts of the project area is the visible manifestation of the underlying conflicts over the present and future use of resources, which involve policy issues at a national and regional level as well as a local one. Countryside management, while adequate for problem exploration and small-scale solutions, was never meant to deal with issues on this scale. While much remains to be done at the practical level, a policy context must be developed and financial resources allocated before countryside management methods can be effective.

Rubbish dumping

4.47   Rubbish dumping still remains one of the most intractable problems in the urban fringe and one which neither of the experiments was able to solve. In Hertfordshire/Barnet, attempts were made to patrol a few well-known fly-tipping sites but, short of making a civil arrest, the only course of action open to the project staff was to report the vehicle licence numbers to the police. However, very often the police were unable to trace the vehicle and no action was taken. In cases that were taken up, the penalties were not sufficient to deter a repeated offence. In Havering, most farmers thought that the opening of a Greater London Council Civic Amenities tip in their area would help to reduce the problem, but farmers immediately adjacent to the site found that their problems were increased, particularly from wind-blown rubbish and from the activities of gypsies. Better management of existing sites and an increase in their number might help to improve the situation.

Gypsies

4.48 The aim of the legislation (Caravan Sites Act, 1968) on the provision of sites for gypsies was to prevent unauthorised camping in areas of open land in order to reduce nuisance to the local inhabitants, particularly those immediately adjacent to those areas, and to prevent harassment of the gypsies. However, unless sites make provision for the gypsies' activities, e.g. sorting scrap metal and grazing horses, as well as for their accommodation, the problems are likely to remain. The Cripps Report[40] drew attention to the possibilities for increasing provision for gypsy sites on the urban fringe, where both urban and rural areas are accessible. The two project areas would appear to provide such an opportunity.

The management of publicly-owned land

4.49 In previous Countryside Commission experiments[3-8], the aim has been to achieve public objectives on privately-owned land but, in London's urban fringe, there was such a large amount of publicly-owned land that the role of countryside management on such land in the Hertfordshire/Barnet project area was examined. There is evidence from both the Hertfordshire/Barnet and Havering experiments that the ownership and management of large areas of countryside around London provides the only real opportunity of achieving the objectives of the Green Belt along the inner urban edge on a strategic basis. The justification for public authorities continuing to hold this land and purchase new land in this location includes the following:

   i.   to demonstrate, by practical example, how land in public ownership can be managed so as to achieve a balance of activities and uses, agricultural, recreational, conservation and education, in fulfilment of Green Belt objectives;

   ii. to safeguard land from development and from being under-used or falling vacant in the hope of development;

   iii. to prevent the fragmentation of estates into small, uneconomic farm holdings;

   iv. to make available a large reserve of land for countryside recreation, both now and in the future;

   v.   to maintain and improve public access;

   vi. to perform an educational role in the provision of a wide range of countryside facilities, especially for the young and underprivileged.

4.50 With the move towards a more positive attitude to the maintenance of the Green Belt and the achievement of its objectives, it is increasingly important that publicly-owned land, particularly along the urban edge, is seen to set an example of how this can be carried out in practice. At the same time, especially in this time of economic constraint, a high priority is placed on obtaining a reasonable income and an adequate return on capital invested in the land. These two aims need not necessarily conflict; the report of the Management of Publicly-owned Land Working Party, set up by the Hertfordshire/Barnet Steering Group, gives some indication of how this might be resolved[34].

4.51 Although the report was specific to the situation found in Hertfordshire/Barnet, the problems and opportunities identified are common to all parts of the urban fringe, although at varying intensities. The conclusions that may be drawn from the report are:

   i.   there is a need to think about the better management of existing resources and their positive use, especially at a time of economic constraint, when a high priority is placed on the adequate return on capital invested in the land;

   ii. the local authorities have a special responsibility to set high standards as an example to others, particularly in showing how agricultural, recreation, conservation and education objectives can be reconciled;

   iii. there is a need for and there are positive advantages to co-operation across local authority boundaries and between departments within those authorities, in order to devise common management objectives and programmes of works.

4.52 In both experiments it was found that the achievement of countryside management objectives was most difficult on land in public ownership. The decision-making process in local authorities is protracted because it involves both officers and elected members and proposals have necessarily to be long-term, so that it is unable to operate in quite the same way as it can on private land in the short term, i.e. on a *quid pro quo* basis or by persuasion. In addition, in an urban-oriented authority, countryside objectives may be well down in the list of priorities for expenditure. However, countryside management can be useful in identifying areas where remedial action is necessary, or where policies can be implemented or changed. Phase Two of the Hertfordshire/Barnet experiment is examining more closely its role on publicly-owned land. Meanwhile, one of the main achievements has been to make the statutory land managers and the statutory planners work together, where liaison in the past has not always been adequate. The countryside management service must be able to call upon both planning and land management expertise and to work across ownership and administrative boundaries. Liaison is an essential element of the approach.

The use of volunteers

4.53 Various forms of manpower were used on an experimental basis (Table 7). The employment of volunteers has long been an accepted part of the countryside management approach in order to involve the local community, to help them develop a knowledge and understanding of their surroundings, to relate to schools' environmental education programmes, to keep costs to a minimum, and to provide an enjoyable and constructive leisure activity. However, the educational and social benefits of working with volunteers, particularly children and young adults, must be set against their general low rate of productivity and, in a three year experiment designed to produce results, productivity was an important factor.

4.54 There are relatively few organised volunteer groups active in the countryside, the most well-known being the British Trust for Conservation Volunteers. There are considerable advantages in employing skilled volunteers. They are capable of undertaking fairly arduous and difficult work and their standard of work is high because they are well-trained and highly motivated. No tasks have to be specially designed or organised because their range of skills allows them to adapt to any type of work. They complement the use of the lesser-skilled volunteers from schools and amenity groups.

4.55 A description of how use was made of volunteers in each project area is found in Parts Two and Three. The main limitation to using voluntary labour was the need to provide a high level of organisation and supervision. Secondly, volunteer labour was much better-suited to some jobs than others, e.g. tree planting rather than building a stile. Thirdly, consideration had to be given to their motivation, e.g. routine scrub clearance would not attract them for long periods. Two other points should be made—skilled volunteer labour, e.g. the British Trust for Conservation Volunteers, is not free, and there are costs attributable to the tasks carried out by unskilled volunteers in terms of supervision, hiring tools etc.[41] In devastated areas like part of Havering, a major transformation is not going to be achieved by an army of volunteers. However, the educational and social benefits are enormous and this highlights one of the fundamental differences between countryside management and conventional estate management: while cost-effectiveness is the all-important factor in the latter, countryside management is evaluated in terms of its overall benefits to the numerous competing interests in the countryside.

4.56 While the tendency was to make the best use of help from voluntary organisations and individuals, a careful and vigorous selection of tasks was undertaken before volunteers were approached. The relative merits of using machinery or professional expertise against voluntary, unskilled manpower was assessed before any project started and attempts were made to achieve a balance between them in the overall work of the experiments. Contractors were hired for some of the large-scale practical work. While using volunteers was very desirable politically, in that it enjoyed widespread public support and was a cheap method of labour, the pressure to achieve visually acceptable results in a short space of time was an equal consideration and the more 'professional' finish obtainable with machinery was considered important in convincing the farming community of the value of the work at the beginning of the experiment. Most of the major projects successfully combined the use of volunteers, the skills of the project staff and hired contractors (Appendix 2).

Educational benefits

4.57 In neither experiment was the educational role of the work fully exploited at primary and secondary level, largely because of the enormous amount of time needed in the organisation and follow-up work, particularly as a contribution from the teachers was not always forthcoming. The local education authority should be more closely involved with any long-term countryside management service. However, at the higher education level, involvement with the experiments has been mutually beneficial, both at the practical and the project level, and is something which should be continued and strengthened. Education in its broadest sense should include community involvement as well as the normal structured channels.

Publicity

4.58 Both experiments were publicly launched with a meeting to which local interest groups and members of the press were invited. Later, the apparent lack of knowledge displayed by people interviewed in the recreation site surveys[33] about the experiments was particularly surprising in Havering, where there had been a fairly wide coverage by the local press as well as some limited leaflet distribution. The Hertfordshire/Barnet project officer, however, had deliberately chosen not to publicise the work locally as he felt that this would be counter-productive in the establishment stage of the experiment. In Phase Two of the Hertfordshire/Barnet experiment, consideration is being given to publicity, particularly in order to get the local community involved.

4.59 A substantial amount of the time of each of the project officers was taken up in communicating the results of the experiments outside the project area, e.g. preparing and giving lectures, organising and guiding tours of the area, attending and addressing conferences and visiting national agencies. In this the Havering project officer spent almost as much time as the Hertfordshire/Barnet officer who had been employed specifically as the Countryside Commission's Countryside Management Adviser (paragraph 5.4). In this way, a lot of interest and discussion was generated on a national and an international basis.

Summary

4.60   The overall conclusion at this stage in the development of countryside management is that small-scale practical work can have considerable success in effecting local improvements, alleviating irritating conflicts and mobilising the resources of volunteers effectively. There is scope for much more of this type of work in the urban fringe.

4.61   Given the resources available and the complexity of the problems encountered, three years was not really long enough to test the countryside management approach to its full potential, particularly in its relationship with the planning process and its ability to change the attitudes of landowners, user groups and others involved in the area. The most difficult decisions for the project officers were choosing priorities when under pressure to achieve practical results. The solutions attempted therefore tended to be those which could achieve success in the short-term although an analysis of some of the intractable problems also took place. In a permanent countryside management service, priorities would be different and the more difficult problems might be tackled on a long-term basis.

4.62   The experiments were not always successful in solving problems in areas where the causes of those problems were more fundamental and where there was a need for a comprehensive planning and management framework for countryside management to be effective. Good examples are provided in Appendices 1 and 6. However, in other cases, information gained through the small-scale approach led to the identification of opportunities for major improvements: e.g. the acquisition of land in Havering by the local authority (paragraph 13.18) illustrates how project staff, while making practical improvements on the ground, can also identify opportunities and outside sources of finance and inform the local authority, or other responsible organisation, who can then, given the political will and the financial resources absent in the case studies in Appendices 1 and 6, take advantage of them. This in turn provides the context in which practical improvements on the ground can be carried out. This process improves the flexibility and responsiveness of local authority planning and management. An appreciation of the underlying conflicts serves to put the small-scale countryside management approach into perspective but by no means invalidates it. It can be both an effective response to small-scale problems and a successful method of problem exploration.

4.63   Local authority support and co-operation from the landowners and land managers is crucial if countryside management is to function successfully; and their attitudes and action following consideration of this report will be important. The adoption by the local authorities of positive policies for the planning and management of landscape, recreation and conservation and their implementation on land in their ownership will mark a change in attitude which will have been stimulated by the operation of a countryside management approach. A pre-requisite for an effective response along the immediate urban edge, particularly in areas like parts of Havering, will be a willingness to face up to the fundamental problems and, given the political will, to make the necessary financial investment for the development and management of a valuable environmental resource.

The future of countryside management in the urban fringe

4.64   The experiments in Hertfordshire/Barnet and Havering were chosen as representing a different range of the more complex problems in London's urban fringe. Methods of improving the urban fringe landscape and of making it more accessible to the urban population were tested while, at the same time, measures to assist in the reconciliation of recreation and agriculture were promoted. They started with the same set of objectives (paragraph 3.2) and, in response to the different problems encountered, developed along very different lines. The original approach of small-scale management began to develop a more clearly-defined role in relation to the planning policies and resource management of other organisations working in the same area, e.g. local authorities, Ministry of Agriculture, Fisheries and Food, Department of the Environment, water authorities etc.

Organisation

4.65   The future development of countryside management in the urban fringe, where the public authorities are closely involved with planning and management and where much of the land is publicly-owned, is inextricably linked with the local authority framework, which can provide the context in which the methods are able to work. However, the project officer can respond quickly to things which are both of a smaller scale and changing on a much shorter time-scale than those in which the machinery of public authorities can normally operate. The essence of countryside management is the apparent independence of the project team and its ability to short-cut local authority procedures and to achieve effective results more quickly. These are essential pre-requisites to its success and there are still some doubts about the ability of the project team to be integrated into the local authority system without losing its autonomy and speed of action. A comprehensive planning and resource management framework to which it can relate must be developed at the same time.

Costs

4.66   These experiments have shown that value for public money can be achieved in countryside management through simplified administration, delegation of authority to the project officer, and the use of voluntary and other available labour. However, it must be noted that although the costs of particular tasks have been shown (Chapter 13 and Appendices), there is insufficient information on the costs of running a long-term countryside management service in a local authority. It is hoped that this will be available soon from current research and the implementation of such services by local authorities such as Havering.

Response to countryside management

4.67   In both project areas, a longer-term commitment after the initial three-year experimental phase was considered. The sponsors agreed that the Hertfordshire/Barnet area was too large to test the approach on a comprehensive basis, particularly in its application to publicly-owned land, within such a short time-scale. At the same time, Hertfordshire County Council were developing a permanent countryside management service along different lines in two other parts of the county and it was not clear how the work of the experiment would be integrated into the local authority framework, particularly across the Hertfordshire/Barnet boundary. The experiment was extended for a further three-year period, with the emphasis on the relationship of countryside management to the management of publicly-owned land and a remit to look at the long-term administrative framework most suitable for a permanent service. It was particularly encouraging that the district councils in Hertfordshire felt that the benefits of the work were such that they agreed to become additional financial sponsors.

4.68   In Havering, there was a fundamental need for the organisations with responsibilities in the area to develop a comprehensive planning strategy which would provide a context within which countryside management techniques could be applied. The Countryside Commission took the initiative and began negotiations with the Greater London Council and the London Borough of Havering for a second five-year experimental phase, involving a major input of resources, and the participation of both the Ministry of Agriculture, Fisheries and Food and the Department of the Environment, so that possible solutions to the problems identified could be tested in the context of an overall approach, linking planning and management. Unfortunately, the economic climate resulted in the withdrawal of funds by the Countryside Commission and a valuable opportunity of developing the planning/management relationship was lost. However, a permanent countryside management service is being set up by Havering to cover the whole of its Green Belt area to tackle the small-scale conflicts and to be complemented by the development of a local planning context.

4.69   There have also been encouraging responses to our earlier work. The work of the Upland Management[3,4] and Bollin Valley[8] projects has been taken over by the local authorities, and other schemes have been initiated in other areas. Structure plans have acknowledged the need for countryside management, as have the Countryside Review Committee, who saw countryside management as "the best means of tackling resulting conflicts . . . on an area basis",[24] a view shared by the Advisory Council for Agriculture and Horticulture in England and Wales[23], with particular reference to the urban fringe. The Standing Conference on London and South East Regional Planning (SCLSERP) was sufficiently convinced of the conciliatory role of the countryside management approach to recommend its adoption by all the Green Belt authorities[14].

Future assistance

4.70   The Countryside Commission are initiating and assisting further projects in the urban fringe but are exercising caution in commending the approach in a complex area like parts of Havering, where problems beyond the scope of countryside management have been identified which cannot be solved in the absence of a local planning context, within which all government agencies, both local and central, would have a framework in which to improve their management of existing resources. There is no doubt, however, that given this context, countryside management can reduce small-scale conflicts effectively and economically. In Havering, the project officer developed further the planning liaison role—he worked within an evolving planning context which he was helping to develop, as well as to implement. This two-way flow of information proved to be invaluable and its further development in the permanent countryside management service being set up by Havering will provide some interesting lessons.

4.71   In both experiments, there were pressures on the project staff to carry out comprehensive area-wide solutions, e.g. landscape improvements but, given the time-scale and the experimental nature of the project, this was never a practical possibility. However, in a long-term countryside management service, such an achievement, by means of a management plan and a positive contribution from all local authority departments, should be the objective, with a commitment to the long-term maintenance of the works carried out. It may be much later, in fact, that the real benefits of countryside management work can be evaluated.

Overall evaluation

4.72   The aim of the experiments was to test a means of injecting into the management decisions of both private and public landowners greater concern for the landscape and for access for recreation, while safeguarding areas in primary productive use. In these two project areas, they have shown by example what improvements can be achieved which people can see and experience. Equally rewarding in the short time available have been some changes of attitude in the local authorities and in groups and individuals whose interests were previously considered to be irreconcilable. Much has been learned and remains to be learned. It is too early to recommend a method if, indeed, an activity depending essentially on simplicity and flexibility merits such consideration. However, the Countryside Commission now believe that countryside management offers real benefits to the following:

    i.   Local planning authorities—by
      a. providing a means of putting broad planning objectives into practice;
      b. clarifying countryside issues and identifying the need for planning initiatives, particularly in urban-oriented authorities, and thus making an input into Local Plans;
      c. encouraging a multi-disciplinary approach to countryside issues;
      d. providing a closer link with local farmers and communities on matters of landscape conservation and recreation provision;
      e. highlighting problem areas where action needs to be taken.

    ii.   Farmers—by
      a. helping to reduce the problems caused by visitors on their land;
      b. wardening and providing other facilities for recreation;
      c. assisting with conservation work;
      d. providing a general source of advice and liaison.

    iii.   Local residents and amenity and recreation groups—by
      a. helping to reduce the impact of visitors in the area;
      b. enhancing the local landscape;
      c. providing an opportunity for their involvement in the conservation management of the area;
      d. providing well-managed informal recreation facilities in an attractive environment without conflicting with other uses of land in the area;
      e. providing information about what other organisations are doing in the area.

    iv.   Visitors—by providing well-managed informal recreation facilities in an attractive environment without conflicting with other uses of land in the area.

4.73   In areas where there are underlying strategic land use and land management problems and where the overall climate is one of uncertainty and speculation, its potential is limited and, in areas like parts of Havering, there is even a danger that the resulting cosmetic improvements, by obscuring the real nature of the problems, might be counter-productive, unless they are put in the context of a much more comprehensive planning and management approach. In both project areas, it was found that lasting practical improvements could best be achieved on sites where there were no underlying strategic problems, e.g. Rainham Lodge Farm in Havering (paragraph 13.6 *et. seq.*) and Little Munden Farm in Hertfordshire/Barnet (Appendix 3) illustrate how effective small-scale countryside management can be in a situation where co-operation is forthcoming from the land-owner, and where uncertainty of land use and land tenure does not exist. Appendices 1, 4 and 6 illustrate very clearly how countryside management can respond successfully to day-to-day problems and can point the way to the solution of large-scale problems outside its own remit, but implementation then depends on political will and the allocation of financial resources. Countryside management was never meant to be a substitute for adequate policies for planning and strategic land management.

4.74   Both experiments in their different ways developed away from the original objectives of problem identification and resolution to the creation of opportunities within a comprehensive planning and management framework. Many aspects of the countryside management approach have been successful and cost-effective but, in order to maximise the benefits, they cannot go on working in a vacuum or on a short-term basis. The range of problems found in the urban fringe cannot be solved either by countryside management or planning alone—what is needed is a comprehensive approach in which countryside management plays a vital role.

PART TWO

HERTFORDSHIRE/BARNET URBAN FRINGE MANAGEMENT EXPERIMENT

Chapter 5: Organisation of the Experiment

Introduction

5.1 The Hertfordshire/Barnet Green Belt Management Experiment started in October 1975 with the appointment of a project officer for an initial period of three years, which was later extended for six months so that the first phase ended at the same time as the Havering experiment, on 31 March 1979. The sponsors were the Countryside Commission, Hertfordshire County Council, the Greater London Council and the London Borough of Barnet, who contributed 75 per cent, 10 per cent, $7\frac{1}{2}$ per cent and $7\frac{1}{2}$ per cent of the funds respectively.

Objectives

5.2 The objectives of the experiment were outlined in paragraph 3.2. Later, more specific objectives were defined by the project officer:

Agriculture	i. to help reduce the conflicts and irritations associated with farming in the urban fringe;
	ii. to identify derelict or underused areas and to encourage their restoration to viable agriculture or other acceptable uses;
Countryside recreation	iii. to improve existing facilities and identify further needs for all forms of countryside recreation;
	iv. to co-ordinate practical field work by voluntary organisations in the improvement of recreation facilities;
Wildlife and landscape	v. to secure visual improvements by screening or removing eyesores, removing accumulated rubbish and encouraging its proper disposal;
	vi. to improve small woodlands and other natural cover;
	vii. to improve the farmed landscape by amenity planting of trees and hedgerows.
Education and advice	viii. to pass on information from the work to the Countryside Commission and local authority departments participating in the experiment, to local amenity and voluntary societies, local education establishments and other local authorities and organisations expressing interest in the work.

The project staff

5.3 Because of the large area involved and the complexity of the problems, it was decided that skills were needed at two levels: the project officer would have administrative skills and would be responsible for conducting negotiations, liaising with local authority officers and other organisations and managing the project, including the other project staff; two assistant project officers, with practical skills, would be appointed to organise the implementation of practical work, as two pairs of hands were required for many of the tasks and this left the project officer to get on with the other aspects of the work.

5.4 The project officer appointed had previously worked in a similar position in the Bollin Valley experiment and because of this experience was given the post of Countryside Management Adviser to the Countryside Commission, in order to distinguish his seniority and the nature of his role. This meant that the Countryside Commission could utilise up to 25 per cent of his time on advisory work, both to the Commission and to other local authorities and organisations interested in countryside management. He also had a general supervisory role, which was never clearly defined, in relation to both the London experiments. For ease of comparison, the term project officer is used for both experiments throughout the report.

Steering arrangements

5.5 Overall policy guidance and budget review was provided by the Chairman's Review Committee. This was a committee of elected members nominated by the sponsoring local authorities and also by the district councils of Hertsmere, St. Albans, Welwyn/Hatfield and Watford in Hertfordshire and was chaired by the Chairman of the Countryside Commission. It met on an annual basis.

5.6   Technical supervision of the work of the experiment was provided by a Steering Group and although, for administrative purposes, the project officer was employed by Hertfordshire County Council, he was directly responsible to that Steering Group. It was made up of officers from the sponsoring authorities and from the district councils of Hertsmere, St. Albans, Welwyn/Hatfield and Watford in Hertfordshire and chaired by the Principal Assistant County Planning Officer of Hertfordshire County Council. It met on a quarterly basis. Its functions are outlined in paragraph 3.18 and its responsibilities delegated to the project officer in paragraph 3.19.

5.7   Membership of the Group consisted predominantly of representatives of the respective planning departments, but also included one representative from the Hertfordshire County Council Land Agent's Department (although not initially), one each from the Parks and Land Agent's Departments of the Greater London Council and one from the Countryside Commission. In addition, each Hertfordshire district nominated one representative to cover the Treasurer's, the Secretary's and the Leisure Departments. The project evaluator also attended. Towards the end of the initial three-year experimental phase, a member of the National Farmers Union, (agreed by the Country Landowners Association), was co-opted onto the Group to provide the experience of a working farmer.

5.8   Day-to-day line management contact was with the Principal Assistant County Planning Officer (as Chairman of the Steering Group), in co-ordination with an officer of the Countryside Commission. The project officer also developed close working relationships with the other departments of the local authorities concerned.

Resources

5.9   Table 1 shows the experiment's annual expenditure during the first three and a half years. The initial cost was estimated to be £60,000 over three years, arranged as three annual allocations of £20,000, with no provision to carry over unspent funds. This would have involved the individual sponsoring authorities in the following expenditure per annum (approximately): Countryside Commission £15,000, Hertfordshire County Council £2,000, Greater London Council £1,500 and London Borough of Barnet £1,500. No allowances had been made for inflation so, after the first complete financial year, the sponsors approved an increase to £23,000.

Table 1: Expenditure

	1/10/75–31/3/76	1/4/76–31/3/77	1/4/77–31/3/78	1/4/78–31/3/79
	£	£	£	£
Staff salaries	3,966	14,466	15,873	15,009
Travelling and running expenses	363	1,894	2,858	2,586
Tools and materials	930	3,119	3,790	2,870
Administrative expenses	39	521	442	299
Vehicle purchase	2,164	—	—	1,243
Total	**7,462**	**20,000**	**22,963**	**22,007**

5.10   The most important item of expenditure, which absorbed 70 per cent of the budget, was staff salaries, including superannuation and national insurance contributions, for the project officer, the two assistants, and a sandwich student. The fairly high expenditure on travelling and running expenses which covered the project officer's essential car allowance and the running and maintenance of two project vehicles, a Land Rover and a van, partly reflected the special role of the project officer (paragraph 5.4) and his attendance at seminars and conferences, and partly the size of the project area.

5.11   Only a small proportion of the budget was spent on tools and materials, the sum varying from year to year and proving difficult to estimate in advance. Over the three and a half years, a number of basic tools (chain saws, spades, hammers, scythes etc.) was acquired for the use both of the assistants and of the volunteers, and a supply of readily-available materials (timber, nails etc.) was built up. Over the same period, approximately £3,000 was spent on hiring contractors and plant to carry out specialist work, e.g. ditching and dredging, where local authority machinery was unavailable or unsuitable.

5.12   The staffing level of three, plus a sandwich student from Seale-Hayne College for six months of each year, allowed wardening and volunteer supervision to be carried out at weekends. They were often assisted by volunteer help, including trained volunteers from the Hertfordshire Voluntary Ranger Service and the British Trust for Conservation Volunteers and from pony clubs, as well as young offenders with Community Service Orders. Contractors were also used.

5.13   The project officer was provided with office accommodation in Hertfordshire County Council's Planning Department, where administrative and secretarial services were available. However, so that he would be more easily identified with the local community, and also to accommodate farmers and voluntary organisations who would wish to contact him outside office hours and at weekends, it was agreed that he should work from home, using a special experiment letterhead, giving his home address and both home and office telephone numbers.

Chapter 6: The Project Area

Introduction

6.1　The project area is situated to the north of London, in the Metropolitan Green Belt (Figure 1). It includes 130 sq. km. of rural land, 110 sq. km. in the southern part of Hertfordshire and 20 sq. km. in Barnet, stretching from the urban edge of Mill Hill, Totteridge and Edgeware in the south and bounded by the densely-populated Hertfordshire towns of Potters Bar, Hatfield, St. Albans and Watford (Figure 2), but excluding the built up area of Borehamwood.

6.2　The main geographical features are the Dollis and Totteridge Valleys in the south and modest ridges at Shenley, Elstree, Totteridge and Mill Hill. The rivers Ver and Colne flow through the project area. Geologically, it falls within the London Basin and lies on the fringe of the great London Clay belt. The soil is therefore mainly heavy clay, but with extensive gravel deposits in the Vale of St. Albans. The majority of the land is classified as Grade 3 by the Ministry of Agriculture, Fisheries and Food.

Land use

Table 2: Land use in the project area

Land use	Hertfordshire (110 sq. km.)	Barnet (20 sq. km.)
	%	%
Agriculture	66.0	65.4
Recreation	7.4	32.4
Woodland	6.6	*
Urban	6.0	—
Institutions	5.2	—
Mineral extraction	3.3	—
Utilities	1.0	—
Airfields	1.0	—
Others	3.5	2.2

*Woodland in Barnet is included under 'Agriculture' and 'Recreation'.

Agriculture

6.3　The major overall land use is agriculture (Table 2). The arable farming of the northern section merges gradually into the horse-grazing which is characteristic of the heavier soils in Barnet, with occasional dairy herds scattered throughout. Small-scale, intensive production of pigs, poultry and beef cattle also occurs and the special market conditions of the urban fringe are reflected in farm shops, self-pick crops, hay production and grazing lets for horses. There are 85 farms in the area, with a mean size of 98 hectares. In Hertfordshire, 64 per cent of the farmers are tenants, reflecting the large amount of land in the ownership of public and private estates and institutions. A further 10 per cent are owner-occupiers, the rest are of mixed tenure.

Recreation

6.4　Much of the area given over to recreation in Hertfordshire (Figure 4) is in the form of private golf courses with only one third of these allowing unlimited public access. The figures also include several areas held by private angling clubs, private playing fields and other facilities for private use. The high proportion of recreation land in Barnet includes woodlands, most of which are privately-owned and managed. So, although the project area seems to be well-provided with open land, very little of it is available to the general public.

6.5　The major areas used for informal recreation are Scratchwood Open Space (40 hectares, including woodland), Moat Mount Open Space (22 hectares including woodland), Aldenham Country Park (72 hectares including 12 hectares of water) and Colney Heath (28 hectares). These, with the exception of Colney Heath, are all owned and managed by the respective local authorities and are all in the south of the project area; Colney Heath is owned and managed by the Parish Council.

6.6   Although there are other isolated pockets of common land and informal parkland within the area, these are usually not more than about 0.4 hectares in size. In addition to this, there are some areas, not designated as recreational open space, where limited *de facto* access is tolerated, e.g. nature reserves and worked-out gravel pits.

6.7   Public access into the countryside is via the extensive rights of way network (Figure 9). While there is still a reasonably comprehensive network of public footpaths in varying condition, allowing access onto private land, there has been a steady decline in the number of bridleways in the area over the last 20 years or so. Many routes have been severed or totally lost with the development of the major road and rail network radiating out of London. The problems that this has created are discussed in Chapter 7.

Woodland

6.8   The distribution of woodland throughout the project area is shown on Figure 4. About 80 per cent of the woodlands in the Hertfordshire area were surveyed by the County Council in 1975. This showed that there were few major woodlands, over half being less than 2 hectares in size. These were mainly broadleaved woodland with the larger areas either conifer plantations or managed for commercial timber. Nearly all the conifer plantations were managed under Forestry Commission dedication and approved schemes. The small, mostly broadleaf, woodland was not managed for shelter, game or timber, which would yield a financial return, and much was in a deteriorating condition and in need of management for amenity purposes. In Barnet, the woodland figures are included under "Agriculture" and "Recreation" in Table 2, but the major woodlands are associated with the public open spaces in the area and amount to about 48 hectares, whereas only about 1 per cent of all woodland over the project area as a whole is in public ownership. From the wildlife point of view, the oak and coppiced hornbeam woodlands were found to be the most valuable as they exhibited a wide diversity of species and ecological habitats. Like other parts of the country, the project area has been badly affected by Dutch elm disease.

6.9   The Hertfordshire Survey estimated that some parts of the project area, particularly in the centre, where arable farming predominates, had lost about 80 per cent of their hedgerows. The area to the east of Borehamwood was the least affected, where traditional pasture land remained. Hedgerows bordering old bridleways and parish boundaries were usually the oldest and the richest in wildlife. Elm was one of the most important

Dutch elm disease has destroyed this line of hedgerow trees near Mill Hill

hedgerow trees until Dutch elm disease took its toll and this may also have had the effect of increasing hedgerow removal. Of those that remain, many have been allowed to grow rank and weak, as maintenance is carried out less frequently because they no longer serve an agricultural function and the costs of labour are so high.

Settlements

6.10   Radlett is the major built-up area to be found within the project boundary. However, the majority of the population live in the many small villages scattered throughout the area. Much of this settlement was established before full planning control came into force and recently only in-fill development has been granted planning permission.

Communications

6.11   The area is fragmented by the major roads radiating from London, the M1, A1, A41, A5 and A6; by the north orbital routes, A405 and the proposed M25; and the main railway lines out of St. Pancras and Kings Cross (Figure 2). It is estimated that the area contains at least 50 km. of trunk roads and a substantial network of B and other minor roads.

Institutions

6.12   The large number of institutions occupying land, 5.2 per cent of the project area, is accounted for mainly by hospitals, either private hospitals or psychiatric institutions. One per cent of the area is occupied by schools, mainly private, and colleges of education.

Mineral extraction

6.13   Mineral extraction, while considered to be a temporary land use, accounts for 3.3 per cent of land in the area, but relates only to the Vale of St. Albans, which is rich in gravel reserves. There are no gravel workings in the Barnet part of the project area. Hertfordshire County Council's policy is not to exceed the 3 million tonnes per annum of sand and gravel presently extracted and to "seek to secure effective control over the longer-term use of land for mineral extraction and appropriate after-use of the sites", including restoration to agriculture and water-based recreation. At the same time, the construction of a rail depot for aggregates at Radlett will help to supply local needs by importing aggregates, particularly for the construction of the proposed M25 motorway.

Utilities

6.14   An assortment of utilities, which are not appropriate to open countryside but require a location near to the population they serve, is found in the project area: rubbish tips, electricity sub-stations, power lines, pipelines etc., all of which are typical uses of land in the urban fringe.

Land use change

6.15   Surveys carried out by Hertfordshire County Council and the London Borough of Barnet reveal that there have been both losses and gains of agricultural land since the 1950s and suggest that there is continuing pressure for urban development in spite of the general presumption against development in the Green Belt. During the last 30 years, at least 560 hectares of agricultural land, affecting 36 farmers, have been lost, mainly to housing, industry, gravel extraction and the development of the extensive road network. Land which has been returned to agriculture has been mainly restored after gravel extraction. A survey of horse-keeping[39] shows that since 1972, 80 hectares have been converted from agriculture to horse-keeping.

6.16   The pressure for development is greatest along the urban edge and it has often been in the form of extensions to established uses rather than new building sites. There is considerable pressure for change of use from agriculture to other acceptable Green Belt uses and the development of a number of local leisure facilities has been allowed. This pressure is reflected in the speculative value of land, at upwards of £6,250 per hectare for agricultural land without planning permission in October 1978, and is well illustrated by the case study of Bury Farm in Appendix 1.

Land ownership

6.17   The sponsoring authorities alone own more than 25 per cent of the land in the project area as a whole (Table 3 and Figure 8). Much of this land was acquired as a result of the 1938 Green Belt (London and the Home Counties) Act, in order to preserve open space and farmland from urban development. The majority of this land is in agricultural use and leased to farming tenants although the woodlands have remained largely under the direct control of the local authorities.

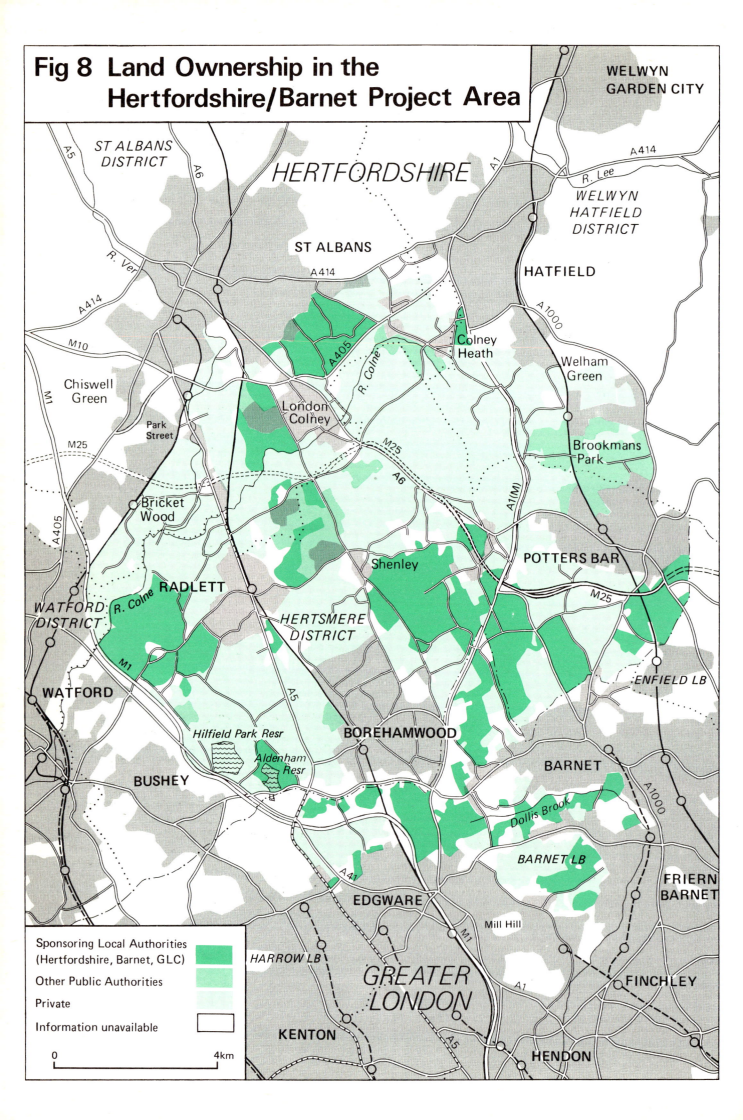

Fig 8 Land Ownership in the Hertfordshire/Barnet Project Area

WELWYN GARDEN CITY

ST ALBANS DISTRICT

HERTFORDSHIRE

WELWYN HATFIELD DISTRICT

ST ALBANS

HATFIELD

Colney Heath

Welham Green

Chiswell Green

Park Street

London Colney

Brookmans Park

Bricket Wood

POTTERS BAR

RADLETT

Shenley

HERTSMERE DISTRICT

ENFIELD LB

WATFORD DISTRICT

R. Colne

WATFORD

Hilfield Park Resr

Aldenham Resr

BOREHAMWOOD

BARNET

Dollis Brook

BUSHEY

BARNET LB

FRIERN BARNET

EDGWARE

Mill Hill

FINCHLEY

HARROW LB

GREATER LONDON

KENTON

HENDON

Sponsoring Local Authorities
(Hertfordshire, Barnet, GLC)

Other Public Authorities

Private

Information unavailable

0   4km

Table 3: Land owned by the sponsoring local authorities in the project area

Sponsoring authority	Public open space		Agricultural holdings		Woodlands	
	Area (ha.)	% project area	Area (ha.)	% project area	Area (ha.)	% project area
Greater London Council	—	—	1,280	9.6	—	—
Hertfordshire County Council	194	1.5	1,019	7.7	72	0.5
London Borough of Barnet	236	1.8	458	3.4	48	0.4
Total	**430**	**3.3**	**2,757**	**20.7**	**120**	**0.9**

Table 4: Land ownership in the project area

Land ownership	% Project area	
	Hertfordshire (110 sq. km.)	Barnet (20 sq. km.)
Large agricultural estate owners, leasing farmland to tenants	21.5	20.0
Owner-occupiers of farmland	20.5	5.0
Local authorities	18.5	33.0
Other private landowners	11.0	6.0
Gravel companies	4.5	—
Owners of private recreation facilities	4.0	5.0
Universities, private schools and institutions	4.0	1.0
Department of Health and Social Security	3.5	—
Public utilities	1.0	1.0
Official receiver	1.0	—
Unknown ownership	4.5	27.0
Urban areas	6.0	2.0

Administrative pattern

6.18   The pattern of administration is complex, with a range of central and local government organisations applying their own policies in the project area; on any one issue, many of their departments may be involved. At central government level, the Departments of Environment and Transport, the Ministry of Agriculture, Fisheries and Food, the Countryside Commission and the Nature Conservancy Council have all been involved with the experiment to a greater or lesser extent. At county level, many different departments in Hertfordshire County Council and the Greater London Council have responsibilities in the area, the latter owning and managing 1,280 hectares of agricultural land within Hertfordshire's boundaries (Figure 8). The second tier of local government involves the London Borough of Barnet and four district councils—Hertsmere, St. Albans, Welwyn/Hatfield and Watford—and within each of these, the Planning, Highways, Parks, Recreation, Estates, Education, Legal, Treasurer's and Environmental Health departments have had some involvement with the experiment. In addition to these, other statutory bodies, such as the health authorities, the water authorities, the Electricity Board etc., and the parish councils all have interests in the area. With such a complex pattern of policy-making over such a small area, it is not surprising that confusion and contradictions occur.

Chapter 7: Analysis of the Problems

Introduction

7.1   An initial analysis of the problems in Hertfordshire had been carried out by the County Council prior to the inauguration of the experiment; similar work, including a farmers' survey and a land use survey, was carried out by the London Borough of Barnet in their area after the experiment had started. A detailed analysis of individual problems was continued by the project staff at ground level and students were encouraged to focus their project work in the area, e.g. Appendices 2 and 3. Some aspects of the work were taken up by the Steering Group, which appointed two working parties to look at the particular problem of bridleways (paragraph 8.13) and the opportunities presented by the public ownership of land (paragraph 8.18). The evaluation exercise provided survey material—including a recreation survey[33], a horse-keeping survey[39], and a neighbourhood study[42]—as well as monitoring the experimental work.

7.2   The previous chapter has shown that the urban fringe is an area where complex systems of inter-relationships exist. Conflicts of interest and competition for land create problems. The problems are seen differently by the various interests in the urban fringe and can be defined as conflicts of land use or of land management, but often these are inter-related and one can be the symptom or the cause of the other. The source of all the conflicts is the competing demand for a limited and therefore valuable resource.

7.3   The following problems were identified in the project area:

i.   problems for farmers—trespass and vandalism, partly as a result of the lack of alternative recreation space, and the competing demands for agricultural land;

ii.   problems of access—the lack of a co-ordinated bridleway network, integrated with riding areas, resulting in the misuse of footpaths and adjoining land by horse-riders, the over-use of certain bridleways, and conflicts between horses and pedestrians;

iii.   the lack of recreation facilities;

iv.   the deterioration of the landscape, particularly as a result of Dutch elm disease and the removal of hedges, with consequential effects on wildlife;

v.   the uncontrolled behaviour of gypsies without adequate site provision;

vi.   indiscriminate rubbish dumping.

Problems for farmers

7.4   Some 93 per cent of the farms are well within 1.5 km. of an urban area and are therefore very accessible to a large population and influenced by urban activities. The problems as understood by farmers in the project area fall into two categories:

i.   those which disrupt farming operations, e.g. trespass, vandalism, livestock worrying;

ii.   those which make farming impossible, e.g. competing demands for agricultural land for development such as for roads, housing, gravel working.

7.5   A survey of the recreational use patterns in the project area[33] showed that, while urban intrusion onto farmland for recreational purposes was not intense, it was fairly consistent over any period of time. Much of this was legitimate, i.e. on recognised footpath or bridleway networks, but enough was illegitimate to create an anxiety, almost a fear, in the farming community, about the potential effects of such access. Other types of intrusion were more tangible and had immediate effects on farming, e.g. illegal gypsy camp sites, fly-tipping and unauthorised shooting and poaching.

7.6   Most farmers suffer trespass problems in one form or another. Taken in isolation, these problems may not appear to be very significant but, when combined together over a period of time, they represent a serious physical constraint to the farmers, who have to spend time and money repairing any damage caused, often unwittingly, by the urban population. Table 5 summarises the types of problems resulting from trespass that affected farmers in Hertfordshire.

Table 5: Problems of trespass in Hertfordshire

Problem	% farmers affected
Trespass	88
Trespass resulting in damage	78
Rubbish dumping	71
Horseriding	36
Gypsies' activities	26
Theft of crops and livestock	16
Unauthorised shooting and poaching	14
Motorcycling	11

7.7   Damage to fences, gates and water supplies were the most common incidents although, occasionally, burning down barns and tampering with expensive machinery also occurred. The most serious damage and the highest levels of trespass (200 cases or more per year per farm) were found on farms immediately adjacent to the

Making a footpath where there isn't one, near Borehamwood

urban edge. Farmers attributed most of this to the local children, although evidence shows that local adults were also sometimes responsible. The recreation survey[33] indicated that 90 per cent of the people using farmland, including those on the footpath network, came from adjacent housing areas.

7.8   Livestock worrying, particularly by dogs, is another major problem. Sheep are particularly sensitive, 12 out of 41 farmers interviewed having given up keeping sheep for that reason[30]. Only three farmers still keep sheep in the area. The effects of worrying of cattle are reduced milk yields, abortions, serious injury and sometimes death. The most serious recent incident involved a group of cattle escaping through a damaged fence onto the M1, when a motorist was killed as well as the cattle, and the farmer was left with long-term insurance problems.

7.9   While some of these problems are caused by deliberate acts of vandalism, many are the results of ignorance and not all public access onto farmland results in trespass. There is an extensive rights of way network through the project area but, in the mind of the farmer, this encourages people to wander onto his land, particularly when the paths are in poor condition (Appendix 2). Many farmers therefore prefer not to have footpaths or bridleways on their land and even take active measures to obstruct them, although this is rare in the project area. The problems of access are discussed in paragraphs 7.13 *et seq.*

7.10   Intense development pressure can result in land going out of agricultural production altogether and 560 hectares of the project area had disappeared over the last 30 years. Development often causes fragmentation or severance of a holding which can make it non-viable as a farming enterprise, although one farmer said that the creation of a road through his farm had actually reduced his trespass problems because the new road had acted as a barrier to urban intrusion. Sometimes the loss is only temporary, as with gravel extraction—although previous crop yields are rarely achieved, the record of restoration in the project area has been good compared with Havering (paragraph 12.8).

7.11   Green Belt designation does not imply a guarantee against development, particularly in the urban fringe. Evidence of land being held in the hope of development is found, e.g. repeated planning applications for change of use at Bury Farm, Barnet (Appendix 1). Land is also lost to roads, e.g. one farmer lost 40 hectares for the widening of the A6; another farmer lost land for the widening of the A1, which also resulted in over half his farm (18 hectares) being isolated from the rest and this Grade 2 land has now been developed as playing fields.

7.12   Effects of such land loss can be drastic. It has been estimated that a 30 per cent reduction in acreage on a farm of 40 hectares can result in a fall in net income of 70 per cent[43]. In addition to the physical and economic effects, the threat of land loss has a psychological impact. It creates uncertainty in the area generally and influences the management decisions of both tenants and owners. The farmer becomes reluctant to invest in the land or in new machinery and this can lead to a general decline in both farming output ('farming to quit') and in the appearance of the landscape, through lack of maintenance of hedges, ditches etc. Another response along the urban edge is often either to sell or to lease out small pieces of land, e.g. for horse-grazing, which in land use terms is classified as agriculture and therefore does not need planning permission as a change of use to recreation.

Problems of access

7.13   Many footpaths and bridleways in the project area have been severed by the construction of major roads and there are also examples of the status of rights of way changing at the administrative boundaries, e.g. from footpath to bridleway in Arkley Lane. The resultant network (Figure 9) does little to provide for the needs of the walker or rider, both of whom require circular routes that link with the transport system. Work carried out by farmers on field enlargement, consistent with modern farming methods, particularly on arable land, can cause problems, as the removal of traditional landscape trees and hedgerows to facilitate the use of heavy mechanical equipment has left many rights of way following non-existent field boundaries, with old stiles and signposts disappearing through lack of maintenance. The farmers argue for a rationalisation of an outdated system, while the rights of way societies argue for its preservation. At the same time the local authorities do not allocate funds to maintain the full network and many paths fall into disuse. As a result, many arguments are now being waged over the exact status of routes shown or not shown on the County Definitive Map, which is presently under review.

7.14   In Hertfordshire, the amenity societies have responded to the conflicts over rights of way by forming a Federation of Rights of Way Societies, involving the Ramblers' Association and the British Horse Society and other organisations connected with rights of way, including the local landowners. The need to reconcile the interests of land occupiers and those seeking access for the public was embodied in a Rights of Way Charter which they asked all public authorities and all persons who have vested interests in the land and its resources to acknowledge and respect.

7.15   The problems of horse-riding arose from the large number of horses in and around the project area and the inadequate provision of riding facilities, particularly bridleways (Figure 9), e.g. there were only five (including two very short sections) Roads Used as Public Paths (RUPPs), which were badly-drained and overgrown, in the whole of Barnet's Green Belt. This had the following effects on farmers, riders and walkers:

    i.   Farmers: many farmers in the project area had complained to the project officer of horses trampling on their crops and of gates being left open as riders were forced to ride on fields to avoid damage to themselves and their horses on the badly-maintained bridleway surfaces.

    ii.   Riders: the horse-riders were concerned about the lack of bridleway networks in the area. In order to use the few badly-maintained existing routes, riders had to negotiate busy and hazardous trunk roads, such as the A1 and A41, to reach the open countryside. Many road verges were obstructed with fly-tipping, potholes and the planting of trees, posing additional dangers. Inadequate maintenance and bad drainage, together with heavy use of the bridleways, were responsible for the deterioration of bridleway surfaces and consequent trespass onto farmland.

    iii.   Walkers: walkers are legitimate users of bridleways but bad surface conditions made them unsuitable for walking.

7.16   The current pressures are the result of a number of factors which have been outlined in paragraph 2.18. From data provided by the British Horse Society and the Barnet Riding Establishment Owners Association, it has been estimated that more than 2,600 horses are stabled in the project area and its immediate surroundings, including the boroughs of Harrow and Brent. In fact over 3,000 horses actually use the area for riding and the Greater London Recreation Survey[44] showed that this activity had further potential for growth.

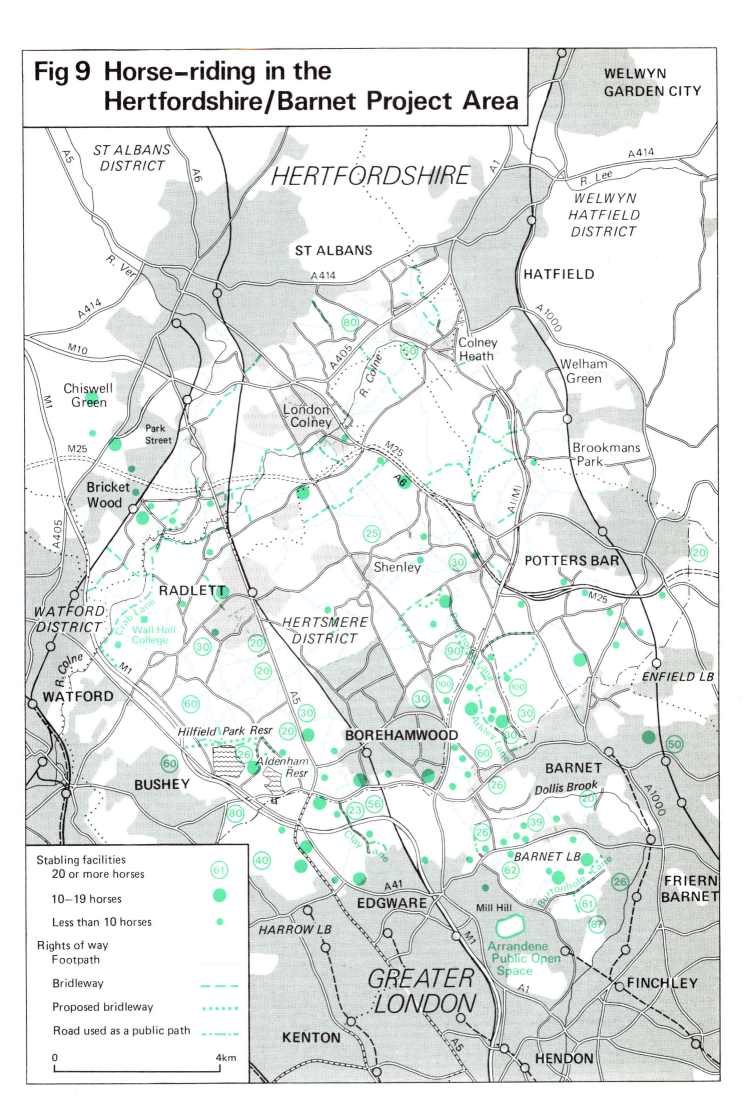

Fig 9 Horse-riding in the Hertfordshire/Barnet Project Area

Stabling facilities
20 or more horses
10–19 horses
Less than 10 horses

Rights of way
Footpath
Bridleway
Proposed bridleway
Road used as a public path

0   4km

Insufficient bridleways force horse-riders onto the roads, causing danger and frustration. Galley Lane on the Hertfordshire/Barnet boundary

7.17   Figure 9 illustrates the distribution of these stabling facilities and it can be seen that most of them are concentrated in the southern area. Most of the stables accommodate fewer than ten horses and frequently fewer than five, while only 14 stables have 50 or more horses. Some of these stabling facilities are riding schools, requiring planning permission, and they own the horses and sometimes provide paddocks and indoor riding facilities. However, many stables provide only livery facilities to private horse-owners, with minimal grazing and riding areas, if any, and this puts additional pressure on the rights of way system and on adjacent farmland. The 'rent a box' system, where the horse-owner hires a loose box, does his own stable management and buys fodder, either from the proprietor or on the open market, is increasing and its distribution and standards of management are difficult to control because it is subject neither to planning legislation nor to welfare controls under the Riding Establishments Acts of 1964 and 1970.

7.18   Figure 9 illustrates the small number of existing bridleways in the project area and the only Public Open Space which provides for riding is Arrandene, in Barnet, outside the project area. The main demand for horse-riding appears to be generated from London, and the British Horse Society points to a demand for bridleways that will take riders out of London, away from the busy and dangerous main roads, into the Hertfordshire countryside. In addition, the local riding stables and schools need many varied circular riding networks near the stables. Some stables have negotiated their own 'permissive' paths with adjacent landowners but few farmers are sympathetic to the needs of riders because of the problems previously encountered.

7.19   These problems have been exacerbated by the poor condition of existing bridleways. The Highways Act 1959 gives the Highway Authority a discretionary duty to maintain them; at a time when resources are limited, this is given a low priority, resulting in bad surfaces, bad drainage—particularly on the London Clay in the south—and overgrown routes. Old bridleways have thus fallen into disuse and the legal status of many of them is in doubt, e.g. some footpaths used to appear as bridleways on older maps. There is obviously a need to determine their legal status and to improve their management as well as to provide new routes. A further complicating fact was that the two organisations responsible for grant-aiding recreation facilities, the Countryside Commission and the Sports Council, did not have defined policies on provision for horse-riding, although the Countryside Commission now has a grant-aid policy on bridleways[45].

Recreation provision

7.20   The project area is not generally well-provided with Public Open Space and the larger sites, Scratchwood Open Space, Moat Mount Open Space and Aldenham Country Park are concentrated in the south (Figure 4). The recreation survey[33] gave the general impression that all these sites had the potential to absorb more visitors. In fact, the overall level of recreation use in the project area was lower than expected. The pattern of distribution appeared to be one of dispersal rather than concentration on these sites, which were relatively

Plenty of space for more visitors

At Scratchwood Public Open Space, the siting of this picnic table is hardly inviting

Moat Mount Public Open Space is sited on the busy A1, but with no parking facilities

unknown even to local residents, difficult to find and not easily accessible. Smaller public open spaces adjacent to housing areas, while few in number, were comparatively more popular and, where boundaries between these areas and farmland were clearly defined, they appeared to serve as useful 'buffer zones' to protect the agricultural land from urban intrusion.

7.21   The two principal owners of Public Open Space in the project area are Hertfordshire County Council (194 hectares) and the London Borough of Barnet (236 hectares). Hertfordshire County Council adopt a low key policy, the aim being to keep the areas as natural as possible, thus ensuring access for quiet, passive enjoyment of the countryside, with adequate car parking and provision for safety and for maintenance of the areas in a clean and tidy condition. They have resisted any promotion of the use of Aldenham Country Park. The London Borough of Barnet had no specific recreation policy in the project area.

7.22   The Greater London Council do not own any Public Open Space within the project area but there are opportunities for recreation, mainly in the form of farm open days, on their Green Belt estates. In addition, two of their privately-leased golf clubs have provision for public play. While other statutory bodies own a substantial amount of land in this area, e.g. the Department of Health and Social Security, the Thames Water Authority, the Electricity Board etc., none of this is open to the public, except on rights of way.

7.23   While a few people use the limited number of recognised recreational facilities in the area, there is a significant use of private land for informal recreation. Some farmland adjacent to housing areas, where there were few play areas and little open space in general, was used by large numbers of school-aged children, who saw it as an extension of the open space associated with the housing, regardless of ownership or rights of access. The recreation survey[33] thus supported the assumptions on trespass and demonstrated a need to control or manage public access in those areas where it was unauthorised and damaging.

7.24   In general, informal recreation activity is widely dispersed throughout the project area and is of a relatively low intensity so that, although recreational pressures are not heavy, they are fairly persistent. Much of the use is by local residents out for a short stroll or exercising the dog and few visits are part of an organised day trip into the countryside. Many people preferred to walk to local sites rather than to get into a car and travel further afield and public transport, where it existed, was rarely used. Opportunities, therefore, exist for attracting a greater number of people and from a wider catchment area to the facilities in the project area and this has implications for their management.

7.25   Private recreation areas played an equally important part in the overall pattern of recreational use of the area, with an apparent high demand for exclusive rights to land for fishing and shoots etc. by many clubs and societies, although the area is less well-served in facilities for casual day fishing. The specialised requirements of motorcyclists, campers and model aeroplane fliers were poorly-served in relation to the potential sites in existence, e.g. old gravel pits.

Landscape and conservation

7.26   The landscape in the project area is generally of a reasonably high quality but has no outstanding features, although an area around Shenley and Ridge has been designated as an Area of Great Landscape Value by Hertfordshire County Council, where special development control measures will apply. However, there is a general decline in the overall appearance of the landscape, which will need careful maintenance and the creation of new features if its quality is to survive. In addition, there are areas immediately along the urban edge where urgent remedial action is required.

7.27   There are two major causes for the deterioration in the landscape adjacent to the urban areas. The first is the uncertainty surrounding the future use of the land, making capital investment and long-term maintenance less economically worthwhile, and even, in some cases, the deliberate running-down of an area in the hope of

Motorway construction left a cul-de-sac road inviting rubbish dumping, which adds to the general uncared-for appearance of the landscape

increasing the possibility of development. The second is the rapid change in land ownership and the fragmentation of holdings, which again decreases the likelihood of a long-term management approach. The problems associated with trespass, vandalism and rubbish dumping add to the general uncared-for appearance of the landscape, which is dominated by the large scale of the urban development, generally badly-sited and poorly-designed.

7.28   The grazing of horses in the project area presented different problems and the local authorities, in particular, expressed concern about the loss of land for food production and the consequences for the landscape and wildlife. It has been suggested that horse-keeping is associated with farm fragmentation. Once a farm is sold off into smaller plots of land and used for grazing horses it is no longer a viable agricultural enterprise and the land is then threatened with a further change of use. It can also lead to abuses such as the application for planning permission for a dwelling on 'agricultural' grounds. The problems have been recognised by the Standing Conference on London and South East Regional Planning who proposed discussions with the Department of the Environment and the Ministry of Agriculture about amendments to the 1947 Agriculture Act and the 1971 Town and Country Planning Act, in which the grazing, keeping and breeding of horses, other than those needed for agricultural purposes, would be deleted from the list of permitted changes of use currently included within the definition of agriculture in the General Development Order.

7.29   It has been estimated that about 800 hectares, representing 6 per cent of the project area, is kept for horse-grazing and this represents 10 per cent of all agricultural land in the area, without including land used for growing hay for the horses, so that the total amount of land involved in horse-keeping may be much higher[39]. Since 1966, nine farms, mainly dairy farms, have been converted to horse-keeping and, in addition to this, nearly 50 per cent of all the farms in the project area have some land grazed by horses. While some of this conversion has been for horse-breeding, the majority has been for recreational purposes. This change in agricultural patterns had not previously been revealed in any land use statistics because such a change does not need planning consent.

7.30   Land grazed by horses and the stables, jumps and loose boxes associated with it tends to detract from the appearance of the landscape. Unless integrated with a farming enterprise or as part of established riding schools and stables, it is generally poorly managed with unkempt hedges and selective grazing. This tends to be on those small parcels of land formed when agricultural holdings are split up and which are then rented or bought by individual horse-owners.

7.31   In the project area the landscape has also been allowed to decline where the land use and land ownership patterns are relatively stable. The major elements in the landscape are the woodlands and hedgerows and these have suffered from the effects of Dutch elm disease, old age and little or no management, as they no longer have an agricultural function. Many internal hedges have disappeared with the advent of modern farming methods and the remaining boundary hedges are usually trimmed mechanically as the cost of labour is so high. While this may not damage the hedge, it does little for its appearance and may be detrimental to wildlife. Ponds form another diminishing feature.

7.32   The numerous small woodlands which form an important element in the lowland landscape, are not usually included in the farm tenancies and many are too small to be managed commercially for timber or game. They are largely unmanaged and deteriorating through over-maturity or uncontrolled access. Although grants exist for the management of woodlands, the cost can be prohibitive as they do not include the costs of removing the dead or dying trees and the timber value of these trees cannot always compensate for the costs of felling them. Even on publicly-owned land, resources are not available to reverse the process of landscape decay, e.g. in 1979 the Greater London Council had a totally inadequate tree planting budget of £2,000 to cover the whole of the Metropolitan Green Belt area and £1,000 for the replacement of dead elms. The decaying woodlands are still attractive features in the present landscape and are of considerable benefit to wildlife. Their renovation involves substantial clearing and replanting which are both costly and of long-term benefit. The landowners often prefer the present modest amenity value to harsh action in pursuit of a long-term aesthetic and financial gain.

7.33   Old lanes, which are represented by a variety of unsurfaced tracks varying between 3 metres and 9 metres in width, are usually hedged on both sides. Several are old drovers' roads and many are of great antiquity. Their hedges provide lines of continuous vegetation which form distinctive features in the landscape, but they are deteriorating both in access and landscape terms through lack of maintenance, e.g. Crab Lane and Packhorse Lane have become like elongated copses.

7.34   Landscape management was considered a priority for the experiment, not only because of the visual benefits that this would produce, but also because concern was expressed about neglect of the woodlands leading to their invasion by ecologically less-desirable plant and tree species, thus reducing the existing wildlife interest of many areas.

Gypsies

7.35   Gypsies were considered to be a particular problem to farmers in the project area. Those farmers with land adjacent to the main roads, the A1, A6, A41 and the A405, were most seriously affected. Farmers had a very clear idea of the problems caused by gypsies: fences and gates removed and burned; illegal grazing by goats and horses; rubbish dumped in fields is a risk to machinery and livestock and encourages vermin; access roads and gateways obstructed by caravans, cars and rubbish; crops trampled and stolen; ditches blocked by rubbish and water polluted by waste; and the visual effects of what was left behind. Hertfordshire County Council has three official gypsy caravan sites, housing only 120 families, to cater for the 300 gypsy families living within its boundaries; the London Borough of Barnet has none.

An unofficial gypsy encampment at Park Street roundabout

Rubbish dumping

7.36   The fly-tipping of household waste and garden rubbish and the dumping of builders' waste occurred indiscriminately in woodlands, fields, lanes and gateways and caused a severe problem throughout the project area.

Chapter 8: The Approach

Introduction

8.1   The essence of the countryside management approach, which has been described in detail in Chapter 3, is to place a small group of people with practical skills, a knowledge of agriculture and land management and limited financial resources, into an area to identify and to alleviate land management problems. This chapter describes the methods used in the Hertfordshire/Barnet experiment and how they were developed and refined in the light of the complex problems encountered.

The learning phase

8.2   The initial phase of the experiment was essentially exploratory, identifying the problems and the resources in the area and forging essential links with the great variety of organisations active in the area, e.g. National Farmers Union, Country Landowners Association, officers of local authorities, amenity societies, schools, voluntary groups etc. While many of the contacts made were at an official or a formal level, others were largely or wholly personal, helped by an ability to work from home and outside office hours. These introductory meetings served two purposes: to identify and understand the problems and conflicts from different points of view and to explain the aims of the experiment. Many led to regular attendances at meetings, e.g. Hertfordshire Federation of Rights of Way Societies, thus consolidating the initial contacts made.

8.3   Although the local authorities had carried out surveys before the experiment started, the contacts with organisations and individuals uncovered a wide range of issues, not all of which fell within the experiment's remit, so priorities for action had to be carefully selected. These discussions were an essential part of both the early and the continuing work of the experiment. At first the project officer met with mixed reactions. Not all organisations welcomed this new initiative: some were very suspicious, while others were sceptical about what could be achieved. However, expectations were often high and the pressure on the project officer to establish his credibility and to achieve results was considerable.

8.4   Assessing priorities for action was a particularly difficult task because so many interests were in conflict with each other and all were competing for scarce resources. Those chosen initially were, for various reasons, different from priorities that might have been chosen by a long-term local authority countryside management service. Within a relatively short time, project staff were expected to produce examples of problem-solving work, which was seen as a major part of the experiment. Pressure came from the organisations working within the area as well as from the sponsoring authorities, who were anxious to see evidence of the productive use of their resources. Important early factors included accessibility to the work sites by visitors, as well as visually dramatic results that would lend themselves to putting across a message photographically. Illustrated talks and tours of the area became an essential means of achieving the information and education objective (paragraph 3.2).

8.5   The essential priority, therefore, in the early work was to establish credibility by achieving results on the ground. Solving a variety of problems was the obvious course although, inevitably, a number of issues arose which, for financial or political reasons, was not capable of solution in the short term, e.g. Bury Farm (Appendix 1) and the creation of a comprehensive bridleway network. Maintaining a balance between the various competing interests was crucial and solutions providing benefits to all parties concerned were highly desirable. The *quid pro quo* principle was established from the outset although, in the short term, works were often carried out which were primarily in the interests of the private land occupier in order to create a climate in which, in the long term, amenity improvements in the public interest could be more favourably considered on his land.

Small-scale practical work

8.6   A series of small-scale, low-key practical works was carried out throughout the project area (Figure 6). These were mainly at the suggestion of the landowner or of the amenity societies, but all were tasks that would not involve lengthy negotiations with many interested parties so that all could be carried out quickly and effectively, e.g. stile improvements, bridge-building, scrub clearance, fencing, waymarking, on footpaths and bridleways. Specific examples included fencing repairs at a farm to reduce damage caused by motorcyclists, the replacement of a stile that had been damaged by vandals, improvements to a popular walk across two farms between St. Albans and Park Street, and the erection of stiles and a small footbridge on two farms to reduce trespass. A summary of the practical work carried out up to 1980 is contained in Table 6.

Table 6: Summary of completed tasks

Task	Number of projects
Stiles/bridges/fences/gates	65
Scrub clearance	33
Tree planting and maintenance	28
Tree felling and surgery	12
Rubbish clearance	10
Bridleway: ditching/grading/surfacing	9
Woodland management	5
Nature conservation	5
Recreation play areas	2
Education	4
Total	**173**

8.7   Within three months of the appointment of the assistant project officers which marked the start of most of the practical work, project work had been carried out on 11 different farms, 14 tours of the area had been made with visitors, 63 meetings with farmers, local authorities, schools and amenity societies had been held to discuss problems and a wardening service had been set up. In addition to the assistant project officers, the Hertfordshire Voluntary Ranger Service and the national branch of the British Trust for Conservation Volunteers had been involved in several tasks and, at the request of the British Horse Society, members of a local pony club had helped to clear a bridleway of scrub.

8.8   Once the experiment's effectiveness and rapidity of response was recognised, requests from farmers and amenity societies for solutions to small-scale problems intensified considerably, so that this aspect of the work became self-generating and, although larger schemes later took an increasing amount of the project staff's time, it remained a necessary and important part of the work throughout the three and a half years. The staff's ability to respond quickly lay in their easy access to resources: the ability to spend up to £300 on any one task, the store of tools and materials and the practical skills of the staff. However, not all the problems were solved with practical work and the liaison and mediation role of the project officer became increasingly important, e.g. in rights of way disputes and in the development of education programmes with local schools.

Small-scale improvements were carried out quickly and effectively: a new stile, waymarking and improved path north of Borehamwood

8.9   The experiment was able to provide fairly simple answers to irritating problems and this, together with introductory meetings with different interest groups, represented an initial learning phase: the project staff were learning to understand the problems from all angles and to appreciate the different viewpoints expressed and also to identify the opportunities available to fulfil the experiment's objectives, which had by that time been made more specific (paragraph 5.2), to emphasise those aspects of the work which were not solely to do with problem-solving.

Analysis of larger-scale problems and opportunities

8.10   Obviously not all the problems identified could be solved quickly or by small-scale practical work alone. The project officer had to determine what involvement countryside management could have in the resolution of the more intransigent problems and to explore opportunities for the development of major schemes that could be implemented in the long term and this became an integral part of the approach in dealing with the problems of the area. The important feature of the work was its ability to take a comprehensive view of all the complex inter-relationships between activities, land uses and policies within an area and, in achieving this, the expertise available in the various local authority departments made a vital input, as did the long-term and intimate knowledge of the area provided by the local voluntary organisations.

8.11   As the work developed, therefore, priorities changed and the balance of the work altered. Several factors affected this. Each sponsoring local authority expected a reasonable proportion of the practical work to be carried out in their area so that, in the short term, priorities were not necessarily linked to the greatest problems in the worst areas. The local planning authorities were anxious to see their policies being implemented and to obtain information to feed into their monitoring exercises and for the formulation of new policies. The work of the experiment made a positive contribution to both, albeit on an *ad hoc* basis.

Horses

8.12   One of the first priorities identified by the project staff was to try and resolve the conflicts between farmers, horse-riders and footpath users, by testing methods of improving conditions on existing routes, by opening up overgrown lanes, by up-grading some footpaths and by suggesting suitable new routes and negotiating 'permissive' agreements, all of which would help to create a viable network that would cut across country and take riders away from busy trunk roads. Examples of the approach used are given in the case studies (Appendices 2 and 3) which illustrate how an overgrown bridleway was opened up as part of a wider network of rides and how a 'permissive' ride was created, in an attempt to rationalise a rights of way system that was causing problems for farmers, riders and walkers. Both the reinstatement of existing routes and the creation of new ones involved a large proportion of the time and financial resources of the experiment.

8.13   In order to make action more systematic, the Steering Group set up the Bridleways Working Party to examine in more detail the problems associated with the large number of horses using a diminishing and deteriorating bridleway network, and to suggest comprehensive solutions capable of implementation by the project staff at the practical level and by the local authorities at policy level. The local horse-riding organisations as well as the local authorities were represented on the Working Party, so that its recommendations would be acceptable to all concerned, the project officer representing the practical farming interest.

8.14   The Working Party made recommendations on the creation of bridleway networks, the maintenance of existing bridleways and the control of riders and riding establishments. They identified several areas where increased bridleway provision would be both desirable and possible (Figure 9). Some of the proposed routes, co-ordinated with exercise fields, were on publicly-owned land, the major proposals being across Public Open Space, so that additional conflicts with the farmers could be avoided. However, this was met with some scepticism by some local authority officers, who felt that riding was equally incompatible with other recreation users, safety being one of their main concerns, although they admitted that segregation from the rest of the public would alleviate those fears. These routes were referred to the Management of Publicly-owned Land Working Party (paragraph 8.18) for their consideration and recommendations for future action. It was hoped that the local authorities, given their commitment to recreation provision, would agree to the proposals on their land, both to help in reducing the pressure on existing bridleways and to set an example to private landowners.

8.15   The report of the Bridleways Working Party[36] was endorsed by the Steering Group and referred to the local authorities and other organisations concerned for their approval and action on the policy issues. Their reactions are outlined in Chapter 9. The project staff then concentrated their practical effort on increasing bridleway provision, by testing low-cost means of opening up overgrown lanes (Appendix 2) or by negotiating 'permissive' routes on both private (Appendix 3) and publicly-owned land. Following the recommendations in the report, priority was given to the southern part of the project area where the problems were most severe. By the end of the first phase of the experiment, five-and-a-half bridleways or RUPPs had been improved, one had been added to the existing network and one had been successfully negotiated across private land as a 'permissive' bridlepath.

8.16   The problems of horse-grazing were examined in a study[39] carried out by a student from Hatfield Polytechnic and its conclusions are given in Chapter 9.

The management of publicly-owned land

8.17   The issue of the management of publicly-owned land was first raised at the Chairman's Review Committee by the Countryside Commission, whose previous experiments had concentrated on achieving public objectives on privately-owned land, with the co-operation of the landowners and tenants. The Countryside Commission were concerned that private landowners, particularly farmers, had little or no incentive to conserve and maintain the landscape when such work was no longer necessary for efficient farming, when they could see

This poorly-managed land, owned by the London Borough of Barnet and 'farmed' by a tenant, gives little incentive to private landowners to conserve and maintain landscape features

little evidence of the land owned by the sponsoring authorities being managed in this way. The Countryside Commission suggested that publicly-owned land should set an example of how to achieve the experiment's objectives by maintaining a high quality landscape as well as improving public access while continuing to farm the agricultural holdings efficiently. At a national level the Department of the Environment and the Nature Conservancy Council were also concerned about the need for public authorities to set an example of comprehensive estate management.

8.18   In order to debate these issues more fully, Hertfordshire County Council's Land Agent was invited to be represented on the Steering Group, the Greater London Council's Land Agent already having representation. In addition a Working Party was set up, chaired by the Countryside Commission, and including representatives from the Land Agent's Departments of all three sponsoring authorities and from the London Borough of Barnet's Parks and Engineer's Department, as the majority of Public Open Space was concentrated in Barnet and on its borders. Its brief was to make an assessment of the contribution which land owned by the sponsoring authorities could make towards achieving the objectives of the experiment.

8.19   The Working Party's objectives were identified as follows:

i.   to quantify the resource, i.e. the agricultural land, woodland, and Public Open Space owned by the sponsoring local authorities in the project area;

ii.   to identify and analyse the problems and opportunities;

iii.   to make recommendations on
   a. public access, particularly bridleways
   b. landscape management
   c. recreation provision
   d. educational facilities;

iv.   to identify short-term solutions which could be implemented by the project staff and provide guidelines for their work;

v.   to identify long-term solutions and provide guidelines for local authority countryside management policies on public access, landscape and wildlife conservation, recreation and education provision.

8.20   The amount of land owned by the sponsoring local authorities in the project area is shown in Table 3 and its geographical distribution is shown in Figure 8. Some 25 per cent of the total project area is owned by the sponsoring local authorities, but in the London Borough of Barnet, 33 per cent of the Green Belt is owned by the local authority. As can be seen from Table 3 this is mostly held in agricultural holdings, which comprise one third of all the agricultural land in the project area, but it also includes woodland and Public Open Space.

8.21   Progress made by the Working Party was very slow, its report being presented to the Steering Group 20 months after its first meeting. This was partly because of the concern felt by the Land Agents that there was a lack of commercial realism in the management objectives being suggested for their agricultural land, thus putting their tenants at a disadvantage compared with the tenant on privately-owned land, and, in the case of Public Open Space, that increased use of these areas would detract from their rural character. However, they agreed to examine their existing policies to see how they related to the experiment's objectives.

8.22   In their existing policies, the Greater London Council were the most progressive in their attitude to the management of their land. Some positive action had been taken to ensure that the public had reasonable access and landscape and conservation objectives were being pursued although, in spite of having endorsed the Countryside Commission's "New Agricultural Landscapes" proposals[46], the financial resources needed to act on this had not been allocated, e.g. in 1979 only £1,000 had been found for the replacement of dead elms over the whole of the Metropolitan Green Belt area. Both Hertfordshire County Council and the London Borough of Barnet, while not being opposed to the policies advocated on landscape and recreation, had done little to incorporate them in their management planning, so that no resources were committed to their implementation.

8.23   The problems identified in paragraph 7.3 are not specific to publicly-owned land, and it was agreed that 7.3 v. and vi. were not within the Working Party's remit. However, the opportunity presented by sponsoring local authority ownership for testing their possible solutions was recognised thus:

i.   By taking advantage of the ownership of agricultural holdings—to combine the following objectives in positive land management: the maintenance of good farming standards with the receipt of a reasonable income and an adequate return on capital; the conservation and enhancement of the landscape; the maintenance and improvement of public access; the conservation of wildlife.

ii.   By taking advantage of the ownership of woodlands—to combine good forestry practice with the objectives of conservation and enhancement of the landscape, the maintenance and improvement of public access and the conservation of wildlife.

iii.   By taking advantage of the grants available from the Countryside Commission—to maintain the valuable features of the landscape and to create new features and recreation facilities, e.g. by amenity tree planting, bridleways, recreation footpaths.

iv.   By making use of information from the recreation site surveys—to suggest new recreation facilities and to improve the use of existing Public Open Space to take pressure away from farmland.

v.   By making use of the educational role of the local authorities—to create new facilities, such as farm open days and educational visits, and to encourage students at all levels to make a practical input into the work of the experiment.

8.24   The Working Party then analysed the problems and opportunities for public authorities owning land in the project area and made recommendations for action, both for the project staff and for the local authorities. Its conclusions are given in Chapter 9.

Landscape improvement

8.25   The main efforts at landscape improvement were directed at implementing tree-planting schemes. During the course of the experiment, about 1,000 young trees were planted in various locations in the project area. The objectives to be achieved by tree planting were to secure visual improvements by screening or removing eyesores and discouraging rubbish dumping, to improve small woodlands and natural cover and to improve the farmed landscape by amenity planting of trees and hedgerows. Tree planting was carried out at every opportunity, often as part of other schemes such as bridleway improvements, but five projects, where landscape improvement was the sole objective, were undertaken to illustrate tree planting in different situations:

i.   on grazing land;

ii.   on arable land;

iii.   on Public Open Space;

iv.   along old lanes;

v.   in copses and small woodlands.

8.26   **The scheme on grazing land** involved the felling of 150 dead and often dangerous elm trees along the banks of the River Ver, south of St. Albans, in an area identified as being in need of urgent remedial action. It also formed part of a scheme to create a recreation footpath, designed by the Ver Valley Society, along the Ver from

St. Albans to Watford. In addition, the boundary between the farm and an adjacent housing estate was reinforced with tree planting and fencing in order to soften the urban edge and act as a barrier to urban intrusion.

8.27 **The scheme on arable land** was designed to reinforce the line of a footpath in an area where trees would have a significant visual impact. This was part of a programme arranged with a local school and the farmer to enable the children to plant trees in the winter and to visit the farm in the summer. Negotiations were also initiated with the landowner for the management of the small woodland on the farm as this too was a valuable landscape feature in the area.

8.28 **Planting on Public Open Space** was restricted to those areas adjacent to housing, in order to soften the visual intrusion of the urban edge—thus making the open space more attractive—and to reinforce the boundary between the housing and farmland. Feathered trees were used in these schemes but they were damaged or vandalised and the survival rate was below 50 per cent, in spite of using local schoolchildren to do the planting.

8.29 **Tree planting along old lanes** included a variety of unsurfaced tracks and old drovers roads, between 3 metres and 9 metres wide, and usually lined with hedges, some of which were of great antiquity and provided

Volunteers assisted with tree planting schemes. Burtonhole Lane

distinctive features in the landscape. Work included felling dead elms, replanting hedgerow trees, clearing scrub growth and ditching to allow better drainage both of the path itself and of the adjacent fields.

8.30 **The first scheme in a small area of woodland** was at Mill Hill, where the wood was cleared of dead or dying trees and invasion by young sycamores was halted. The area was planted with young oak and maple transplants with the help of boys from Mill Hill School.

Experimental solutions

8.31 One of the aims of the experiment was to find new solutions to some of the problems. Informal management agreements with landowners or tenants were developed as a vehicle to test compromise solutions for an interim period, e.g. 'permissive' bridleways (Appendix 3). This allowed the land occupiers flexibility in their future management and was more likely to be accepted by them than a legally-binding agreement, which could seldom be obtained in the short term and involved resources which were difficult to justify in a three-year experiment. It was hoped that in the long term formal management agreements would be negotiated where appropriate.

8.32 The assistant project officers attended training courses on countryside management, tree surgery, chain saw work etc. to develop their skills and expertise but, as there were no stereotyped procedures for carrying out some of the work, the ways in which it was performed were often experimental themselves, e.g. a cheap but sound and maintenance-free surface had to be found for the bridleway in Burtonhole Lane, Barnet, which had severe drainage problems associated with the London Clay—ditching was carried out and the surface covered in hardcore donated by the local authority; alternative methods of scrub clearance, including the use of weed-killers, were always being tried out (Appendix 2); new types of machinery were tested; and cheap sources of tools and materials were sought as an alternative to the accepted local authority channels for purchase.

Experimental solutions were tested using criteria such as costs, manpower and skills required, e.g. the usefulness of volunteers, educational benefits and the consequent maintenance commitment (Appendix 2).

Experimental solutions at Burtonhole Lane, jointly financed by the London Borough of Barnet and the experiment. After ditching and grading, an improved surface was laid using hardcore donated by the borough

8.33   Inevitably, problems arose and opportunities occurred which were beyond the resources of the experimental budget or would command a very high proportion of it. In this case, work was often undertaken on a small scale to demonstrate the feasibility of similar work on a larger scale, should resources permit at a later stage, e.g. the management of old woodland for amenity purposes. Two other alternatives were also available: a costed programme of action could be prepared and submitted to the local authority or other body concerned, indicating sources of grant aid, for adoption and implementation, e.g. a bridleway across the Dollis Valley, Barnet; or a programme of joint action could be undertaken, employing the resources of the experiment together with those of other interested parties, e.g. the adventure playground at Edgwarebury (Appendix 1). The time and resources available were the prime determinants in the choice of action taken.

Sources of labour

8.34   Various types of manpower were used on an experimental basis. The employment of volunteers has long been an accepted part of the countryside management approach in order to involve the local community, to help them develop a knowledge and understanding of their own environment and to keep costs to a minimum. Footpath societies, the pony club and the British Horse Society groups, school and youth groups have all made an important contribution on a fairly regular basis. Hertfordshire County Council's Voluntary Ranger Service and the British Trust for Conservation Volunteers have been a valuable source of trained and supervised volunteers, although their volunteers were not usually from the immediate local area. A regular arrangement with the local probation office provided a number of selected young workers under Community Service Orders. The number and variety of volunteers with different interests and levels of skills necessitated careful task selection and arrangements for insurance, first aid etc. An evaluation of their use is included in Chapter 9.

8.35   Machinery was hired for some of the large-scale practical work, e.g. ditching, thus exploiting the skills of the project staff, although contractors were used for tasks requiring the use of heavy equipment and specialist skills or where the suitability of different kinds of machinery was being tested.

Non-practical elements

Education

8.36   An extension of the volunteer work was the development of school-based activities. Where children from a particular school were known to be creating problems on nearby farmland, talks, farm visits and conservation work were arranged, aimed at developing a continuing relationship between farm and school. However, the development of this work on a wide scale was beyond the resources of a short-term experiment and only a few selected schools were involved.

8.37   Contacts were made with students and staff of colleges and universities, including foreign institutions. College students were employed as part of their sandwich courses and each year an undergraduate from Seale-Hayne College spent from four to six months doing practical and project work in the area (Appendices 2 and 3). Other undergraduate and postgraduate students were also encouraged to carry out project work in the area (Appendix 1).

Publicity

8.38   Publicity for the work of the experiment had two main purposes:

    i.   the need for information and education at a local level, to encourage a better understanding of the problems of the urban fringe among the local communities and to create and promote a political climate in which change and compromise solutions could be accepted;

    ii.   to promote the work on a regional and national level, to encourage the development of countryside management and to provide a forum for discussion on issues related to countryside management in the urban fringe.

8.39   At the local level, the work included talks to local community and amenity groups and organisations such as the National Farmers Union. It also involved liaison with schools and amenity groups as sources of volunteer help for practical tasks, such as tree planting and footpath clearance, with encouragement for the long-term maintenance of the facilities thus created. Tours of the project area for officers of local organisations, local authorities and government departments formed an important part of the introductory phase.

8.40   Contact with the local press was carefully controlled so that the local population's expectations were not too high and to avoid creating a recreation demand with which the experiment could not cope. Local publicity did bring positive benefits, e.g. volunteer labour from schools and amenity groups, but it was seen as part of an overall programme to educate the local population and to obtain their co-operation in the management of their own environment and the provision and maintenance of their own facilities. This aspect of the work can be very time-consuming and was not practised on any large scale.

8.41   At the national level, there were frequent tours of the area with officers and members from other local authorities and from central government. The project officer attended and spoke at national conferences and occasional interest was shown by the national press and the television network.

Summary

8.42   The countryside management approach in the Hertfordshire/Barnet project area attempted, through close co-operation with many different interest groups, to resolve conflict in the area and, in so doing, to change attitudes. This resulted in visible effects on the ground, while the liaison work, monitoring and feeding back of information to the various planning agencies attempted to provide the key element to a unity of administration in the countryside. The success of its operation is analysed in the following chapter.

Chapter 9: Evaluation

Introduction

9.1   The original aim of the experiment was to test the concept of countryside management in an area where complex urban fringe problems prevailed. The overall conclusions and evaluation of the approach adopted in the two Metropolitan Green Belt experiments are to be found in Chapter 4. However, outlined below are the interim conclusions specific to the Hertfordshire/Barnet project area.

Small-scale practical work

9.2   A wide range of practical work was carried out during the first phase of the experiment, a period of three and a half years (Figure 6). While it would appear that the initial small-scale work was most advantageous to the farmers and landowners, the project officer ensured that it was also of benefit to other land users and that a solution fair to all sides of a conflict was achieved wherever possible. In areas such as the Lake District[3] and Snowdonia[4] and the Bollin Valley[8], where the major conflict was between agriculture and recreation, this work had a considerable effect on the area as a whole and even on the economic viability of farming in the area. Here, however, the effects of the work were more localised as, apart from a few serious examples, trespass was just one of the problems faced by farmers in this complex urban fringe area. The practical work helped to gain the confidence of the farming community, creating a climate in which discussions on landscape improvements and concessions to visitors in the form of 'permissive' paths and bridleways were possible.

9.3   The greatest proportion of time and resources was devoted to work on bridleways and, during 1977 and 1978, 46 per cent of the assistant project officers' time was spent on this work, in addition to that spent by volunteers and by the project officer in negotiations and meetings. However, it was the expensive nature of the work, rather than the amount achieved, that accounted for the large expenditure involved. The decision to commit both time and resources to bridleways work was a response to the problems associated with the large number of horses using the area and a recognition that their solution would be of direct benefit to farmers, horse-riders and footpath users alike. In addition, the work could be carried out by the project staff and provided a visual and behavioural impact which could be evaluated.

9.4   However, the project officer was aware of the need to demonstrate in the three-year period the full range of work possible rather than to respond to priorities defined by the scale of the problem. Tree planting, woodland management and footpath work each accounted for about 11 per cent of the practical work, although this also involved more of the volunteers' time. Work concerned specifically with nature conservation, school visits, open space recreation management and rubbish dumping was not given a high priority, partly because in a short-term experiment the reward gained did not justify the large amount of time involved and partly because, in many cases, there were difficulties in getting co-operation to do the work. However, in a long-term countryside management service, these aspects of the work, particularly nature conservation and education, could be fully developed.

9.5   The project staff were under intense pressure to respond to requests from farmers and amenity groups for the alleviation of irritating problems by small-scale tasks. This is one way of assessing the success of the experiment so far, in that this approach obviously succeeded in tackling problems where other methods had failed (Appendices 2 and 3). It put a heavy call on time and resources and the work programme had to be flexible to be able to respond quickly to urgent requests for help. However, it was an essential component of the work in that it established the credibility of the experiment and led to the creation of goodwill and co-operation from the farmers, landowners and local interest groups and provided opportunities to develop larger schemes for environmental and landscape improvements.

Conclusion

9.6   In general terms, the conclusion is that intervention at the level of small-scale practical work has had considerable success in effecting local improvements and there is scope for much more of this type of work. The emphasis has been on testing procedures or techniques in problem-solving situations and in making the most of opportunities. No attempt was made to tackle problems comprehensively on an area basis, e.g. widespread landscape improvements, as, given the levels of staffing and finance over a three-year period, this would have been impossible. However, the incremental effect of small-scale countryside management must not be under-estimated and, over a longer period of time and with the political commitment of the local authorities, much can be achieved with this level of funding. It is not, however, a substitute for inadequate planning and land management and there are areas along the immediate urban edge, e.g. Bury Farm (Appendix 1), where its scope is more limited and short-term, and where the problems demand a much higher policy response and associated financial resources.

Major policy issues

9.7   The project officer had to work with a considerable number of individuals and organisations and, because of the size and complexity of the area, it took a long time before an overall assessment of the problems could be made. This is not to say that the area was too large but, given the resources, the initial foundation phase took longer than would have been the case in a smaller, less diverse area. This left little time to initiate major innovatory schemes and to consider the wider implications of countryside management, particularly its relationship to the planning process. During the last year of Phase One, however, a programme of major schemes was initiated, based on the problems identified in the area. These are outlined below.

Problems of access

9.8   Evidence from the recreation survey[33] showed that only local people used the footpath system and most casual visitors were deterred from venturing too far for two main reasons: paths which were not maintained, especially if they were also used by horses, made walking conditions unsuitable for lightly-shod townspeople, and little or no information was available on where a path went, how to return and how long it might take to get back. There was thus a substantial underuse of the paths in the project area even though a very good network existed. Work carried out by the project staff, e.g. on RUPP No. 51 (Appendix 2) and at Little Munden Farm (Appendix 3), has shown how these problems can be alleviated.

9.9   The Bridleways Working Party was set up to look at the problem on a more systematic basis, involving all concerned in a discussion forum. It produced a report[36] which gave guidelines for the work of the project staff and made policy recommendations to the local authorities. The reactions of the local authorities and other organisations to whom the Bridleways Report was referred are outlined below, including those bridleway proposals which crossed publicly-owned land which had been referred to the Management of Publicly-owned Land Working Party and then to the relevant committees in the local authorities.

9.10   Only the London Borough of Barnet had found resources additional to its contribution to the experiment budget to create a new bridleway route across the Dollis Valley. Hertfordshire County Council agreed to the recommendations in principle, but no action was taken because of the lack of funds at that time. The Greater London Council's policy was to make and encourage provision for riders within the Greater London area, e.g. riding centres at Trent Park, London parklands and the Lee Valley Regional Park, outside the project area, in order to relieve pressures on the agricultural land and to meet recreational demand. They would not allow 'permissive' bridleways across the agricultural land in their ownership. The British Horse Society's policy was to pursue the reinstatement of bridleway rights through the review of the Definitive Maps and they were less sanguine about compromise solutions proposed by the project officer. In practice, it proved easier to improve existing lanes and to get agreement to carry out work on privately-owned land than on publicly-owned land.

9.11   The Report was also referred to the Standing Conference on London and South East Regional Planning and the policy issues were taken up by Surrey County Council who had similar problems.

9.12   There was considerable conflict between walkers and riders on a bridleway on the north-west side of Wall Hall College, especially in wet weather, when the path became virtually impassable on foot. Segregation of the walkers and riders had been carried out by the project staff where the Principal of Wall Hall College gave permission for a separate footpath to run inside the edge of the College wood, parallel to the bridleway. However, this has not been completed as the bridleway continues along land also owned by Hertfordshire County Council, who have so far not agreed to the extension of the permissive footpath through their Dedicated Woodland, another example of how it is often difficult to obtain agreement to work on publicly-owned land.

9.13   The conclusion reached is that while the project staff were able to implement the practical solutions suggested, the policy issues were not dealt with satisfactorily by the authorities concerned. Until a comprehensive policy for the area can be agreed, the opportunist approach will have to continue and should be developed in close collaboration with the riding groups, who will be best placed to indicate the main riding needs. However, flexibility will be required from them too, e.g. negotiating changes to existing routes when considering new ones. From evidence so far (Appendix 3), new routes are more likely to be successful from all points of view if they are 'permissive' initially and, where appropriate, clearly fenced off from other users. Given success over time, these 'permissive' routes may achieve legal status in exchange for giving up an inconvenient existing right of way.

9.14   The major difficulty in creating new routes and in clearing existing ones will be sources of finance. If the present highway authorities and estates departments retain responsibility, their priorities necessarily lie elsewhere. The Countryside Commission have now clarified their position on grant aid[45] and the voluntary sector may provide some of the financial resources. Maintenance requires such a large share of resources that again the voluntary sector will be required to help, particularly on their priority routes.

Recreation provision

9.15   As the large recreation sites in the area had the potential to absorb more visitors, consideration was given to increasing access to them. The Management of Publicly-owned Land Working Party, in particular, made specific recommendations for action. However, in the time available little progress was made.

9.16   Recreational use of private land caused problems which had practical implications for management. Bury Farm (Appendix 1) functioned as a local open space for the adjoining housing estate, which lacks open space and children's play facilities. Much of the activity results in trespass and damage on the adjoining farmland and the dumping of rubbish is clearly related to the direct access from the housing area onto the farmland. The high level of use and the difficulties faced by the farmer may be seen as a direct consequence of poor housing layout and inadequate open space provision. A children's play area has since been constructed by the project staff near to the community centre and this, together with a strengthening of the boundary between farmland and housing, may alleviate some of the pressure on the farmland; its effect should be carefully monitored. The project staff recommended that the local authority should acquire a strip of farmland to act as a clearly-defined recreational 'buffer zone' between the housing estate and the productive farmland. Contact between local schools and the farmers, aimed at increasing the children's awareness of farming activities, would assist in reducing the level of direct damage on the farm. This shows how project staff, while making practical improvements on the ground, backed up by survey information, can identify opportunities and inform the local authorities, thus making possible an improvement in the flexibility and responsiveness of local authority planning and management. Implementation then depends on political will and the allocation of financial resources.

9.17   Equally important is the need to develop an awareness amongst architects, in particular, and local authorities, in general, of the problems that can arise when housing estates are built adjacent to farmland, particularly if inadequate thought is given to the needs and desires of the residents and the difficulties facing neighbouring farmers in urban fringe areas. (See illustrations on page 36.)

The management of publicly-owned land

9.18   The results of the recreation site surveys[33] were considered in depth by the Management of Publicly-owned Land Working Party. The Working Party looked at agriculture, conservation and education objectives as well as at recreation and produced a report[34], the conclusions of which may be summarised as:

  i.   there is a need to think about the better management of existing resources and their positive use, especially at a time of economic constraint, when a high priority is placed on an adequate return on capital invested in the land;

  ii.   the local authorities have a special responsibility to set high standards as an example to others, particularly in showing how agricultural, recreation, conservation and education objectives can be reconciled;

  iii. there is a need for, and there are positive advantages to, co-operation across local authority boundaries and between departments within those authorities, in order to devise common management objectives and programmes of works.

9.19   The Working Party made recommendations for action, both for the project staff and for the local authorities. Like the Bridleways Working Party, the conclusion reached is that, while the project staff have been able to implement some of the practical work, the policy issues have not been dealt with satisfactorily, with the exception of the London Borough of Barnet. The role of countryside management in relation to publicly-owned land is being further examined in Phase Two of the experiment.

Landscape and conservation

9.20   Although a great deal of importance was attached to implementing new tree planting proposals, only a few schemes were implemented, with the help and advice of the local authority landscape architects. Various sites were identified by the local authorities, mainly on sites in public ownership and along the urban edge and trunk roads, where substantial concentrated tree planting could make a dramatic impact on the landscape, with little loss of land for uses such as agriculture or recreation, but the main attempts at landscape improvements in the initial stages were largely remedial—removing and replacing dead or dying elms and rehabilitating decaying woodland sites. This was largely because, in responding to immediate problems, little time was left in a three-year period for any large-scale planting. The project staff showed by example what might be done.

9.21   In persuading farmers to allow tree planting on their land, the project staff did not try to interfere with current farming practices, e.g. if a farmer wanted to remove internal hedges and hedgerow trees as part of a rationalisation programme, he would be encouraged to allow compensation tree planting on odd corners of land, thus creating a new landscape, along the lines of the Countryside Commission's "New Agricultural Landscapes" policy[46], rather than trying to fossilise the old, although the retention of old hedges of particular value to wildlife was encouraged. The general attitude of the farmers towards tree planting varied from indifference to active support, although hedgeline plantings were not usually favoured. Owner-occupiers were usually easier to convince than tenants on privately-owned land. Planting in odd corners and on waste ground received general approval, but getting rid of dead elms was costly and grant-aid for felling as well as for replanting was a frequent plea.

9.22   Tree planting on Public Open Space was less successful than on farmland. It was difficult to design a scheme which fitted into the rural scene, as the local authority insisted on sufficient space being left between the trees to allow a gang-mower to pass for maintenance purposes and, in particular, to discourage rubbish-dumping. The resulting schemes, although using indigenous tree species, took on an urban park-like character. Even where trees were planted by children from schools in the surrounding area, many were lost through acts of vandalism, some accidentally but mostly by their stems being broken and stakes removed. The overall survival rate was about 50 per cent. There is no doubt that greater involvement by the local community helps to solve this problem, although it will be difficult to eradicate it completely.

9.23   The survival rate of trees planted along old green lanes was good. The hedgerow planting meant that hedges could not be trimmed by flail-cutter. Hand-trimming is very time-consuming and therefore expensive and adjacent landowners have been reluctant to commit themselves to this type of maintenance. In the past, farmers adjacent to these lanes have frequently machine-cut only the field side of the hedge, leaving the lane side to grow wild.

9.24   During the experimental period, small, often isolated, pockets of land were identified and planted, with the owner's consent. The overall impact so far is therefore not substantial but, in the long term, the incremental effect should not be underestimated and the experiment has shown what can be achieved with limited resources

Field corner tree planting adjacent to a copse, near Colney Heath

over a short period of time. In order to undertake the comprehensive landscape improvements recommended in the report of the Standing Conference of London and South East Regional Planning[14], a much greater impetus by the local authorities is required, particularly on land in their ownership. The present measures being taken to replace dead elms are completely inadequate and the implementation of major tree planting schemes is of the utmost priority.

9.25   During the course of the experiment, although not because of it, Hertfordshire County Council, with the aid of the Countryside Commission, launched a tree planting scheme offering grant aid of up to 75 per cent towards the cost of approved tree planting. The project staff were able to persuade some landowners, usually owner-occupiers, to take advantage of the scheme and, in some instances, actually carried out the work as agents for the County Council. However, large scale tree planting schemes, which may necessitate ground preparation or scrub clearance prior to planting, are expensive and so it was difficult to persuade farmers to participate. The lack of grant for maintenance and following the first year of planting and for felling costs may also be a deterrent to some farmers, although in the project work, the costs of felling dead trees and the maintenance of new ones were borne by the project budget. Only mixtures of broadleaves with a high proportion of conifers or pure conifer planting offer any hope of a positive return on the scheme; small areas of indigenous broadleaf trees are of high landscape value but are expensive.

9.26   Both Hertfordshire County Council and the London Borough of Barnet operated tree banks but, at the time of the experiment, neither could cope with the demand and there were long waiting lists. The London Borough of Barnet's tree bank, in particular, stocked mainly ornamental species which were inappropriate for planting in the countryside. The project staff therefore bought tree stocks from local nurseries.

9.27   There is a large number of small woodlands in the area. Many of them have received little or no management for many years and, as a result, are deteriorating through over-maturity or uncontrolled access. A few schemes were negotiated with landowners to carry out remedial work on some small woodlands and then to undertake agreements for future management work. In these cases, local schoolchildren were encouraged to

School children from Borehamwood were involved in tree planting on a local farm

carry out the scrub clearance and the replanting and it is hoped that their interest will be retained by the implementation of long-term management plans as part of their environmental studies classes; the project staff worked closely with the local authority officers to identify woodlands close to urban areas where such work could be agreed with the landowners.

9.28   Another aspect which was of concern in landscape terms, as well as in the loss of agricultural land, was the increase in the amount of horse-grazing, particularly in the southern part of the project area (paragraph 7.29). However, where good management is ensured, the result can be far more aesthetically pleasing than, for example, intensive livestock production and other permissible Green Belt uses, such as mineral workings. The study of horse-grazing[39] in the project area indicated that, where it was integrated with a farming system, much of the land so used was fairly well-managed, particularly land owned by established riding schools and stables. The poorly-managed fields tended to be those pockets of land which had been let out or sold to private individual urban horse-owners, who had no opportunity to vary the grazing and had little idea of what needed to be done, although land associated with some of the stables was also very poor and neglected in appearance. It is clear that there are management problems which need to be overcome and Hertfordshire County Council are currently negotiating the implementation of voluntary management guidelines.

Sources of labour

9.29   Various forms of manpower were used on an experimental basis (Table 7). The employment of volunteers has long been an accepted part of the countryside management approach in order to involve the local community, to help them develop a knowledge and understanding of their surroundings, to relate to schools' environmental education programmes, to keep costs to a minimum, and to provide an enjoyable and constructive leisure activity. However, the educational and social benefits of working with volunteers, particularly children and young adults, must be set against their general low rate of productivity and, in a three-year experiment designed to produce results, productivity is an important factor. In addition to the volunteers, other sources of labour included the Community Service Order scheme for young offenders, operated by the Probation Service.

Table 7: Project work carried out by different sources of labour

Task	Project staff	Source of labour (no. of tasks)		
		Volunteers (and project staff)	Community Service Order workers	Contractors
Stiles/bridges/fences/gates	62	3	0	0
Scrub clearance	9	14	10	0
Tree planting and maintenance	16	10	2	0
Tree felling and surgery	11	1	0	0
Rubbish clearance	7	2	1	0
Bridleways: ditching/grading/ surfacing	6	0	0	6
Woodland management	3	2	0	0
Nature conservation	0	5	0	0
Recreation play areas	1	1	0	0
Education	4	0	0	0
Total	**119**	**38**	**13**	**6**

9.30   There were considerable advantages in employing skilled volunteers such as the British Trust for Conservation Volunteers and the Hertfordshire Voluntary Ranger Service. They were capable of undertaking fairly arduous and difficult work and their standard of work was high because they were well-trained and highly motivated. No tasks had to be specially designed or organised because their range of skills allowed them to adapt to any type of work. The disadvantage of these two groups of volunteers was that most of them lived outside the immediate project area and mundane or routine work lowered their motivation, particularly when it was not exploiting their skills to the full. However, they complemented the use of more local, lesser-skilled volunteers from schools and amenity groups.

9.31   School classes and unskilled volunteers can present problems. The practical task must not be beyond their capabilities but needs to be sufficiently interesting to maintain their enthusiasm. They need to see tangible results for their efforts and their motivation is reduced when asked to do routine maintenance work. It therefore usually has to be specially designed and carefully organised, all of which involves the project staff's time in preparing tools and equipment, organising insurance etc., supervising the volunteers and the equipment and cleaning up afterwards. With low output per man and often a lower standard of workmanship, the use of unpaid unskilled voluntary labour is not always as cost-effective as it might appear at first—the relative merits of using machinery or professional expertise against voluntary, unskilled manpower need to be assessed before starting any project and a balance maintained between them in the overall work of the experiment. However, the social and educational benefits from the involvement of volunteers in environmental work far outweigh the disadvantages and, when a school can integrate the work with its educational programme and follow-up studies are made on tree planting or woodland management, the advantages are even more far-reaching.

9.32   Machinery was hired for some of the large-scale practical work, e.g. ditching. This exploited the practical skills of the assistant project officers. While using volunteers was very desirable politically, in that it enjoyed widespread public support and was a cheap method of labour, the pressure to achieve visually-acceptable results in a short space of time was an equal consideration and the more professional finish obtainable with machinery and which, with the exception of the Hertfordshire Voluntary Ranger Service and the BTCV, few volunteer groups could achieve, was considered important in convincing the farmers and landowners of the value of the work.

9.33   One or two Community Service Order workers were taken on to work under the supervision of the project staff, mainly on Sundays, for the number of hours specified. Apart from the lack of transport to and from the work site, which had to be provided by the project staff in the initial stages, the scheme worked well, although they required careful supervision and were not highly motivated. The scheme was then expanded, the Probation Service providing its own transport and supervisor. Five or six workers were involved and the scheme progressed satisfactorily, although they worked separately from other volunteers and no skilled tasks were tackled. If they can be mixed with other groups of volunteers as individuals the benefits are often greater.

9.34 The opportunities presented by the Manpower Services Commission's schemes were not taken up. While the benefits of low-cost labour and providing employment for young people were recognised, the project officer considered that, with all the existing commitments, the staff were not able to take on the additional workload that would be involved in supervising and training in the short timescale of the experiment. However, it is to be hoped that a long-term countryside management service would make use of every opportunity of this kind.

9.35 Projects in other areas have used volunteers in preference to other types of labour on a wide range of tasks. The Hertfordshire/Barnet experiment tried to achieve a balance between the available labour sources, and most of the major projects have successfully combined the use of volunteers, skilled labour and hired contractors.

Non-practical elements

9.36 The non-practical elements of the work were equally important in Hertfordshire/Barnet, whereas in other experiments performance has been assessed only in terms of the visible impact on the ground. The results of many long negotiations with various groups to resolve conflicts or to propose changes in policy did not always result in physical evidence and its results are more difficult to evaluate over such a short time period.

Education

9.37 The educational aspects of the work were not fully exploited. This was because of the time needed to organise and supervise practical tasks and follow-up work, especially where a positive contribution from the teachers was not forthcoming. This could be developed in a long-term countryside management service, in association with the local education authority and with the teachers playing a more positive role. School-children did, of course, act as volunteer labour. The liaison with higher educational establishments for both practical and project work, e.g. Seale-Hayne College and Hatfield Polytechnic, was generally found to be of great benefit to all concerned.

Publicity

9.38 The project officer deliberately chose not to give the experiment general local publicity as he felt that this would be counter-productive while they were establishing their credibility. It is not surprising, therefore, that the recreation site surveys[33] showed that, even on sites where the project staff had carried out a substantial amount of work, very few people had noticed anything taking place and knew nothing of the experiment. Attempts have been made to increase understanding between the farmer and the local community by physical changes but, unless the community is involved in these practical schemes, there will be little alteration in awareness or in their patterns of behaviour. Long-term education should be through community involvement as well as through normal structured channels. Consideration has since been given to publicising the work, particularly in order to get the local community involved in carrying out the work themselves, and has met with varied success.

9.39 A substantial amount of the project officer's time was taken up in communicating the results of the experiment outside the project area in his role as Countryside Management Adviser (paragraph 5.4). In one 18 month period, he gave 30 lectures, of which only 12 were of local significance; 44 tours of the area were conducted, of which 50 per cent were with local representatives; and he attended 21 conferences or visits to national agencies outside the project area.

Summary

9.40 Given the resources available and the size of the area, with such complex problems, the initial foundation phase necessarily took longer than might have been the case with a smaller, less diverse area. This has left little time, in a three-year experiment, to develop major schemes or to test the countryside management approach to its full potential, particularly in its relationship with the planning process and its ability to change the attitudes of landowners, user groups and others involved in the area. The most difficult decision for the project officer was choosing priorities under pressure to achieve results. The solutions attempted, therefore, tended to be those which could achieve success in the short term rather than the more intractable problems. In a permanent countryside management service, priorities would be different and the more difficult problems might be tackled on a long-term basis.

9.41 The countryside management approach, as well as carrying out practical work on the ground, attempts to change attitudes towards caring for the countryside. In this the project officer has an important liaison role, not only between various interest groups but also between different departments of all the local authorities with responsibilities in the area. In a short three-year period, it would be unrealistic to expect any discernible changes in attitude, but there are indications that there is a greater potential for success than the experiment has so far been able to demonstrate, e.g. the district councils in Hertfordshire offered to become additional financial sponsors. The second phase of the experiment will hopefully develop this aspect further.

9.42 The approach is essentially a flexible one which is changing and developing all the time. The first introductory phase and the establishment phase have been completed. A programme of major schemes is currently being developed and implemented based on the problems identified in the area. Phase Two is implementing this programme as well as consolidating, developing and expanding the work as opportunities arise and confidence in countryside management grows. The work is being related to the policy and implementation process to determine more comprehensive solutions to the problems. This was started by the reports of the Bridleways[36] and the Management of Publicly-owned Land Working Parties[34], which form the basis for development of the work in these areas. Phase Two is looking particularly at the role of countryside management on publicly-owned land, the future maintenance commitment and a suitable administrative framework for a long-term countryside management service. A management plan will be produced.

PART THREE

HAVERING
URBAN FRINGE
MANAGEMENT
EXPERIMENT

Chapter 10: Organisation of the Experiment

Introduction

10.1   The Havering Urban Fringe Management Experiment started in February 1976 with the appointment of a project officer, for an initial period of three years. The sponsors were the Countryside Commission, the Greater London Council and the London Borough of Havering, who contributed 75 per cent, 12½ per cent and 12½ per cent of the funds respectively

Objectives

10.2   The objectives of the experiment were outlined in paragraph 3.2. These were to be achieved by the project officer, as defined in his job description:

i.   familiarising himself with the activities, the planning situation, the land uses, the potential conflicts and opportunities, and the organisations, both official and voluntary, within the project area and drawing up a list of priorities for action;

ii.   initiating direct action, where appropriate, to improve the landscape and facilities for recreation by means of agreements or carrying out small practical tasks;

iii.   making the maximum use of voluntary labour but also using small sums of money to employ landowners and tenants to carry out improvements where appropriate;

iv.   encouraging landowners and tenants to provide for public access and recreation;

v.   taking action, where possible, to secure the removal of eyesores and to reduce the impact of vandalism and litter;

vi.   identifying and endeavouring to reduce conflict between users in the project area;

vii.   bringing to the attention of the appropriate authorities the need for action on matters outside the scope of the experiment;

viii. keeping a full and accurate record of all work undertaken and improvements secured and recording failures as well as successes.

The project staff

10.3   It was originally envisaged that the project officer would organise most of the practical work, e.g. tree planting, fencing, etc., himself, with help from volunteers and temporary employees. However, as the work programme developed, it became necessary to employ an assistant project officer to concentrate specifically on carrying out the practical work, under the supervision of the project officer and often with his help. This released the project officer for the liaison and negotiation aspects of the work. In addition to the project officer and his assistant, other staff were employed when necessary, either on a contract basis or as casual labour. These were mainly students seeking temporary employment as part of a sandwich course. Voluntary labour was also used for practical tasks, the main source for this being the national branch of the British Trust for Conservation Volunteers.

Steering arrangements

10.4   Overall policy guidance and budget review was provided by the Chairman's Review Committee. This was a committee of elected members nominated by the sponsoring local authorities and chaired by the Chairman of the Countryside Commission. It met on an annual basis.

10.5   Direction of the work of the experiment was provided by a Steering Group and although, for administrative purposes, the project officer was employed by the London Borough of Havering, he was directly responsible to that Steering Group which was made up of officers of the three sponsoring authorities. It was chaired by the Deputy Borough Planning Officer of the London Borough of Havering, and met on a quarterly basis. Its functions are outlined in paragraph 3.18 and its delegated powers to the project officer in paragraph 3.19.

10.6   Membership of the Group included representatives from the London Borough of Havering's Planning and Recreation and Amenities Departments, the Greater London Council's Planning and Transportation, Parks and Land Agency Departments and from the Countryside Commission. Representatives from other local authority departments were invited as necessary. A representative from the Ministry of Agriculture, Fisheries and Food joined in July 1977 and from the Department of the Environment in October 1977. The project evaluator also attended. The project officer recommended that, as in Hertfordshire/Barnet (paragraph 5.7) the Steering Group should co-opt a representative from the local farmers, but this was rejected on the grounds that farming should not be accorded a privileged position compared with other sectional interests who would also wish to be represented, thus making the Group too large.

10.7   Day-to-day line management contact was with the Deputy Borough Planning Officer (as Chairman of the Steering Group), in co-ordination with an officer of the Countryside Commission. The project officer also developed close working relationships with the staff of the Borough Planning Department, the Recreation and Amenities Department and the Estates Department. He also worked directly with the Greater London Council's Parks Department and the Minerals Section of the Planning and Transportation Department.

Resources

10.8   Table 8 shows the experiment's annual expenditure during the first three years. The initial cost was estimated to be £24,000 over three years, arranged as three annual allocations of £8,000, with no provision to carry over unspent funds. This would have involved the individual sponsoring authorities in the following expenditure per annum (approximately): Countryside Commission £6,000, Greater London Council £1,000, London Borough of Havering £1,000. No allowances had been made for inflation so the budget had to be adjusted, as shown in the table.

Table 8: Expenditure

	15/2/76– 31/3/76	1/4/76– 31/3/77	1/4/77– 31/3/78	1/4/78– 31/3/79
Staff salaries	447	5,127	7,781	10,211
Travelling and running expenses	36	396	408	1,723
Tools and materials	54	2,582	1,604	1,412
Administrative expenses	2	232	327	262
Total	**539**	**8,337**	**10,120**	**13,608**

10.9   The major portion of the budget was devoted to staff salaries and associated costs, including travelling expenses. Tools and materials was the second largest item, accounting for approximately £1,500 annually although, apart from the purchase of a chain saw, there was no need to buy expensive equipment as this could all be hired locally. A range of hand tools was purchased at the beginning of the experiment. A petty cash imprest of £50 was made available to the project officer.

10.10   No vehicle was provided specifically for the experiment and so the project staff purchased light vans for use on experiment work, for which they were entitled to a casual car user's mileage allowance only. The wear and tear involved in the transport of heavy tools and materials and in travelling over rough ground was generally unacceptable and the consequent service bills large.

10.11   The project officer was provided with office accommodation in the Borough Planning Department, where administrative and secretarial facilities were available. However, he worked mainly from home, using headed notepaper with both his home and office addresses and telephone numbers, so that evening and weekend contact with local people was made easier. While many of the contacts made were at an official or a formal level, others were largely or wholly personal. It therefore helped to be able to work from home and outside office hours, as few individuals representing voluntary bodies or farming interests could conveniently attend local authority offices during the day and often preferred meeting in more informal surroundings. The cost of installing a telephone at his flat, allocated by the Borough Council, was covered by the experiment. However, the project officer moved right out of the area half-way through the experiment and this made efficient working more difficult.

Chapter 11: The Project Area

Introduction

11.1   The project area forms part of the approved Metropolitan Green Belt (Figure 1) and lies in the south east of the London Borough of Havering. It covers 1,880 hectares or approximately 19 sq. km. It is bounded on three sides by suburban development—Rainham to the south, Dagenham and Romford to the west and Upminster to the north—while to the east is the relatively open countryside of Essex. Havering is the furthest east of all the London boroughs, and the project area, 21 km. from central London, is actually the nearest open countryside to London's East End population.

11.2   The project area lies within the Lower Thames Valley (Figure 1), at a level predominantly below 30 metres and is generally flat and featureless. The most significant geographical feature is the River Ingrebourne which flows north-south into the River Thames. The land lies over river deposits of sand and gravel and is classified as Grade 1 by the Ministry of Agriculture, Fisheries and Food. The high quality soil is light and free-draining and this, together with the mild climate, gives great flexibility of cropping and an extended growing season, with highly intensive vegetable production the predominant form of agriculture.

Havering's most significant geographical feature—River Ingrebourne

Land use

Table 9: Land use in the project area

Land use	Havering
	%
Agriculture	55
Mineral extraction	31
Recreation	5
Settlements	4
Woodland	2
Utilities	1
Others	2

Agriculture

11.3 Seventy per cent of the project area lies within farm boundaries, although not all of it is farmed. Of the 18 farms, three are owner-occupied, eight are tenanted and the rest are of mixed tenure. They range in size from 5 hectares to 220 hectares, but with 30 per cent of them over 120 hectares, the larger farms having been formed by the amalgamation of small farms for economic reasons in recent years, or from the farmer acquiring additional land elsewhere as and when it became available and running a fragmented holding. Some farmers also own or lease land outside the project area.

11.4 The principal enterprise is vegetable production which, together with cereal crops, accounts for 70 per cent of the agricultural land in the study area (Figure 12). The remainder is predominantly rough-grazing on land that has been poorly-restored after gravel extraction and which carries poor-quality horses reared for the continental meat trade. There is also one intensive pig-rearing unit.

11.5 The project area has become one of the most intensive horticultural districts in the country. Its development has been effected by the quality of the soil, the mild climate, proximity to the London market and the availability of labour in the urban fringe. Careful tillage and the incorporation of London sewage over a long period improved the fertility of the soil to such an extent that by 1941 Scarfe referred to the area as "uncommonly fine for all vegetables and grain crops"[9]. A tendency to drought was the main limitation to cropping, but this has been overcome by irrigation, which can increase yields by up to 25 per cent and enables the cropping programme to be more precisely controlled, giving an advantage in marketing. Vegetables can be harvested two weeks ahead of most other regions and it is possible to grow two or three crops per year on the same land.

11.6 The majority of farmers rely solely upon agriculture for their income, but there is a trend towards integration with marketing particularly among the larger vegetable growers. One farmer has established a packing house, employing 60 people, pre-packing and distributing vegetables direct to supermarket chains. Other farmers have businesses in London wholesale markets, where first-hand market information enables them to gear their cropping programmes to market demand.

Mineral extraction

11.7 Mineral extraction has been taking place for over 50 years and there are still considerable reserves in the area, with four separate companies still in operation at the time of writing. Major extraction is taking place at Bush Farm, where the restoration is in accordance with the restoration experiment sponsored by the Sand and Gravel Association, the Department of the Environment and the Ministry of Agriculture, Fisheries and Food[47]; at Moor Hall Farm, where there will be no in-filling as this site is to be restored at the excavated level; and at Stubbers, where reserves will last for another three or four years and where the land is owned by the London Borough of Havering, who plan to leave a large part of the site as a lake for recreation purposes. Deposits at the East London Quarry at Berwick Pond Road and the adjoining South Hornchurch Airfield are now almost exhausted. Extraction at Gerpins Lane has ceased although minimal reserves remain and will eventually be worked. Filling at the Warwick Lane site is likely to take a long time. Extraction is about to take place at Great Sunnings Farm, adjoining Bush Farm, and further areas are being investigated. In addition, the three main processing sites at Berwick Pond Road, Gerpins Lane and Warwick Lane process gravel extracted from outside the project area as well as from within it.

The scale of devastation can be seen at South Hornchurch Airfield, where the gravel is now exhausted

11.8   After the gravel has been extracted, the hole is sometimes sub-contracted out for filling. There is a great demand in the London area for places suitable for refuse disposal and "it has been known for profits from filling to exceed those from the sale of aggregate extracted from the hole."[28]

11.9   Until recently, companies had little interest or expertise in restoration of the land after extraction and filling. Returning it to high-grade agricultural land costs at least double its restoration to low-grade agricultural land. It appears that, when buying land, companies rarely consider its use once gravel has been extracted and the hole filled. Most companies seem to hold on to their restored land, sub-letting it to farmers at a low rent.

The devastating effect of gravel working

After the extraction, the back-filling causing dust, smell, excessive traffic and more visual intrusion

After restoration, loss of high grade agricultural land

Recreation

11.10   The project area lies next to suburban residential development with a large demand for both informal and formal recreation facilities which is not entirely met from within the urban area. The project area is therefore under considerable pressure to meet this recreational demand, often of a specialised nature e.g. motorcycling. In addition, according to the guidelines published in the approved Greater London Development Plan[16] the London Borough of Havering has some localised areas of open space deficiency.

11.11   There is a relatively small amount of Public Open Space within the project area. Sites devoted specifically to informal recreation include a 19 hectare amenity woodland run by Essex County Council (Warwick, Whitehall, Running Water and Little Brickkiln Woods) and Public Open Spaces at Berwick Pond, Spring Farm Park, Hacton Parkway, Suttons Parkway and Parklands (Corbets Tey) (Figure 5).

11.12   The network of statutory footpaths in the project area (Figure 5) is somewhat fragmented and could be improved, particularly where paths have been destroyed by gravel extraction and have never been restored. In many cases the demand for paths does not coincide with the present routes and, as a result, a number of *de facto* paths and access areas have been created, mostly in open areas adjacent to housing estates, e.g. Hacton, Cranham Hall Farm, etc. No bridleways exist in the project area, although in recent years there has been a considerable increase in the number of horses kept for riding.

11.13   Formal recreation facilities are also sited in the project area (Figure 5). The local education authority has an outdoor pursuits centre at Stubbers (48 hectares), which provides a range of sports facilities for children from Havering and other London boroughs. A large lake with provision for sailing, canoeing, etc. will be developed when gravel extraction at Stubbers is completed. The four schools which lie on the boundary of the study area have sports pitches associated with them. Harwood Hall, at Corbets Tey, is a privately-owned equestrian centre, having a Wembley-sized indoor arena where major national horse-jumping events are held. The only other commercial recreation facility in the study area is a small riding stables and caravan site at Llantrissant Oaks at Aveley Road. A small private airstrip has been created on a farm in the project area and this is used by the farmer and his friends for recreational flying.

11.14   Several recreation clubs use sites in the project area. Only one of these sites (Warwick Lane Fishery) is owned by the club, the remainder being rented on an informal basis, e.g. an angling club rents Berwick Pond on an annual 'word-of-mouth' agreement with the tenant farmer; a clay pigeon shooting club has secured temporary facilities at Bush Farm; and, until recently, a model aeroplane club used a field in Berwick Pond Road.

Settlements

11.15   The project area itself contains no centres of population. The residential population is scattered in farms and private houses. However, the area is bordered on the southern, western and northern sides by areas of suburban housing and beyond these, the urban development of Greater London is continuous. The line of the urban edge was determined by the extent of housing development in 1947, when planning legislation effectively put a stop to any further expansion of the built-up area into the Green Belt. This left certain illogical pieces of development, such as the Parsonage Farm estate, an isolated tongue of housing intruding into an area of open countryside, at Rainham, south of Berwick Pond (Figure 3 and back cover). Such irregularities extend the length of the boundary between town and countryside and exacerbate the associated problems. However, the Green Belt boundary is likely to remain as it is (except for some in-fill development on the northern part of South Hornchurch Airfield, under a scheme agreed between the predecessors of the Department of the Environment and the present planning authorities) until the Local Plan for the area has been finalised, when minor boundary adjustments might be made.

11.16   In addition to the permanent residential population, temporary settlements are created by gypsies. One gypsy site exists in the project area, in Dennises Lane, with spaces for 15 caravans, but with no room for activities from which gypsies earn their living, e.g. sorting scrap metal, although it is laid out to official DOE standards.

Nature conservation

11.17   Although the project area is dominated by gravel workings, poorly-restored land and areas of intensive agricultural production, there are still a number of sites of high conservation value, although none have been officially set aside for nature conservation. A range of habitats, including woodland, ditches, hedgerows, scrub, marsh, streams and open water provide a variety of flora and fauna and the ecological value of Berwick Pond, Cranham Marsh, the Ingrebourne Valley and Warwick, Whitehall and Running Water Woods has been investigated, and is summarised below.

11.18   Despite intense competition from gravel extraction, urban development, recreation and agriculture, part of the Berwick Pond site remains of high ecological value. Records indicate rare species of insect and reptile life and recent surveys have identified a wide range of interesting flora and fauna.

Despite the nearby demands of gravel extraction, urban development, recreation and agriculture, the wetland site at the west end of Berwick Pond remains of high ecological value

11.19   Cranham Marsh is one of the last surviving examples in Essex of a marshy fen that retains the original peat deposits, together with ancient associated vegetation. The site relies heavily upon the high water table for its variety and for the maintenance of rare plant species. A proposal by Essex Naturalists' Trust that Cranham Marsh and the adjacent Spring Wood should be designated as a Site of Special Scientific Interest is likely to be accepted by the Nature Conservancy Council in due course and, at present, the Trust are negotiating with the London Borough of Havering to lease the site and manage it both for conservation and amenity use.

11.20   The River Ingrebourne has produced a flood plain with a fertile water meadow of ecological value. The valley has interesting flora and is used regularly by migratory birds. It is also heavily-used for informal recreation, which conflicts with its conservation value.

11.21   There are only 40 hectares of woodland in the project area. Warwick, Whitehall and Running Water Woods are remnants of a large woodland estate once used for hunting. A variety of tree species exists, many of which are young or semi-mature. The woodland provides a valuable and, locally, very rare habitat for wildlife, associated both with dense woodland and with woodland edge. Hedges and hedgerow trees have been maintained on the perimeter of many farms, but many internal boundaries have been removed.

Utilities

11.22   An assortment of urban uses, which are not appropriate to open countryside but require a location near to the population they serve, is found in the project area. The burial of the dead has an important claim upon land in the area. Two sites exist: a cemetery and crematorium at Corbets Tey serving the local population, and a large Jewish Cemetery at Rainham which serves the East End of London, both of which are likely to need additional land within the next few years. Other claims upon the land in the project area come from sewage, water and gas pipelines, high voltage electricity power lines and sub-stations and from rubbish disposal. A Greater London Council Civic Amenities tip for the disposal of bulky household refuse is located in Gerpins Lane. Initially the site was adjacent to a gravel pit where the rubbish was tipped, but now the rubbish is taken to Aveley by skip lorry for disposal.

Education

11.23   There are three secondary schools and one special school with associated playing fields within the project area, although there are more than 25 schools within 1 km. of the project area's boundaries. Apart from this, educational use is confined to Stubbers Outdoor Pursuits Centre, which occupies a site of 48 hectares.

Communications

11.24   The project area lies between the A12 and A13 trunk roads, which carry heavy traffic to and from London. The A13 is the major route for heavy lorry traffic from the container port of Tilbury and the Thames-side industrial area and the A12 carries a considerable amount of commuter traffic. Within the project area there is a network of B classified roads and secondary traffic routes.

11.25   The Fenchurch Street to Tilbury railway line runs along the southern edge of the project area and to the north is the Fenchurch Street to Southend line. A branch line from Upminster to Grays forms part of the eastern boundary. The London Transport Underground comes within 1 km. of the project area, terminating at Upminster, but there is no railway station within the area and only two bus routes.

Land use change

Table 9: Changes in land use 1933–77

	1933		1962		1977	
	ha.	% project area	ha.	% project area	ha.	% project area
Arable (mainly vegetables)	1,307	70	1,046	56	872	46
Pasture/natural grassland	413	22	414	22	174	9
Open space (cemeteries, playing fields etc.)	2	N	67	4	76	4
Woodland	61	3	41	2	40	2
Natural water	19	1	19	1	19	1
Residential/commercial	73	4	77	4	77	4
Marginal (heath/marsh)	1	N	21	1	45	2
Sand and gravel workings						
Current	4	N	119	6	142	8
Restored to grazing	—	—	32	2	174	9
Waterfilled	—	—	21	1	38	2
Derelict	—	—	23	1	223	12
Total area affected by sand and gravel workings	**4**	**N**	**195**	**10**	**577**	**31**
Total project area	**1,880**	**100**	**1,880**	**100**	**1,880**	**100**

N—Nominal: the percentage figures have been rounded.

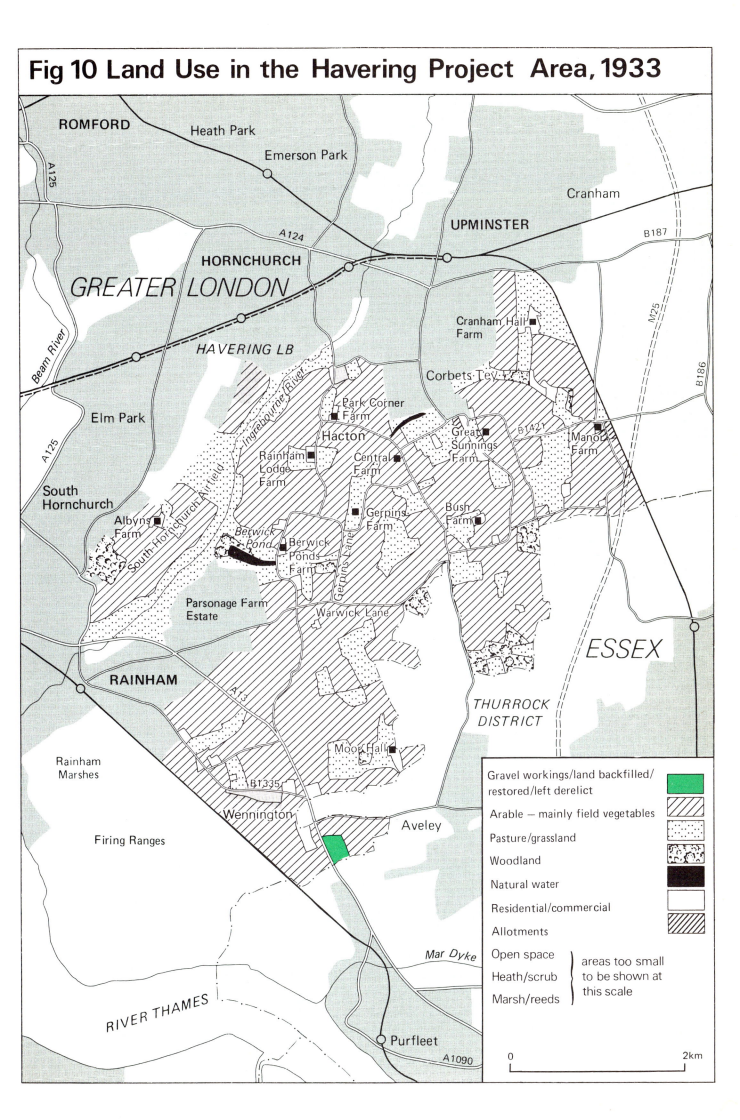

Fig 10 Land Use in the Havering Project Area, 1933

ROMFORD
Heath Park
Emerson Park
Cranham
UPMINSTER
A124
B187
HORNCHURCH
GREATER LONDON
M25
HAVERING LB
B186
Beam River
Ingrebourne River
Cranham Hall Farm
Elm Park
Corbets Tey
Park Corner Farm
Hacton
B1421
Manor Farm
A125
Rainham Lodge Farm
Central Farm
Great Sunnings Farm
South Hornchurch
Albyns Farm
Berwick Pond
Berwick Ponds Farm
Gerpins Farm
Bush Farm
South Hornchurch Airfield
Gerpins Lane
Parsonage Farm Estate
Warwick Lane
ESSEX
RAINHAM
A13
THURROCK DISTRICT
Rainham Marshes
Moor Hall
Firing Ranges
B1335
Wennington
Aveley
Mar Dyke
RIVER THAMES
Purfleet
A1090

Gravel workings/land backfilled/ restored/left derelict

Arable — mainly field vegetables

Pasture/grassland

Woodland

Natural water

Residential/commercial

Allotments

Open space
Heath/scrub   } areas too small to be shown at this scale
Marsh/reeds

0   2km

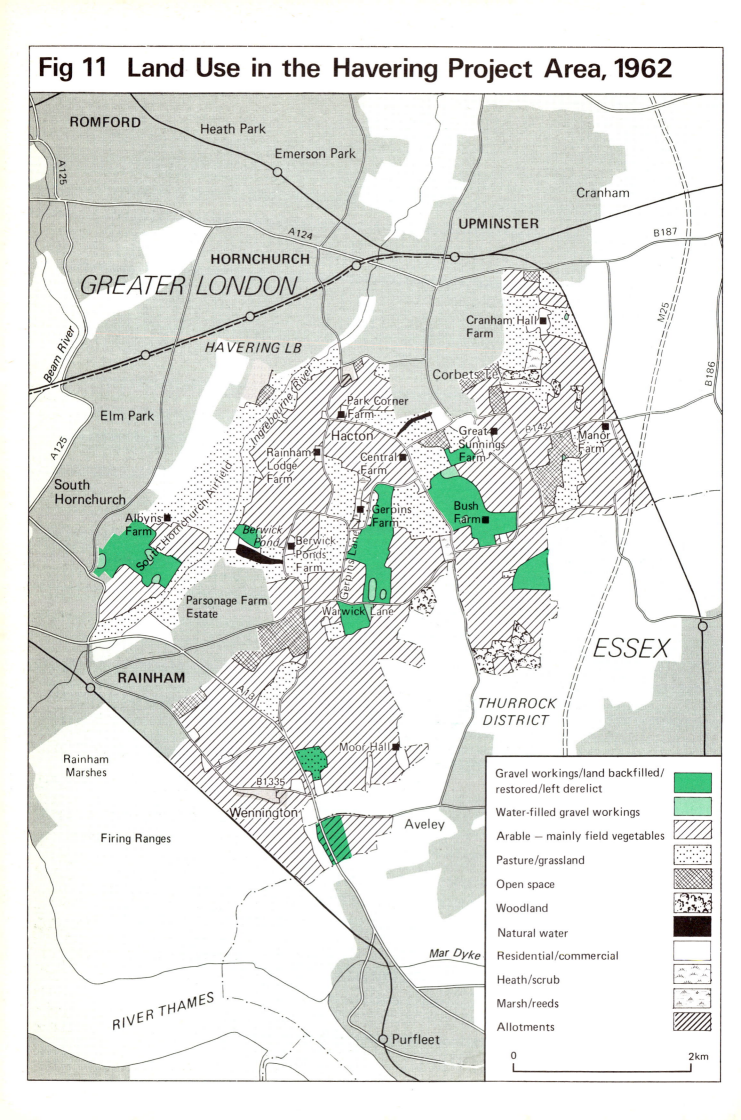

Fig 11 Land Use in the Havering Project Area, 1962

ROMFORD
Heath Park
Emerson Park
A125
Cranham
A124
UPMINSTER
B187
HORNCHURCH
GREATER LONDON
M25
B186
HAVERING LB
Cranham Hall
Farm
Ingrebourne River
Corbets Tey
Elm Park
Park Corner
Farm
A125
Hacton
Great
Sunnings
Farm
B1421
Manor
Farm
Rainham
Lodge
Farm
Central
Farm
South
Hornchurch
Bush
Farm
Albyns
Farm
South Hornchurch Airfield
Gerpins
Farm
ESSEX
Berwick
Pond
Berwick
Ponds
Farm
Gerpins Lane
Parsonage Farm
Estate
Warwick Lane
RAINHAM
A13
*THURROCK
DISTRICT*
Rainham
Marshes
Moor Hall
B1335
Firing Ranges
Wennington
Aveley
Mar Dyke
RIVER THAMES
Purfleet

Gravel workings/land backfilled/restored/left derelict	
Water-filled gravel workings	
Arable — mainly field vegetables	
Pasture/grassland	
Open space	
Woodland	
Natural water	
Residential/commercial	
Heath/scrub	
Marsh/reeds	
Allotments	

0   2km

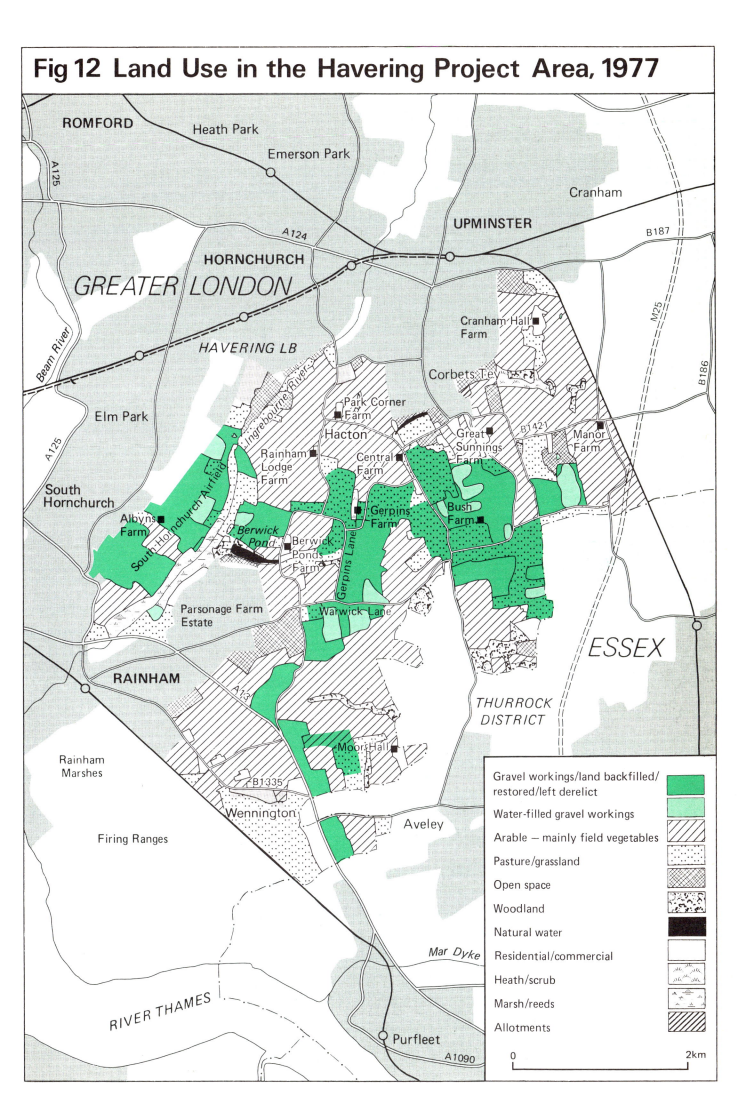

Fig 12 Land Use in the Havering Project Area, 1977

ROMFORD

Heath Park

Emerson Park

Cranham

A125

A124

UPMINSTER

B187

HORNCHURCH

GREATER LONDON

M25

Cranham Hall
Farm

B186

HAVERING LB

Beam River

Corbets Tey

B1421

Elm Park

Park Corner
Farm

Manor
Farm

Ingrebourne River

A125

Hacton

Great
Sunnings
Farm

South
Hornchurch

Rainham
Lodge
Farm

Central
Farm

Albyns
Farm

*Berwick
Pond*

Gerpins
Farm

Bush
Farm

South Hornchurch Airfield

Berwick
Ponds
Farm

Gerpins Lane

ESSEX

Parsonage Farm
Estate

Warwick Lane

RAINHAM

A13

THURROCK
DISTRICT

Rainham
Marshes

MoorHall

B1335

Firing Ranges

Wennington

Aveley

Mar Dyke

RIVER THAMES

Purfleet

A1090

Gravel workings/land backfilled/ restored/left derelict	
Water-filled gravel workings	
Arable — mainly field vegetables	
Pasture/grassland	
Open space	
Woodland	
Natural water	
Residential/commercial	
Heath/scrub	
Marsh/reeds	
Allotments	

0   2km

11.26   A time-series analysis of the changing land use patterns in the project area over the past 45 years reveals that there has been an enormous reduction in the amount of arable land (Table 9 and Figures 10–12). Since 1933, one third of it, 435 hectares, has been lost, 174 hectares of this since 1962.[48,49] This represents a loss of almost 12 hectares per annum, equivalent to one small farm a year. The area affected by mineral workings is now 577 hectares, although only from 120 hectares to 200 hectares are actually being worked at any one time. There has been a direct transfer of high-grade agricultural land to that degraded by mineral workings. By 1977, only 174 of the 577 hectares had been restored to any form of agricultural use, mainly for keeping unhealthy-looking horses and, as such, their classification as agricultural land is debatable. In 1977, 397 hectares of Grade 1 land (21 per cent of the study area) had been rendered agriculturally marginal or sub-marginal by the legacy of the sand and gravel workings. Table 9 indicates that 55 per cent of the project area (1,046 hectares) is devoted to agriculture and 31 per cent is, or has been, affected by sand and gravel workings. These rapid land use changes give rise to widespread uncertainty and underly a series of conflicts which are described in the next chapter.

11.27   The demand for land for formal recreation in the project area is likely to increase. A survey carried out in 1979 showed that, in recent years, there has been a considerable growth of interest in space-using outdoor activities, such as sailing, motorcycle-scrambling, riding, fishing and model aeroplane-flying.

11.28   Land is unlikely to be lost to building development in the project area, provided that Green Belt legislation is as strictly enforced as it has been in the past, but future road-building programmes such as the M25 and the possible north/south link road across South Hornchurch Airfield will involve loss of land, e.g. the M25 will take 28 hectares of high-quality agricultural land from Manor Farm, Upminster.

Land ownership

11.29   Figure 13 shows land ownership in the project area. The three major landowners are the gravel companies, the farmers, some in fragmented holdings, and the public authorities. The latter include the London Borough of Havering, Essex County Council, the Department of the Environment and the Greater London Council, which between them own 28 per cent of the project area. Table 10 shows the use of this publicly-owned land, 32 per cent of which appears to lie vacant.

Table 10: Publicly-owned land in the project area

Land use			ha.	%
Agriculture			260	49
Vacant land			166	32
Public Open Space			43	8
Woodland			26	5
Education			25	5
Cemetery			7	1
Total			**528**	**100**

11.30   Market forces would probably ensure that land in Havering would be extracted for gravel, filled with rubbish and then developed for building. The planning system and government policy for the protection of agricultural land have gone some way to preventing this process. Nevertheless, land ownership patterns (Figure 13) and the fragmentation of holdings illustrate the pressure under which agriculture finds itself and this, together with the large amount of vacant land, contribute to the very poor quality of the landscape generally.

Administrative pattern

11.31   The pattern of administration is complex, with a range of central and local government organisations applying their own policies in the same area and, on any one issue, many of their departments can be involved. At central government level, the Departments of Environment and Transport, the Ministry of Agriculture, Fisheries and Food, the Countryside Commission and the Nature Conservancy Council have all been involved with the experiment to a greater or lesser extent. At county level, many different departments in the Greater London Council have responsibilities in the area, e.g. for applications for mineral extraction on sites over 2 hectares. The second tier of local government involves the many departments of the London Borough of Havering, most of which have had some involvement with the experiment. In addition to these, other statutory bodies, such as the Water Authority and the Electricity Board, have interests in the area. With the involvement of so many authorities with conflicting objectives, there is such a complex pattern of policy making and of land ownership in this small area that it is not surprising that confusion and contradictions occur.

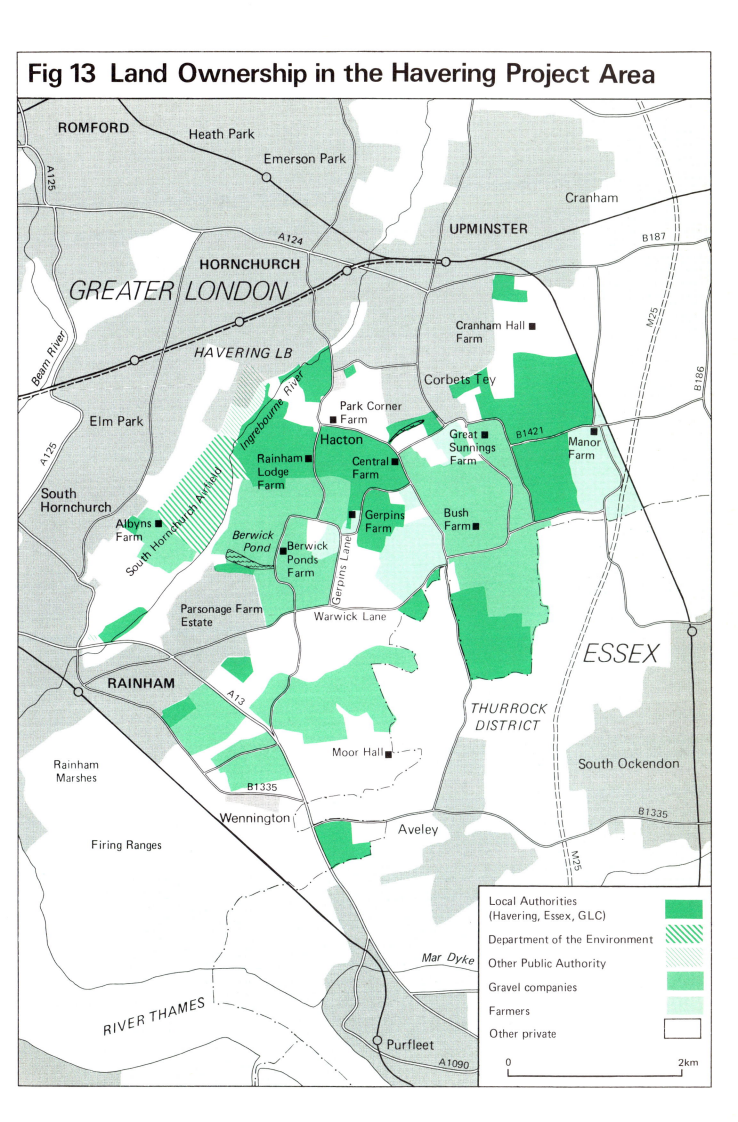

Fig 13 Land Ownership in the Havering Project Area

ROMFORD
Heath Park
Emerson Park

UPMINSTER
Cranham

A125

A124

HORNCHURCH
GREATER LONDON

B187

M25

Beam River

HAVERING LB

Cranham Hall
Farm

B186

Elm Park

Corbets Tey

Ingrebourne River

Park Corner
Farm

A125

Hacton

Great
Sunnings
Farm

B1421

Manor
Farm

South
Hornchurch

Rainham
Lodge
Farm

Central
Farm

South Hornchurch Airfield

Albyns
Farm

Berwick
Pond

Berwick
Ponds
Farm

Gerpins
Farm

Bush
Farm

Gerpins Lane

Parsonage Farm
Estate

Warwick Lane

ESSEX

RAINHAM

A13

THURROCK
DISTRICT

South Ockendon

Rainham
Marshes

Moor Hall

B1335

B1335

Firing Ranges

B1335

Wennington

Aveley

M25

Mar Dyke

RIVER THAMES

Purfleet

A1090

Local Authorities (Havering, Essex, GLC)	
Department of the Environment	
Other Public Authority	
Gravel companies	
Farmers	
Other private	

0   2km

Chapter 12: Analysis of the Problems

Introduction

12.1   The proximity of urban development is the dominating feature of the project area and the main reason for setting up the experiment. It is the urban influence which gives rise to many of the problems in the area, as genuine conflicts of interest arise. It is thought that fragmentation of farm holdings results from the pressure of the urban land market and the same pressure creates 'hope value', i.e. land held vacant in the hope of development. It is the nearby urban demand for aggregates which causes pressure for gravel extraction and the consequent conflict with agriculture. Likewise the problem of trespass and vandalism on farms originates from the adjacent urban population. Finally, the local authority is strongly influenced by urban values and considerations, because the majority of the local electorate live in the surrounding urban developments, and in the past has had difficulty in dealing effectively with the problems of the Green Belt.

Underlying pressures

The land market

12.2   Close proximity to London, the high price of land and capital intensive enterprises necessitate a highly commercial attitude on the part of farmers. The high value of the underlying gravel has tempted them to agree to extraction for short-term benefits, in spite of the inevitable reduction in the quality of the land after restoration in the long term. The high value of land can also make farmers susceptible to property speculation. The buoyant market for land encourages the landlord and tenant to circumvent tenancy arrangements, e.g. large payments have been made to tenants to give up agricultural tenancies (Appendix 6). The high level of tenurial uncertainty, especially where farms are owned by gravel companies, or property companies, can disrupt long-term investment and management decisions, e.g. as farm acreages are diminished by gravel extraction the unit becomes progressively less viable. High capital and labour costs and the shortage of land necessitate very intensive cropping, made possible by the quality of the land, so that every last piece of land is used and hedges and footpaths are removed. High labour costs also necessitate the mechanisation of operations, e.g. the use of flail-type hedge trimmers, and cutting hedges down to ground level to minimise operations. The large nearby population encourages farm gate sales, e.g. potatoes, Christmas trees, logs, and non-agricultural activities, e.g. storing caravans, depots for construction companies.

12.3   High capital investment and the very strong demand for gravel makes for a highly commercial attitude on the part of gravel companies and encourages rapid exploitation, where short-term interests predominate over the long-term concern for adequate restoration and the effect on the landscape. There are few commercial incentives to carry out high-quality restoration, e.g. the high cost of hired machinery, which means that machines do not stop work in wet weather when moving the soil completely destroys its structure, and the shortage of suitable fill material at an economic price.

12.4   The high value of land and high level of uncertainty, encouraged by occasional successful planning appeals, favours property speculation and can result in the fragmentation of farm holdings and the retention of land in an unused condition in the hope that it will be released for building development. The absence of a Local Plan for the area does not help the situation.

12.5   The large local market gives rise to pressures for the development of non-agricultural uses, e.g. car-breakers yards, building and construction depots, riding stables, caravan sites. This causes deterioration in the landscape, traffic problems and puts pressure on the enforcement procedures of the local planning authority.

Complexity of administration

12.6   Problems arise from the complex multi-level administration and from the administration of a non-urban area from an urban base. These include the following:

   i.   the apparent inconsistencies between government policies on agriculture and environmental planning e.g. arising from the dilemma of balancing transport costs of gravel extraction against agricultural losses;

   ii.   the inadequate conditions attached to many gravel extraction planning permissions up to the mid-1960s;

   iii.   the division of responsibilities for minerals planning—the local planning authority (the London Borough of Havering) receive applications for mineral extraction, but only make recommendations to the Greater

London Council, who deal with all applications for any site over 2 hectares and are also responsible for enforcement procedures for gravel and the licensing and control of waste disposal and tipping operations; but insufficient numbers of trained staff result in very infrequent site visits and thus inadequate enforcement procedures;

iv. the rigidity of the Ministry of Agriculture, Fisheries and Food policy on gravel extraction and restoration to agriculture in the past has prevented the reassessment by local planning authorities of poorly-restored land for other uses;

v. the lack of a Local Plan for the project area;

vi. the lack of a clear public policy for the acquisition of land along the urban edge in the project area.

12.7   These underlying pressures are manifested in a number of conflicts between land uses and activities which give rise to the problems described in the following paragraphs.

Problems for farmers

12.8   The main cause for concern is uncertainty about the future of the land, both because of speculative acquisition and of gravel working, in an area where 48 per cent of the land is owned by property companies and gravel companies. The very thing which has helped the development of agriculture is also in demand for the construction industry in London and there is constant pressure for its extraction: 37 per cent of the land is owned by gravel companies and much is leased to farmers so that a high degree of uncertainty prevails, which tends to weaken the long-term agricultural industry. So far, land which has been extracted for gravel has not been returned to a reasonable agricultural standard and, in 1977, 397 hectares of Grade 1 land, 21 per cent of the project area, had been rendered agriculturally marginal or sub-marginal by the legacy of the sand and gravel workings (Table 9 and Figure 12). In addition, there is the problem of the decline and loss of the specialist agricultural work-force in areas subjected to prolonged mineral extraction.

12.9   As inadequate conditions on old planning permissions have technically been complied with or are now unenforceable, there is little likelihood of forcing owners to make improvements. Moreover, the land does not appear to come within the official definition of 'derelict land'. However, where appropriate, the local authorities might be able to enter into planning agreements with the gravel companies which would provide them with opportunities for achieving environmental improvements when negotiating further planning permissions. Any such agreement would have to be attractive from a planning point of view and provide a number of community benefits.

12.10   As far as current restoration practice is concerned, back-filling with rubbish makes the implementation and enforcement of conditions very difficult, but a major effort to apply recently-researched techniques is taking place at the Department of the Environment/Ministry of Agriculture/Sand and Gravel Association jointly-sponsored Bush Farm Experiment[47] site in the project area where initial results indicate restoration costs of £12,500 per hectare at 1978 prices. However, elsewhere in the project area, restoration of a very poor quality is still taking place. Farmers who had acquired restored land from the gravel companies at a reduced rent, in an attempt to grow grass and corn, have found that their efforts outweighed the economic return. At the end of the Havering experiment the Ministry were intending to carry out a land capability survey on badly-restored land.

12.11   During the process of extraction and back-filling with refuse, there are other environmental problems. Noise and dust are generated and wind-blown rubbish is strewn along roads and hedgerows. The extraction process can cause a temporary lowering of the water table, which has had an adverse effect on woodlands in the vicinity, where trees have become stag-headed or have died. Farmers allege that, on occasions, the water has been polluted, although this claim has never been substantiated. The Greater London Council's new Minerals Sub-Committee and the strengthening of its enforcement staff, on both planning and site licence conditions, will hopefully improve the situation.

12.12   Over the years then, there has been a steady attrition of agricultural land in favour of mineral extraction, despite the fact that the national agricultural policy is to expand production by $2\frac{1}{2}$ per cent per annum[50]; and that the Ministry of Agriculture currently objects to all gravel applications on Grade 1 land, unless it can be shown that the land will be returned to its original quality after extraction and unless there are no other suitable deposits beneath land of lower quality. Even though the London Borough of Havering's policy is to oppose gravel extraction where the road network is unable to cope with the traffic and on Grade 1 agricultural land unless satisfactory restoration can be guaranteed, it seems likely that land will continue to be released, because they are not the planning authority dealing with all the applications; the final arbiter is often the Department of the Environment. The demand for gravel in the London region is very strong, especially where the source of supply is close to the market, as in Havering, with the consequent saving in transport costs. The report of the Verney Committee[51] favoured a continuation of supplies at roughly the present rate in the south-east and this would imply the release of 800 hectares per annum in the region as a whole, with the Havering area making its due contribution. The construction of the M25, north of the Dartford Tunnel, will add to the pressure for extraction in Havering.

12.13   In spite of these problems, today's buoyant horticultural industry gives farming in the area a strong economic base in the short term. This enables the industry to have a higher tolerance of urban intrusion—trespass and vandalism—which, although high, has not resulted in any farmer giving up farming and leaving the area, as has been cited elsewhere in the country, although it has been a contributory factor in one such decision (paragraph 13.21). However, some farmers have changed their farming patterns to accommodate this nuisance factor, e.g. sheep are no longer kept and the growing of vegetables is kept away from the immediate urban edge. The production of high-value crops means that crop loss or damage must be very severe before the economic viability of the farm is affected.

12.14   Since provision of facilities for outdoor informal recreation is small compared with the demand in the locality and the footpath network is fragmented, *de facto* access to private land is common. Much of this trespass is accounted for by children and teenagers seeking opportunities for adventurous activities, such as shooting air guns or riding unlicensed motorcycles. The major landowners, the farmers and gravel companies, suffer a high level of vandalism, particularly fires, because of this.

Recreation provision

12.15   The project area is not generally well-provided with Public Open Space (Figure 5). The recreation survey[33] gave the general impression that all these sites had the potential to absorb more visitors in an area where the overall level of recreation use was low. This is not surprising in such a degraded environment where local people use such sites in the absence of any suitable alternative. The pattern of use on the urban edge, e.g. Hacton Parkway, is similar to that of urban parks. The potential for environmental improvement and for the provision of recreation facilities which would serve a wider catchment area would seem to be enormous.

12.16   There is a significant use of private land for informal recreation where no clear boundary exists between public and private land, e.g. at Berwick Pond, which is particularly intensively-used, and at Park Corner Farm. Children see farmland as an extension of the open space associated with housing and the design and layout of the urban edge encourages this. There is also a need for improvements to the rights of way system which has suffered from widespread interruption by gravel extraction. There is no coherent network and there are no bridleways at all. The existing routes are poorly-maintained and waymarked, leading to trespass problems.

12.17   In addition to the conflict which exists between recreation-seekers and farmers, there are conflicts between different groups of recreation users, e.g. at Berwick Pond (Appendix 4) and along the River Ingrebourne, where children on bicycles and motorcycles disrupt other more peaceful recreation activities.

12.18   There is also a strong demand for formal recreation in the project area. However, landowners of the large amount of unused land and water seem reluctant to close their options on these vacant sites, even on a temporary basis. This, together with problems of noise and access has, in most cases, prevented the demand from being met.

Landscape and conservation

12.19   The evolution of the landscape in Havering has increased in pace over the last 40 years as agricultural land has disappeared with the advent of gravel working. Before that, the modernisation of agriculture had produced changes but at a much slower pace and on a much smaller scale. The uncertainty about the future resulting from this rapid land use change makes investment decisions difficult; speculative land acquisition occurs; farm holdings are split up into uneconomic units; high quality land is left vacant. The result is a degraded, unattractive landscape, badly affected by Dutch elm disease and overgrazing by horses.

12.20   Where agriculture is still the main activity, traditional landscape features remain, to create a varied landscape of reasonable quality, with a high visual absorption capacity. However, intensive horticultural practices, where productivity takes precedence over the landscape, have had their effect in some areas. Some of these farmers maintain the hedges on their perimeter boundaries to restrict public access, but many internal hedges have been removed as they are no longer needed as shelter for stock, to increase the cultivated acreage and to improve visual supervision of the crops; those that remain are either neglected because of the high cost of maintenance or are mechanically-maintained. Small woods have been neglected and trees felled for firewood because they attract visitors and increase the threat of trespass.

12.21   Although the project area does not contain any commercial forest, ten small amenity woodlands fulfil an important role within the landscape. A number of small blocks of trees exist on farmland and a number of trees

The few hedges that remain are mechanically maintained. This hedge has been almost flailed out of existence

remain in the hedgerows, although Dutch elm disease has dramatically reduced the tree cover. The loss of trees has opened up the landscape, making the intrusive nature of urban and industrial developments more obvious. No substantial replanting is taking place.

12.22 Gravel extraction, particularly over the last 15 years, has caused rapid and noticeable changes. Areas where this land use is dominant show a landscape transformed by the removal of field boundaries, hedges and trees and by the frequent reshaping of land contours. The visual absorption capacity has been severely reduced, e.g. 24 per cent of the trees have been lost in the Berwick Pond area over the last few years and 18 per cent of those that remain are dead or dying because of the lowering of the water table during gravel extraction, so that the flat open landscape is dominated by poorly-restored land, gravel tips, silt ponds and rubbish dumps.

12.23 On the Public Open Space sites owned by the local authority (Figure 5), urban park-type management prevails, with extensive areas of mown grass. Some modification of this management regime would result in a more rural environment, but so far there has been no significant change.

12.24 Other features which have affected the landscape are the influence of residential and industrial development and the proliferation of power lines, amongst which the three 275kv and three 132kv lines are the most prominent. The proposed M25 motorway will make a major impact.

12.25 Sites which have been identified as being of high ecological value are Cranham Marsh, Berwick Pond, the Ingrebourne Valley, and Warwick, Whitehall and Running Water Woods. The woods are managed for amenity purposes by Essex County Council but no management regime exists for Berwick Pond or the Ingrebourne Valley. In an area of intensive and specialised land use, there is an obvious need to protect and develop some habitats which will provide a wide variety of flora and fauna. The existing derelict areas, such as old settling pits, might also present opportunities to do this.

Traffic problems

12.26 Many of the minor roads have been damaged by the considerable number of heavy vehicles associated with mineral workings. All the gravel leaves the area by road and lorries also bring in the backfilling material. In addition, some of the gravel works contain readymixed concrete plants which generate their own traffic of mixer trucks and bulk cement lorries. In general, the narrow lanes are inadequate for heavy lorries and the local residents are constantly complaining, particularly along Upminster Road North.

12.27 Heavy congestion on both the major and the local roads has led to proposals for new roads, such as the possible north/south link across South Hornchurch Airfield, which would have a significant impact on the project area. The M25, which is intended to connect the Dartford Tunnel with the M11 and M2, will pass through the eastern edge of the project area. Some of these proposals will put pressure on land in the project area, through direct competition with other land uses, particularly agriculture, and through demand for sand and gravel.

Gypsies

12.28 A large unofficial gypsy site, containing 80 caravans, was established on South Hornchurch Airfield until local residents complained and council officials ejected the caravans and a great deal of bitterness and hostility was caused. The gypsies earn their living from dealing in scrap, from small contract work, e.g. laying tarmac driveways, and from seasonal farm work and therefore need to live in a place where both rural and urban environments are accessible. The Cripps Report[40] drew attention to the possibilities for increasing the provision of gypsy sites on the urban fringe and this area could provide such an opportunity.

Rubbish dumping

12.29   The siting of a GLC Civic Amenities tip in Gerpins Lane was expected to rid farmers and local residents of the problems of fly-tipping, and there was indeed a noticeable decrease throughout the project area. However, the site generates high levels of traffic, both private cars and lorries, causing congestion in Gerpins Lane, and can attract up to 9,000 cars at busy weekend periods. Farmers and local residents near the site suffer considerable nuisance, not only from traffic but also from wind-blown refuse. Additional disturbance is caused by 'totters', who congregate at the site at weekends and at night during the week. The site is also very intrusive visually.

Chapter 13: The Approach

Introduction

13.1   The project officer began work in February 1976 with the broad objectives outlined in paragraph 3.2, a small budget sufficient to cover minor works, travelling expenses etc., and access to information from the Countryside Commission's other countryside management work, on which the experiment was to be based. Experience in these areas[3-8] had suggested that a low-key approach, centred on a project officer, could deal effectively with a wide range of small-scale conflicts and problems in the countryside.

The learning phase

13.2   The role of the project officer was to get to know all the interested parties in the area, including the farmers, amenity groups, and the public authorities and, having gained a good understanding of their problems, to act as a mediator in the inevitable day-to-day conflicts which arise and as a catalyst for action. He had the resources for quick and effective practical intervention where necessary, e.g. mending a broken fence, clearing a footpath, repairing a footbridge. The approach to work on the ground was flexible and included the landowner or tenant doing the work themselves, voluntary labour, such local authority staff as might be available and appropriate and also giving a hand himself when circumstances allowed. In addition to this day-to-day work he could, where necessary, carry out wardening of intensively-used areas and also do some small-scale landscaping work, such as tree planting. Another of his roles was educational: interpreting the problems of farmers and landowners to schoolchildren, amenity groups etc. and explaining the needs of these groups to the farmers in the interests of more harmonious relationships which, in the short term, would lead to compromise solutions in conflict situations, but which, in the long run, would hopefully create a climate in which it would be less likely that conflicts would arise or at least develop to an advanced stage.

13.3   No detailed information base was available and so the project officer became involved in survey work in conjunction with the project evaluator. This also enabled the project staff to get to know the area and the people who lived there.

13.4   A farmers' survey provided a good indication of where small-scale practical work was required but it also highlighted major problems and conflicts confronting the farmer and the agricultural industry, namely the conflict between mineral extraction and highly-productive agriculture, uncertainty of tenure and fragmentation of ownership. These major problems became more apparent during the course of land use and land ownership surveys. The land use conflicts identified were then studied in depth by post-graduate students from the Bartlett School of Architecture, University College, London[28].

Small-scale practical work

13.5   While the survey work and the further studies were being carried out, small-scale practical projects, identified during the farmers' survey, were initiated where immediate action on the ground, using the low-key methods typical of other countryside management experiments[3-8], was possible; within the resource constraints of the experiment, a programme of work was carried out (Figure 7). Examples are given in paragraphs 13.6–13.10.

Rainham Lodge Farm

13.6   Rainham Lodge Farm is one of a group of six small-holdings in the project area owned by Essex County Council (Figure 13) which, before London local government reorganisation, was the authority administratively responsible for the area. Unlike other farms in the area, these holdings have security of tenure, as the county's policy has consistently been one of retaining the land in agricultural use. This stability makes management decisions easier and the scope for small-scale countryside management and landscape improvement work is therefore greater, as both the landlord and the tenants are able to take a positive long-term attitude.

13.7   At Rainham Lodge Farm, a total of 550 trees and 400 metres of hedge material were planted on both the outer and internal boundaries of the farm and in the meadowland adjacent to the river. The trees and hedge material were supplied by the Forestry Section of Essex County Council (who donate trees to their tenants as part of a scheme to combat the effects of Dutch elm disease) and the planting itself was done by the project staff,

95

Tree planting at Rainham Lodge Farm

The gravel company were all set to destroy Bramble Farm, a listed building, but the London Borough of Havering stepped in the nick of time. Although the land was restored it was flat and featureless and devoid of trees and interest

aided by the British Trust for Conservation Volunteers. The cost to the experiment was £222. An agreement was made with local members of the Essex Naturalists' Trust to undertake routine maintenance. One of the lines of new trees runs alongside a public footpath through the farm so that, in addition to improving the landscape in general and providing a useful wind-break, the trees have an immediate amenity value to members of the public using the footpath. While working at the site the project staff took the opportunity of improving the footpath, restoring its original route to avoid damage to crops, and installing two footbridges and a footpath notice. There were plans for an extension of tree planting along the footpath and along the River Ingrebourne.

13.8   On another part of Rainham Lodge Farm, a boundary fence was erected between the fields and the car park of an adjacent public house to prevent trespass by the visitors to the pub. The owners of the pub paid for the fencing material, project staff and volunteers erected the fence and the tenant farmer undertook to maintain it. Having been fenced, the car park, which contained a grassed area, was improved by planting trees, and picnic tables were installed.

Bramble Farm

13.9   In 1977, a 2-hectare site which had been extracted for gravel was restored at Bramble Farm, Corbets Tey, and the present owners began to farm on a small scale, while renovating their seventeenth century farmhouse, which had been saved by the London Borough of Havering from destruction by the gravel company because it was a listed building. A scheme was devised to improve a landscape devoid of trees after gravel extraction, to show what might be achieved. The project staff and conservation volunteers planted 50 trees, donated by the Greater London Council from Hainault Forest, and the owners agreed to maintain the trees and to allow their land to be used as a tree nursery for the project. A large number of the trees have survived, although some of the standards did not withstand transplanting. The landscape in the area has been much improved—an example of what can be achieved on a small scale on reclaimed land, given the co-operation of the owners. Further proposals included the removal of dead elms and the provision of a shelterbelt and a boundary hedge. Advice was given on the establishment of farm visits for children and on the acquisition of the adjacent pond, its organisation for fishing and on the design and implementation of a landscape plan for the pond area.

Warwick Lane Fishery

13.10   The owners of Warwick Lane Fishery, Thurrock Angling Club, approached the project officer for advice on tree planting. A Greater London Council Landscape Architect was commissioned, at no cost to the project, to produce a plan for the landscape improvement of the site, which was visible from roads and footpaths, taking into account the needs of the anglers. With Countryside Commission grant aid at 75 per cent of the total cost of £700, 104 trees were planted by volunteers from the club, supervised by the project officer and the contractor. Future work involving club members would complete the implementation of the plan, including the creation of a recreation area for informal use and hedge and tree planting on the part of the site recently excavated for gravel.

Analysis of larger-scale problems and opportunities

13.11   The aim of the practical work, such as that outlined above, was to effect immediate small-scale improvements. However, the analysis of a particular problem and subsequent practical involvement on the ground often revealed a group of related problems at different levels, ranging from simple practical solutions to major planning issues. The project officer therefore approached the carrying out of minor works with a view to identifying the more fundamental problems in the area so that the results of the work should not be purely cosmetic.

13.12   Once the project officer had identified these fundamental problems and had realised that they were not capable of solution by an experiment designed to operate at a low level with minimal resources, he was faced with an immediate dilemma: under the guidance of the Steering Group, he had to divide his time between small-scale practical works on the ground and in-depth analysis and presentation of the problems identified. The fundamental problems, although not capable of solution by countryside management techniques, could not be ignored.

13.13   It was at this point that the Countryside Commission began the long drawn-out negotiations with the other sponsors and with the Ministry of Agriculture, Fisheries and Food and the Department of the Environment for setting up a new large-scale experiment, involving a more comprehensive area approach. This is outlined in paragraph 14.23. Meanwhile, the project officer was told by the Steering Group, which now included representatives of MAFF and later DOE, to work on two levels: to continue the cosmetic exercise on a small scale and to tackle a major, complex and visually significant problem to demonstrate the advantages of intervention. The preceding paragraphs, without cataloguing every activity, have indicated the effects of the small-scale work; paragraphs 13.14–13.27 and the case studies (Appendices 4, 5 and 6) outline what happened at the higher level of operation.

The Ingrebourne Valley

13.14   The approved Greater London Development Plan[16] identified the Ingrebourne Valley as an "area of opportunity" which has potential for recreation activities and visual enhancement. The River Ingrebourne, which has a tendency to flood and remains relatively wet during the summer months, forms a natural barrier to the majority of urban residents and the valley forms a corridor between urban development and farmland which could provide a wide range of formal and informal recreation facilities. Careful zoning would help to avoid conflict between different recreation activities and between recreation and agriculture. The idea of creating and managing a 'buffer zone' between residential development and agricultural land along the Ingrebourne Valley (Figure 14) evolved from small-scale practical schemes and illustrates how practical involvement can result in the recognition of major opportunities for improvement.

13.15   The practical work began at Hacton Parkway, a 4-hectare linear site between residential development and the River Ingrebourne. It is owned and managed as a district park by the London Borough of Havering and regularly used by both adults and children for informal recreation. The objectives of a tree-planting and rubbish-clearing scheme were to improve the landscape along the river banks, to educate volunteer schoolchildren in tree planting and understanding the countryside, and to monitor the effects of vandalism on planting along the urban edge. Both the local authority and the Water Authority were consulted. The latter objected to the scheme at first because the trees would prevent mechanical trimming of the river banks. Work included clearing out the river by the British Trust for Conservation Volunteers and the planting of 676 trees, using local contractors and schoolchildren, at a cost of £416. Whips and transplants were used to make the trees less noticeable but once they had grown it was hoped that people would regard them as a visual barrier and would be encouraged to stay in the improved environment of the park rather than to cross the river onto productive farmland. The trees improved the visual appearance of the open space but, as expected, half of them were lost by vandalism in the first few months. The pattern of vandalism indicated that anything new attracted attention, but that the trees near the houses, those planted by the children and those planted in larger groups were not so badly affected. It was a useful education exercise as far as it went but the children were supposed to maintain the trees and on the whole this was not followed up. Here the role of the teachers was important. Their attitude must be positive if this sort of work is to become part of the education programme.

13.16   Park Corner Farm is a holding of 73 hectares, owned by two property companies. The tenant farmer produced cereals and vegetables and suffered from the loss of crops by visitors straying from the footpaths. The project officer constructed a footbridge and three signposts, at a cost of £84, to encourage walkers to stay on the footpaths; and distributed 1,500 leaflets, at a cost of £45, explaining the work to the residents of the surrounding housing area (Figure 14) and the result was a partial reduction in crop damage. Similar work carried out on the other footpath on the farm had the same result. However, the signposts were immediately destroyed and should have been made more vandalproof. A damaged sign which was replaced remained intact.

13.17   Project staff then embarked upon a practical exercise to reinforce the boundary between the agricultural and non-agricultural land uses along part of the western side of the farm where trespass, particularly by motor-cyclists, from adjoining scrubland was causing particular problems. The aim was to confine informal recreation to the fields in the valley bottom, by making an impenetrable barrier between these fields and the adjacent agricultural land along a length of 819 metres. This part of the Ingrebourne Valley would then be managed as a 'buffer zone' between the urban area and the farmland, allowing informal recreation of decreasing intensity towards the agricultural land. In return for this, the farmer agreed to provide the labour for landscape improvements on his land in the form of tree planting along the outer boundary and internal boundaries where

Hedge-laying reinforces the boundary between first class agricultural land at Park Corner Farm and recreation use on adjoining land

This aerial view of the River Ingrebourne demonstrates how the river forms a natural barrier between urban development and farmland

Fig 14 The Ingrebourne Valley, Havering

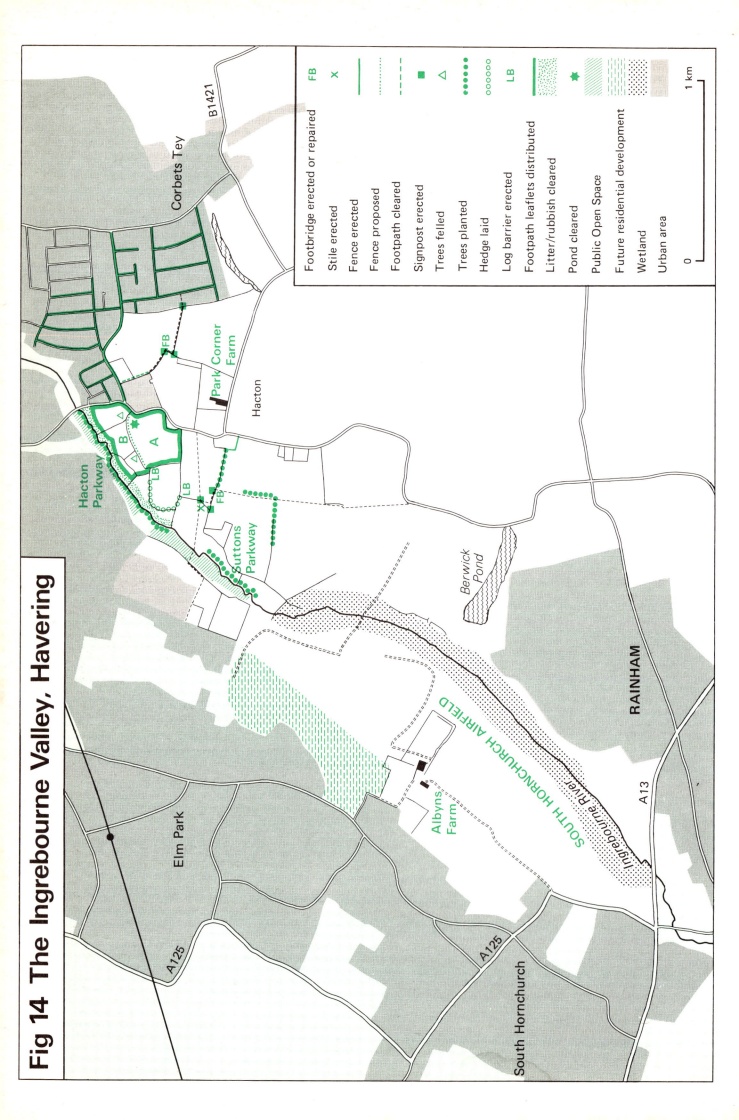

Legend:

FB	Footbridge erected or repaired
X	Stile erected
—	Fence erected
⋯	Fence proposed
– –	Footpath cleared
■	Signpost erected
△	Trees felled
●●●●	Trees planted
○○○○○	Hedge laid
LB	Log barrier erected
▓	Footpath leaflets distributed
★	Litter/rubbish cleared
▨	Pond cleared
▦	Public Open Space
▨	Future residential development
▒	Wetland
░	Urban area

0 ___ 1 km

Map labels:

Corbets Tey
B1421
Park Corner Farm
FB
Hacton
Hacton Parkway
A
B
LB
LB
LB
FB
X
Suttons Parkway
Elm Park
A125
Berwick Pond
Albyns Farm
SOUTH HORNCHURCH AIRFIELD
Ingrebourne River
South Hornchurch
A125
RAINHAM
A13

this did not interfere with the visual supervision of fields, and to screen caravans, an electricity sub-station and a sewerage inspection house. A barrier was created by fencing, hedge-laying and felling dead trees to provide tree trunks which were laid lengthwise to deter trespassing motorcyclists. These measures proved effective, at a cost of £900, including labour, compared with the farmer's unsuccessful efforts by digging a large ditch, which the motorcyclists immediately filled in. They also gave the land a more cared-for look, poor maintenance being a contributory cause of trespass according to a user survey carried out on this site.

13.18   Work was then held up when 15 hectares of the adjacent land was put up for sale because its owners could not obtain planning permission for residential development. The project officer proposed that the London Borough of Havering should buy the land. He submitted a plan showing how public acquisition would enable the boundary-strengthening work to proceed and would prevent fragmentation into smaller lots. It could also lead to an improved management regime with low maintenance costs, whereby half the land, (A on Figure 14) currently idle, could be returned to productive agriculture and the remainder (B on Figure 14) could be managed for informal recreation, thus reducing conflicts between different recreation activities e.g. walkers and motorcyclists, as well as between recreation and agriculture. The scheme would also improve the landscape and conserve the wildlife of the area. The London Borough of Havering, with the help of grant aid from the Countryside Commission, responded positively to this proposal and purchased the land, thus enabling the plan to be implemented although, at the time of writing, no work had been initiated.

13.19   At the other side of the Ingrebourne Valley, the site of South Hornchurch Airfield exemplifies some of the most intractable problems to be found in the project area. The site of a former fighter station, it covers a flat area of Green Belt land of some 200 hectares adjacent to the urban edge. Most of the site has been extracted for gravel and back-filled with refuse and the landscape has been devastated, with no tree cover and, in many parts, no topsoil.

13.20   The southern part, south of Albyns Farm, approximately 80 hectares, is an area of vacant and derelict land. Gravel extraction took place about 30 years ago and the standard of restoration is very poor, there being no topsoil. It is now mostly owned by a development company and is being held vacant in the hope of a successful planning application for development although, so far, all applications have been refused as the site forms part of the approved Green Belt.

13.21   Albyns Farm, owned by a gravel company, is in the middle of the airfield and was, until recently, a successful commercial vegetable-growing unit in spite of the severe trespass and vandalism problems associated with the nearby housing estates. However, the uneconomic size of the holding as gravel extraction progressed, together with the trespass problems, caused the farmer to leave. Farming activities were suspended and the farm house was sold. It remains to be seen whether farming with a new occupier can begin again after mineral extraction, when the quality of the land will be much lower and the holding will have no farm house.

13.22   The northern part of South Hornchurch Airfield, an area of 87 hectares, formerly the site of the runways, is owned by the Department of the Environment and is to be purchased by the London Borough of Havering. It extends east from South Hornchurch housing estate to the River Ingrebourne. It presents the same bleak picture, with backfilling in progress after gravel extraction. Fires from burning rubbish cause regular annoyance to local residents. Children, particularly on unlicensed motorcycles, use the site as an unofficial play area, in the absence of alternative open space and recreation facilities in the neighbourhood. Large mounds and small hillocks, together with derelict wartime installations and acres of open space provide an ideal adventure play environment. The incidence of vandalism, particularly arson and damage to contractors' equipment, is very high. In addition, 80 families of gypsies were camping on the site until they were ejected by local residents and council officers after a protracted and bitter conflict. The landscape after gravel extraction includes an extensive area of water with a well-established flora and fauna, but is being restored by the gravel company in accordance with planning conditions. Twenty three hectares will be developed for housing, 7 hectares of which can be started immediately, but the remainder will have to wait for the land to settle, unless special stabilisation techniques are used.

13.23   The project officer realised that public ownership of the northern 87 hectares presented an opportunity to demonstrate the improvement of a derelict landscape and the creation of recreation facilities in an area with poor provision. He adopted a liaison role between the various interested parties and produced outline proposals, to be followed up by a landscape design and management plan which would enable this site to be of benefit to the local population and to complement the existing environment: the residential development to the west, intensive farming on the eastern side of the river, a wetland area and the existing informal recreation use. It would also provide an example of what could be done given the commitment of the landowner, in this case the London Borough of Havering.

13.24   The objectives of the proposals were:

i.   to create a 'buffer zone' between urban development and farmland, thus reducing trespass, and making it an integral part of a proposed 'buffer corridor' running parallel with the River Ingrebourne;

ii. to provide both formal and informal recreation facilities, aiming for a decreasing formality and intensity of use away from the urban development, but taking account of existing recreation activities on the site;

iii. to improve the existing landscape by retaining existing features of value and creating new ones where appropriate.

13.25 The effective demand for recreation on South Hornchurch Airfield, as represented by those currently taking part in outdoor activities, is for walking, adventure play areas for children, and for the use of unlicensed motorcycles. The creation of a new environment would disrupt the current activities and force them to look for new areas, which might include farmland, unless alternative provision were made. The provision of facilities for existing uses is therefore as important as the creation of new facilities for potential users if the site is to act effectively as a 'buffer zone' and to absorb urban activities. Any scheme should therefore take account of the general pattern of present use and of existing landscape features.

13.26 The intensity of use should gradually decrease away from urban development so that the incidence of trespass on adjacent farmland is reduced and the 'buffer' can absorb urban pressures effectively. Low key management of informal recreation areas should also reduce conflict between users, e.g. between walkers and motocyclists. Landscaping of the site should enhance the urban fringe environment and the design of the new urban edge should enable the provision of a strong structure of integrated uses and should aim to minimise conflicts. Any scheme must be part of an integral plan along the whole valley so that trespass and vandalism problems are not passed further along where management is lacking.

13.27 The idea of a 'buffer zone' along the Ingrebourne Valley thus evolved from two practical projects at separate sites and from the opportunity presented by public acquisition of land to develop and manage the whole area in such a way as firstly to separate the activities, e.g. agriculture and informal recreation, by strong boundaries, and then to integrate them, where possible, in a controlled way. The conclusions drawn are set out in paragraph 14.6.

The use of volunteers

13.28 One of the aims of the experiment was to harness local enthusiasm for environmental improvements, particularly by making use of voluntary labour. There was no shortage of groups willing to take on voluntary work in the project area. The following organisations were most closely involved: British Trust for Conservation Volunteers (national and Havering Branches), Brentwood and District Young Farmers Club, a Hornchurch cub pack, Scotts Primary School, Essex Naturalists' Trust and local secondary schools, through the schools' work experience programme. A wide range of practical work was available and there was no shortage of tasks for volunteers to undertake, e.g. repairing pond banks, clearing ponds, clearing litter and rubbish from recreation sites, tree planting, fencing and scrub clearance. The most effective way of using volunteers was to have a fairly small number working alongside project staff so that there could be adequate supervision. Voluntary labour was also used in conjunction with labour from a local contractor, again taking advantage of the contractor's experience in organising the work. The Manpower Services Commission's schemes were not exploited because, in a three-year experiment, the amount of time spent in administration could not be justified.

Non-practical elements

Education

13.29 Contact between the project officer and local educationalists indicated that, apart from outdoor pursuits a demand existed for the following:

i. field studies sites

ii. practical conservation tasks

iii. farm visits

iv. facilities for individual project work (at senior school and college level).

Many of these needs could be met within the project area if facilities were provided and activities co-ordinated. However, one of the problems is that schools have a traditional idea of farming and the countryside. They prefer to take children to see animals rather than to introduce them to the processes of vegetable production and cereal growing, which is what they need if they are to understand their own environment.

13.30 One particularly successful tree planting exercise, involving a class of children from Scotts Primary School, was organised, but these projects require a high level of supervision, e.g. one adult to four children in this case, so that it was not possible in the context of the experiment to do more than test the idea because of the limitation of project staff time. There is a good supply of suitable work in the project area, provided that adequate supervision can be arranged.

13.31   Some interest has been shown in the land use problems of the area by 'A' level students, and the project officer contributed to the 'A' level Human Biology course at a local comprehensive school.

13.32   Interest in land use problems has been strongest at the level of further education and the experiment has received a constant flow of enquiries and visits from students both in this country and from abroad. The project officer has also given lectures to university groups on several occasions. The benefits from these contacts are reciprocal: project staff benefit from the ideas suggested at meetings with university students and staff and, in some cases, student projects produce useful reports, e.g. the report by students from University College London on land use conflicts in the project area[28], which collated and analysed much of the raw data collected by the project staff during the first 18 months of operation.

Publicity

13.33   The project officer spent a large proportion of his time on promoting and publicising the work of the experiment. It was publicly launched in June 1976 with a public meeting to which representatives of local interest groups and members of the press were invited. The experiment was presented by the local press as a cheap and effective 'clean up' exercise, with the project officer acting as the catalyst to local goodwill and voluntary help. It was emphasised that the cost to local ratepayers would be only £1,000 per annum, i.e. 12½ per cent of the running costs. The experiment therefore represented good value for money as far as the London Borough of Havering was concerned.

13.34   The response of the local press remained favourable throughout the course of the experiment. The project officer was dubbed "Mr. Countryside" and pictured carrying out tasks with volunteers and local schoolchildren such as clearing up rubbish and planting trees. The project officer himself actively encouraged this coverage by inviting the press to attend volunteer tasks because it was felt that the credibility of the experiment needed to be strongly established locally and that favourable press coverage would increase interest in and support for the experiment from local councillors and the community. However, the results of the recreation survey[33] show that it was not as successful at reaching the general public as it was with organised groups.

13.35   During the course of the first year a portable exhibition was prepared which proved to be effective in publicising the experiment. It was shown at local events and to councillors and visitors, e.g. Countryside Commissioners, and was updated and used regularly throughout the course of the experiment. At the beginning, the project officer embarked on a series of talks/slideshows to local clubs and societies and these continued to be a regular feature of his work, covering a wide spectrum of local interest groups, with some engagements further afield as the work attracted wider interest.

Summary

13.36   The countryside management approach in the Havering project area attempted, through close co-operation with many different interest groups, to resolve small-scale conflicts in the area, and, in so doing, to change attitudes. This resulted in practical work on the ground but also helped to identify strategic land use problems. The liaison work, monitoring and feeding back of information to the various planning agencies pointed to the need for co-ordinated administration in the urban fringe. Its operation at both these levels is analysed and discussed in the following chapter.

Chapter 14: Evaluation

Introduction

14.1   The original aim of the experiment was to test the concept of countryside management in an area where severe urban fringe problems prevailed. The overall conclusions and evaluation of the approach adopted both in the Hertfordshire/Barnet and in Havering are to be found in Chapter 4. The aim of this section of the report is to evaluate how effective the approach has been in solving the problems identified in Havering and to provide a basis for action in the future.

14.2   In general terms, the conclusion is that intervention at the level of small-scale practical countryside management has had some success in effecting local improvements and there is scope for more of this type of work. However, given the underlying strategic land use problems and the uncertainty they engender, its potential is limited and there is a danger that the resulting cosmetic improvements, by obscuring the real nature of the problems, might even be counter-productive unless they are put in the context of a much more comprehensive response. This chapter sets practical countryside management in a broader context.

Small-scale practical work

14.3   The small-scale works were carried out with three objectives in mind:
 i.   to make minor practical improvements;
 ii. to explore the problems through practical involvement on the ground;
 iii. to establish the credibility of the experiment so that it could influence decisions at a higher level.

In order to achieve these objectives, the project officer made a positive decision to become involved at difficult sites, i.e. those where the situation was most volatile and where the problems could be seen most clearly, e.g. Berwick Pond and Cranham Hall Farm (Appendices 4 and 6).

14.4   All three above objectives were achieved in some measure. However, lasting practical improvements could best be achieved on sites where there were no underlying strategic problems, e.g. Rainham Lodge Farm (paragraphs 13.6–13.8) illustrates how effective small-scale countryside management can be in a situation where co-operation is forthcoming from the landowner and where uncertainty of land use and land tenure does not exist.

Major policy issues

14.5   In other places where small-scale remedial tasks were attempted, it soon became clear that the causes of the problems were more fundamental and that for countryside management work to be effective, there was a need for a comprehensive planning and management framework, e.g. at Cranham Hall Farm (Appendix 6). However, in other cases, information gained through the small-scale approach led to the identification of opportunities for major improvements, e.g. paragraph 13.18 illustrates how countryside management staff, while making practical improvements on the ground, can also identify opportunities and inform the local authority, or other responsible organisation, who can then take advantage of them. This in turn provides the context in which practical improvements on the ground can be carried out. This process improves the flexibility and responsiveness of local authority planning and management.

14.6   The Ingrebourne Valley proposals (paragraphs 13.14–13.27), which include Hacton Parkway and South Hornchurch Airfield, indicate the opportunities presented by the public acquisition of land in strategically-sensitive areas along the urban edge. Public acquisition gives the local authority the opportunity to manage the land in a coherent way and to avoid the fragmentation of ownership and piecemeal developments which characterise the urban fringe, e.g. at Cranham (Appendix 6). They also indicate the value of developing a 'buffer zone' along the urban edge, firstly to separate the activities, e.g. agriculture and informal recreation, by strong boundaries, and then to integrate them, where possible, in a controlled way. The 'buffer zone' itself can be managed so that the land near the urban edge has an open aspect, becoming gradually more impenetrable, to include a 'wild area', so that the intensity of use decreases towards the agricultural boundary. The Ingrebourne Valley presented an opportunity to develop this idea in practice.

14.7   This approach is the most promising way forward. It opens the way not just to achieving a proper use of public sector land, such as South Hornchurch Airfield, but also to the possibility of negotiating with the private sector to achieve environmental improvements, e.g. at Berwick Pond. An appreciation of the underlying conflicts serves to put the small-scale countryside management approach into perspective but by no means invalidates it. It can be both an effective response to small-scale problems and a successful method of problem exploration.

Liaison with the farmers

14.8   An important result of the experiment was the liaison role that the project officer was able to develop with the farming community. The local branch of the National Farmers Union co-operated from the outset and this resulted in a survey of all the farmers at the beginning, which established relationships on an individual basis, and several subsequent attendances at branch meetings to report on progress or to seek further co-operation. While this has been common to all the Countryside Commission's countryside management experiments, in this case it established an understanding which had not previously existed between the farmers and the urban planning authority. This has been particularly important in relation to the preparation of the Local Plan and is acknowledged by both sides as a great step forward in the future planning and management of the Green Belt in the borough. It is a situation which is not generally typical of the London boroughs as a whole.

14.9   The co-operation of farmers is clearly a key factor in the success of countryside management, based as it is on the idea of a partnership between public and private interests. In order to foster this interest it was perhaps unfortunate that, unlike Hertfordshire/Barnet, and in spite of the eagerness of the farmers to play an active part, the Steering Group did not think it appropriate to include a working farmer in their number for the reasons set out in paragraph 10.6.

Recreation provision

14.10   All the evidence points to the need for more recreation facilities in the area and considerable opportunities exist for its provision—the use of the derelict South Hornchurch Airfield which was to come into public ownership was particularly significant in this context in the choice of the Havering project area. Footpath and bridleway networks, a country park, picnic sites, caravans, golf, boating, angling and motor-cycling should all be considered against a broad overall recreation strategy.

Landscape

14.11   The Havering project area has a greater concentration of severe problems than either of the other urban fringe experimental areas in Bollin Valley[8] and Hertfordshire/Barnet. The scale of physical deterioration over large parts of the project area is the visible manifestation of the underlying conflicts over the present and future use of resources, which involve policy issues at a national and regional level as well as a local one. Powerful commercial interests are involved which existing planning legislation and its inadequate enforcement seem unable to control; countryside management, while adequate for problem exploration and small-scale solutions, was never meant to deal with issues on this scale. While much remains to be done at the practical level, there is a need for more emphasis on the policy issues in order to develop a context within which country-side management can be effective.

14.12   The Havering project area currently has many problems and conflicts which appear insoluble or un-manageable. Nevertheless, there are some positive features which provide unique opportunities. A buoyant agricultural industry provides a strong, economic and social structure in the area and should be protected. The gravel extraction industry gives a temporary economic vitality and dynamism to the area and, while gravel remains in the ground, the planning authority is in a strong bargaining position to use the opportunity provided by the vacant land owned by the gravel companies to create a new urban fringe landscape as well as provision for recreation. Existing geographical resources include natural sites such as Berwick Pond and Cranham Marsh which could be developed for conservation and amenity uses; man-made derelict sites, e.g. South Hornchurch Airfield, provide interesting land forms as the basis for creating new landscapes; the River Ingrebourne provides a natural barrier at the urban edge. The land already in public ownership can be used to provide examples of what can be achieved.

The use of volunteers

14.13   The employment of volunteers has long been an accepted part of the countryside management approach in order to involve the local community, thus helping them develop a knowledge and understanding of their surroundings, to relate to schools' environmental education programmes, to keep costs to a minimum and to provide an enjoyable and constructive leisure activity. There was no shortage of volunteers in this area. However, the educational and social benefits of working with volunteers, particularly children and young adults, must be set against their general low rate of productivity and, in a three-year experiment designed to produce results, productivity was an important factor.

14.14   It was found that the main limitation to using voluntary labour was the need to provide a high level of organisation and supervision. It was sometimes easier and quicker for project staff to do the work themselves. Secondly, voluntary labour is much better suited to some jobs than others, e.g. tree planting is an appropriate task because it is relatively unskilled and labour-intensive, while building a stile can be done more effectively by one or two skilled workers. Thirdly, when using volunteers, consideration must be given to the satisfactions which the volunteers themselves are seeking, e.g. British Trust for Conservation Volunteers are happier doing conservation work, such as tree planting, rather than clearing up litter, and are attracted to sites with some ecological value, such as Berwick Pond, where there are opportunities for bird watching. The cubs wanted work which would qualify them for their conservation badge, the primary schoolchildren needed an educational task and the secondary school pupils wanted work which would provide relevant experience in their search for a job. However, by trying to meet these needs as far as possible, very effective use was made of voluntary labour. An important additional advantage was that volunteer tasks attract interest and publicity and the project officer encouraged the local press photographers to cover such events.

14.15   Two further points should be made. Firstly, voluntary labour is not free. The British Trust for Conservation Volunteers charged £1.50 per man day, plus petrol expenses. In addition, there are expenses attributable to the task in terms of supervision by project staff, hiring appropriate tools etc. Secondly, it would be quite wrong to give the impression that a degraded landscape such as that of this part of Havering can be transformed by means of voluntary labour. As has already been stated, in many cases major problems have to be resolved before any practical work can take place and, even when this has been done, many of the practical projects will be on a scale inappropriate for voluntary labour, e.g. the improvement of badly-restored gravel sites or large-scale tree planting on sites such as Gerpins Lane (Appendix 5).

Non-practical elements

Education
14.16   The educational aspects of the work are outlined in paragraphs 13.29–13.32, from which the conclusion may be drawn that the educational role of the experiment was not fully exploited because of the time needed to organise and supervise practical tasks and follow-up work. This could be a priority in a permanent countryside management service where the local education authority and the teachers should be encouraged to make a positive long-term contribution. The liaison with higher educational establishments for both practical and project work, e.g. Seale-Hayne College, and for problem analysis, e.g. University College London, was generally found to be of great benefit to all concerned.

Publicity
14.17   Initially the work of the experiment was presented in fairly simple terms, with photographs of practical improvements, local volunteers etc. This approach proved to be very acceptable to audiences, was non-controversial and easy to present in visual terms. However, having gained a realistic appreciation of the major problems, the project officer then spent a good deal of time interpreting these issues to landowners, planners and policy makers at local, regional and national level, in the form of lectures, tours of the area and the preparation of a portable exhibition. The main emphasis was on problem interpretation rather than prescribing solutions because it was recognised that the underlying conflicts in the area were complex and not open to quick and easy answers. While continuing to point to the value of the small-scale approach, he attempted to place it in the context of the underlying issues.

14.18   Publicity and promotion of the work of the experiment have proved to be an important factor, giving tangible gains in terms of local support, particularly in the attitude of the local councillors. However, a continued effort needs to be made to put the original simple message of countryside management into its proper context and, as public support is vital to the success of any future work in the area, it is essential to present the public with the real issues and the opportunities that exist for their solution. It is obvious from the results of the recreation survey[33] that half-way through the experiment only 10 per cent of the general public knew of its existence and this is something that should be examined further.

Summary

14.19   The problem has been one of resource management in an environment of pressure, conflict, uncertainty and rapid change. The project area is dominated by competition for the use of land between different groups: farmers, gravel companies, rubbish disposal companies, recreation seekers, local residents, gypsies, road builders, conservationists etc., all of whom have legitimate claims on a diminishing resource. The essential thing is to look at the problem as a whole—one component, such as gravel extraction, should not be singled out, however important, as what matters is understanding the relationships and interactions between them all.

14.20 It is also necessary to accept that there is no final solution nor panacea for the more intractable problems. In spite of the fact that there are opportunities for compromise solutions, some conflicts are inevitable, e.g. agriculture and gravel extraction both need the same resource, and the effective management of conflict becomes more important than seeking a solution.

14.21 Within a strong planning context, there would be a role for a practical countryside management service in developing and maintaining a strong multi-functional structure, acting as a facilitating agency and feeding back information for the monitoring of planning policy and its implementation. It would be involved in the multi-use management of selective sites, the management of publicly-owned land, particularly along the 'buffer zones' and would have a practical involvement on private land.

14.22 The problems and conflicts found in Havering may be latent in other areas where pressures are increasing but where the symptoms, as yet, are not so obvious. A pre-requisite for an effective response will be a willingness to face up to the fundamental problems and, given the political will, to make the necessary financial investment for the development and management of a valuable environmental resource.

14.23 In recognition of the need to solve or to manage these fundamental problems, the experiment's sponsors were negotiating the setting up of a new large-scale experiment, involving both the Department of the Environment and the Ministry of Agriculture, Fisheries and Food, and with substantially increased funding. The aim was to test solutions to the problems identified in the context of an overall approach, linking planning and management. Its objectives were as follows:

i. to examine the relationship between the statutory Local Plan, to be prepared by the London Borough of Havering, and the management plan, to be prepared by the project leader, to demonstrate how a balanced approach of both planning and management might achieve the objectives of the Green Belt;

ii. in association with existing experimental work, to examine methods of achieving the restoration of any future gravel workings to productive agricultural use, and to make recommendations, including the improvement of standards of waste disposal;

iii. in relation to existing areas of badly-restored land:
   a. in association with the Ministry of Agriculture's experimental work, to examine methods of bringing this land back to productive agricultural use
   b. to make recommendations for other land uses, such as afforestation and formal and informal recreation facilities, and to implement proposals as appropriate
   c. to improve the landscape by amenity tree planting;

iv. to examine the effects of the fragmentation of farm holdings on the economics of agriculture, on landscape and on planning control, and to make recommendations;

v. to test the effects of the provision of new informal recreation opportunities on reducing the pressure on highly-productive farmland;

vi. to conserve the valuable landscape and wildlife features of the area and to implement improvement measures;

vii. to test methods of stimulating the interest, awareness and appreciation of the countryside by the local people;

viii. to communicate the results of the experiment, through the Countryside Commission, by means of reports, publications and seminars;

ix. to establish an appropriate administrative and financial framework for the possible long-term implementation of countryside management in the Havering Green Belt.

14.24 Unfortunately, the economic climate resulted in the Countryside Commission having to withdraw its funding and a unique opportunity was lost. Meanwhile the London Borough of Havering, with Countryside Commission grant aid, have set up a permanent countryside management service to tackle the small-scale problems over the whole of their Green Belt area.

Fig 15 Bury Farm, Edgwarebury Lane, London Borough of Barnet

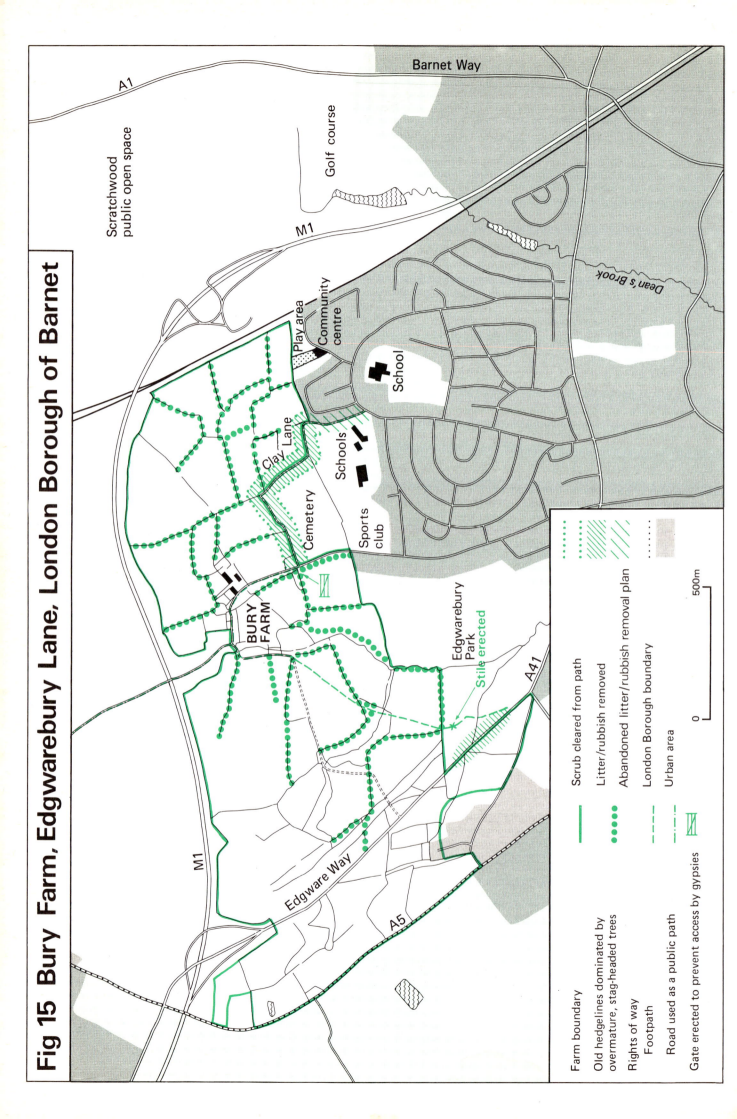

Barnet Way

A1

Scratchwood public open space

Golf course

M1

Community centre

Play area

Clay Lane

Schools

Cemetery

Sports club

School

Dean's Brook

BURY FARM

Edgwarebury Park

Stile erected

A41

M1

Edgware Way

A5

Legend:

Farm boundary

Old hedgelines dominated by overmature, stag-headed trees

Rights of way
Footpath

Road used as a public path

Gate erected to prevent access by gypsies

Scrub cleared from path

Litter/rubbish removed

Abandoned litter/rubbish removal plan

London Borough boundary

Urban area

0   500m

Appendix 1: Case Study: Bury Farm, Edgwarebury Lane, London Borough of Barnet

Introduction

A1.1   To the north of Edgware, in Barnet, is Bury Farm, a holding of 200 hectares in the ownership of an Oxford college and farmed by a tenant. Its western, northern and eastern boundaries are formed by the A41, M1 and the main St. Pancras railway line (Figure 15). It is adjacent to a large housing estate and, as such, on the very edge of urban London but, in spite of suffering from a variety of urban fringe problems, it is still a viable agricultural concern, the principal farming enterprise being beef cattle, with fodder crops of corn and barley. It is used here to illustrate a number of aspects of countryside management work and the extent to which this has been effective in dealing with the problems of this particular farm.

The problems

A1.2   During this century, London housing has steadily advanced right up to the farm's boundary and it has suffered losses of land for the building of the main line railway out of St. Pancras, the A41 and the M1. The farm suffered from problems of trespass and vandalism: damage to crops, e.g. by motorcyclists, damage to buildings and fences, cattle-worrying by dogs, straw-burning, illegal gypsy encampments and rubbish dumping. The results of the recreation survey[33] and the neighbourhood study[42] and frequent observation by the project staff showed that local children, mostly under 11 years of age, were the main culprits, although older children were the cause of damage by motorcycles.

A1.3   The farmer had tried to solve the problems himself. He had asked the police and the London Borough of Barnet to remove the gypsies, but no action had been taken. He had also taken out all the internal hedges, both to increase his arable acreage and to improve supervision of the land adjacent to the housing estate, by increasing visibility across the holding. However, this had left him with the inconvenience of a footpath running across three fields and he had applied for a diversion of the right of way. The removal of hedges had also resulted in a dying landscape, leaving lines of stag-headed oaks, a few of which died and were removed each year, and there was a line of dead elms along the south ridge.

A dying landscape—overmature, stag-headed trees are all that remains of what was once a hedgerow

A1.4   At the same time, the land was the subject of a planning application by a private leisure company, with the agreement of the landowner, for the development of a leisure complex, including a private 18-hole golf course with a membership of 2,000, a public 18-hole golf course, an equestrian centre, 20 tennis courts, a private club house, a public entertainment and leisure area, residential accommodation with 100 rooms and administrative space, a conference centre and car parking for 2,500 cars. This and similar applications were eventually turned down by the local planning authority on Green Belt grounds. A further application for the development of a private hospital and health clinic associated with an organic farming system was refused and the subsequent appeal dismissed. However, the uncertainty continues as, immediately adjacent to this land, planning permission is being sought for a hypermarket.

A1.5   In view of the uncertain future of the holding, no long-term project management was carried out on the farm itself, e.g. although the dying landscape was visible to millions of people from the main railway lines and roads from London, both the landlord and the tenant were unwilling to consider the necessary comprehensive tree planting to improve the situation. Activities were therefore limited to the surrounding area, including the housing estate itself, in order to test short-term solutions to some of the problems such as trespass.

Project work

A1.6   An extensive programme of work began as early as April 1976, with repairs to the farm's boundary fence to prevent motorcyclists riding on the cereal crop. The project staff supported the farmer's approach to the local authority for the removal of the gypsies but without success. Eventually, however, they were persuaded to leave and the lane in which they had camped and left their rubbish was tidied up, and a gate constructed at its entrance in order to discourage its use by vehicles, although access for pedestrians, motorcycles and horses was not hindered. Exhaustive patrolling of the farm area was carried out by the project staff to deter trespassers and to clear the rubbish dumping and fly-tipping in the lanes. Stiles were erected on the footpath. An early plan to clear the rubbish and create a play area in Clay Lane was abandoned because the residents who lived immediately adjacent to the lane were not prepared to take part.

A1.7   At the suggestion of the project staff, the farmer agreed to a series of afternoon visits to the farm by young children from a school in nearby Borehamwood. However, he was not keen to further this invitation to teenagers.

A1.8   The programme of small-scale works led to an involvement with the local community in the adjacent housing estate. A neighbourhood study[42] showed that one of the reasons why the farm suffered so severely from trespass by children was the lack of adequate open space and play areas within the estate, most of the open space that was available being wasteland waiting for further housing development. The large area of Public Open Space on the other side of the M1 was considered to be too far to walk and too near for a car journey, where a car was available. The project officer invited two students from the West London Institute of Higher Education to examine this problem as a landscape project. The study included interviews with estate residents and resulted in the identification of a suitable area for a play space (see illustration below), designed and costed by the students. It was adjacent to the farmland, on land owned by the London Borough of Barnet, and the intention was to create an attractive alternative, where the local children could play, and which would act as a 'buffer' between the housing and the farmland, and at the same time to reinforce the farm boundary.

The high density housing is on the very edge of agricultural land—the open foreground is now housing plus an adventure play area

A1.9   The scheme was discussed with the local residents' association who agreed to the need for additional play areas. They felt that this project would help to diminish the amount of trespass by providing an alternative, by defining a clear boundary between open space and farmland and also by making the urban residents realise the damage to farming that such interference caused. They thought that there was a need for a co-ordinated education programme. In the case of rubbish dumping, they agreed to publicise the location of the legitimate refuse disposal site. They also agreed to help with tidying-up and fencing the lane between the housing and the farm and with tree planting to create a pleasant country walk and to enhance the local environment.

A1.10   The scheme for the play area was presented to the London Borough of Barnet who accepted the design and agreed that it should be implemented by the project staff, using partly local materials, once the housing development had been completed. It was completed during the summer of 1979. However it will not be possible to assess its effectiveness until the complementary work of strengthening the boundary between it and the farmland has been carried out by the London Borough of Barnet.

A1.11   The neighbourhood study showed that the residents' attitude to the planning application for the future development of the land appeared to support its retention as farmland, although they did not understand the land use conflicts involved. They realised that the development of a leisure complex would restrict their free access to the area and reduce the amount of open space. It would be unlikely that many of the facilities would be made available to the public at large, and then only on a payment basis and at a price which most of the local residents would not be able to afford.

Conclusions

A1.12   In order to reduce the uncertainty about the future of the land and to preserve it for agricultural use, the project staff recommended that the London Borough of Barnet should acquire the land, and draw up an integrated farm management plan, embracing agricultural, conservation, recreation and education objectives, thus making it a valuable asset for the community. They felt that if this recommendation were to be accepted, it would indicate the positive input which the experiment had made into planning issues, the local authority's commitment to countryside management objectives and would provide a policy context within which countryside management could be more purposeful.

A1.13   The London Borough of Barnet's stated policy is "to continue with the assistance of the Greater London Council in appropriate cases to buy land in the Green Belt in order to secure its use for Green Belt purposes". However, it does not seem appropriate to use compulsory purchase powers, nor are they likely to have the financial resources necessary to purchase the land from a landowner who is holding it as a long-term investment. The local authority might find the resources to enter into access and management agreements, e.g. for dead elm removal and tree planting, but this again relies on the agreement of the landowner and his tenant which, in this case, has not been forthcoming.

A1.14   This case illustrates how countryside management can respond successfully to day-to-day problems and can point the way to the successful solution of large-scale problems outside its own remit. Implementation then depends on political will and the allocation of financial resources.

Appendix 2: Case Study: RUPP No. 51—Wilkins Green to Colney Heath, Hertfordshire[52]

Introduction

A2.1   The work on this project started after a tenant farmer had complained to the local authority that people were trespassing on his land, causing damage to fences and crops, in order to avoid using an impassable Road Used as a Public Path (RUPP). When the District Engineers could offer no help, he approached the project staff and it was agreed that resources from the experiment could be used to attempt a solution which would benefit the farmer, the riders and the walkers.

A2.2   A RUPP is a highway and therefore may be used by pedestrians, equestrians and motor vehicles but this one, typical of many footpaths and bridleways in the project area, had become impassable to any type of user for much of the year because of the lack of regular maintenance. It is doubtful whether any maintenance had been carried out for 15 years, as the path had become choked with vegetation and access was restricted to a narrow 1.2 metre section through the centre for most of its length of 2.5 km. (Figure 16). The effect of concentrated wear on this section had destroyed the original surface and the area had become waterlogged, because the central depression acted as a water trap where the original drains had become blocked. The adjacent farmland was therefore used as an alternative route.

Fig 16 Bridleway Clearance: RUPP No 51 – Wilkins Green to Colney Heath, Hertfordshire

←1.2 metres→

Dense scrub (now cut back to edge of original path)

Original path shape (now restored)

Original ditch (now restored)

Pitted, waterlogged central area

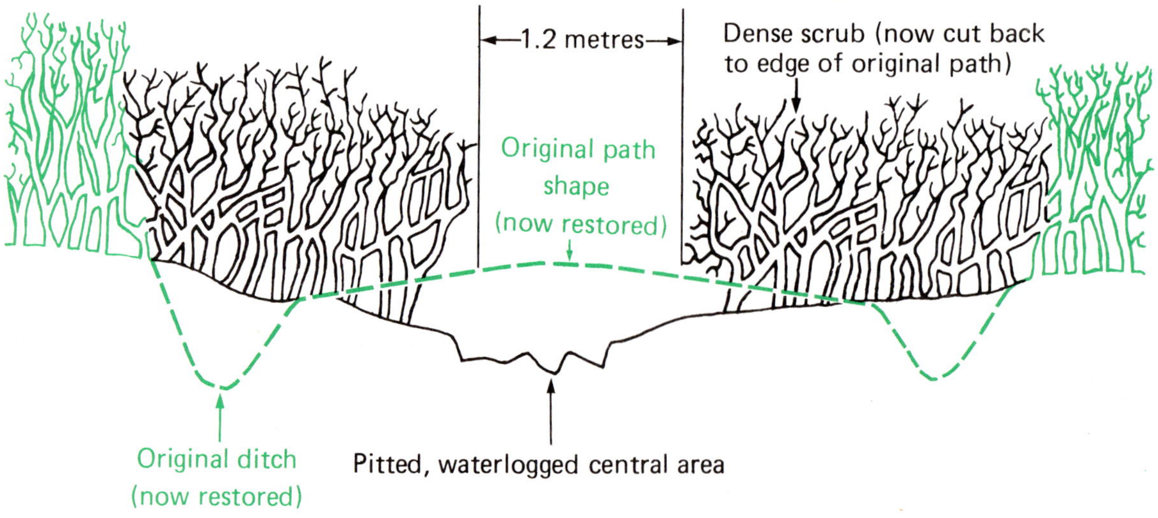

Aims of the project

A2.3   The primary aim was to restore the bridleway to a condition in which access and drainage would remain unimpeded and seasonal maintenance could be carried out under reasonable conditions. Secondly, it was hoped that opening this route to the public would relieve pressure on the adjacent farmland. Finally, a wildlife monitoring exercise was carried out to determine the extent to which opening up the area resulted in species changes.

Project work

A2.4   The first stage was project design and negotiation with the parties involved. It was agreed that the first task would be scrub clearance, followed by ditching and reshaping. In order to determine the most effective method, several ways of tackling the project were investigated.

A2.5   As the farmer regarded the path as being the Council's responsibility which they had neglected and the solution proposed was experimental, he was not prepared to offer any help, e.g. in the form of lending ditching/ hedging machinery, even though he was, hopefully, going to benefit from diminished trespass and improved field drainage. Similarly, the District Council were unable to lend any machinery because the Rights of Way Review was taking place and expenditure on rights of way work was being cut back until its completion.

A2.6   As such a large amount of scrub clearance was necessary before a start could be made on ditching and reshaping, buying or hiring machinery was considered. The two major tasks of scrub clearance and ditching could be tackled with conventional machinery, i.e. flail and back hoe, but the limited access discounted the use of a normal tractor. A number of sales representatives from mini-tractor firms were contacted but without success. (Later, once the clearance and drainage had been completed, a Kubota tractor was used to grade the section between the old railway and the A405.)

Grading was carried out using a hired mini-tractor

A2.7   Scrub clearance by hand seemed the only solution but would have been too time-consuming without the involvement of large numbers, so various local voluntary bodies were asked to help. The Footpath Society already organised clearing parties in the area on a two-weekly basis and were happy to add this lane to their rota. A number of local riding establishments, who were keen to see the work done, were contacted but with little success as they were not well-organised and few were prepared for really hard work. Their interest waned rapidly when they learned of the involvement of the Footpath Society. The other source of labour came from the Community Service Order scheme, where young offenders have to take part in community service as an alternative to prison sentences or fines. They provided four workers on most Sundays. The scrub clearance was thus carried out by hand by the project staff, volunteers and Community Service workers.

A2.8   The work done by the project staff involved three men using power tools, e.g. chain saws and brush cutters, and the result was very efficient work carried out by professionals. They cleared 45.5 metres of dense scrub per day, including the removal of blackthorn, hawthorn, brambles, dead elms, small hazel, oak, ash etc. over a width of 4 metres.

A2.9   The volunteers were usually made up of from eight to ten inexperienced but hard-working individuals, who were very keen but who, unless under supervision, tended to clear only the amount of scrub necessary for passage on foot, instead of the amount required, which extended right across the width beyond the lateral ditches to the lining hedges, where these remained, on both sides. The volunteers had difficulty in burning all the cut vegetation and project staff had to complete the task. However, when properly supervised, the members of the Footpath Society were very useful and were able to clear up to 91 metres of the light scrub per day.

A2.10   The Community Service Order workers needed constant supervision, which sometimes prevented the project staff from carrying out their own work and was an inefficient use of resources. However, a number showed a genuine interest in the work and contributed well, clearing up to 27 metres of dense scrub per day.

A2.11   Having cleared the scrub, the next stage was to solve the acute drainage problem and a local Polytechnic engineering student carried out a drainage survey. An Iseki TX 3000, 4-wheel drive tractor, with a back hoe, was then hired on a weekly basis to carry out the ditching work. Scrub clearance had revealed that in spite of heavy silting, there was a reasonable ditch along most of the path and the mechanical ditching proceeded fairly rapidly. The long-term use by horses had created a U-shape across the lane. The silt and debris removed from the ditch was deposited in the central depression to build this up, to allow the water to drain sideways, and this was compacted by the machinery working over the top of it. Blackthorn stumps, which had been left after scrub clearance, had to be removed as they presented a considerable risk to the tractor tyres. After the ditching work, a scraper blade was fixed to the rear of the same vehicle so that the path could be graded and reshaped. Finally a lorry-load of earth and rubbish was removed from the entrance to the lane and a gate was erected to discourage rubbish dumping occurring in the future, although access was not hindered. New signs were sited at both entrances to the lane to promote its usage.

Labour and costs

A2.12   Labour and costs are summarised as follows:

April	Project staff and Community Service workers—clearance of scrub and of trees in ditch; removal of fly-tipping and construction of gate.	4 man days
July	Project staff and volunteers—scrub clearance	11 man days, 8 volunteer days
August	Project staff, Community Service workers and Footpath Society—scrub clearance and burning	4 man days, 16 volunteer days
September	Project staff—300 metres ditching by using hired self-operated digger/dumper (£150) and hand ditching	8 man days
October	Project staff—hand ditching	1 man day
November	Project staff and volunteers—300 metres ditching by using hired self-operated digger/dumper (£150), hand ditching and hand clearance	19 man days, 18 volunteer days
December	Volunteers—scrub clearance	18 volunteer days
January	Project staff—ditch clearance—and pipe-laying contractor—200 metres ditching by machine (£160)	1 man day
Summary:	**Scrub clearance and ditch work by hand**	**48 man days, 60 volunteer days**
	Cost of ditching by machinery for 5 weeks along 800 metres (1978 costs)	**£460**

Maintenance

A2.13   The main problem was the rapid regrowth of blackthorn and hawthorn scrub, although this will be minimal once the scrub roots are removed and with constant use. Meanwhile, spraying with selective herbicide from ultra-low volume hand sprayers was found to be very effective, but great care is required to prevent misuse. Hedges will need to be trimmed every two years, using a conventional flail mower. The ditches should require only a light mechanical treatment within five years. Grading the path would be within the capability of machinery used by any highways department, although the limited width might cause difficulties.

Conclusions

A2.14   The project has been evaluated against its original aims, the first of which was to make the lane accessible. Since the public have become aware that the path has been cleared, it has been used quite extensively and an article has appeared in the local parish magazine advertising the work. Regular usage has a self-maintaining effect, as constant wear prevents the regeneration of scrub.

A2.15 Clearing the path had two conflicting effects on the trespass problem. A certain amount of random wandering was halted by providing a pleasant well-marked path, but its increased attractiveness encouraged young children in particular to use the land as a play area. The narrow hedges left after scrub clearance provided no deterrent and trespass onto the adjacent farmland by this section of the public may actually have increased in places. The solution will be to ensure that in future hedges are kept as wide and as impenetrable as possible so that the boundary between open space and farmland is clearly defined.

A2.16 Finally, the wildlife monitoring exercise showed that the effect of clearance was to increase the range of wildlife in the lane, especially small mammals and, in spite of encouraging more people into the area, the wildlife was flourishing, plant life benefiting from the increased amount of light reaching the floor of the lane. However, the loss of blackthorn and hawthorn affected the nesting sites for birds; at least one badger family left while the work was being carried out; and an unforeseen problem was a small increase in the number of rabbits, which had been restricted by the dense undergrowth and the lack of burrowing sites.

A2.17 An understandable friction existed between the riders and walkers as they were both competing for the same facility. However, with co-operation, both can be accommodated successfully on the same path. The local authority will have to accept responsibility for regular long-term maintenance if this is to continue.

A2.18 The relative merits of scrub clearance by hand and by mechanised means were not able to be assessed because the machinery was not available. However, although hand clearance is slower and therefore more costly in man hours, it has the inestimable value of involving local people in the management of their own resources and, in general, people are more likely to have continued respect for something in which they have been involved. This highlights one of the fundamental differences between countryside management and conventional estate management, where cost effectiveness is the all important factor. Countryside management techniques are evaluated in terms of their overall benefits to the numerous competing interests in the countryside.

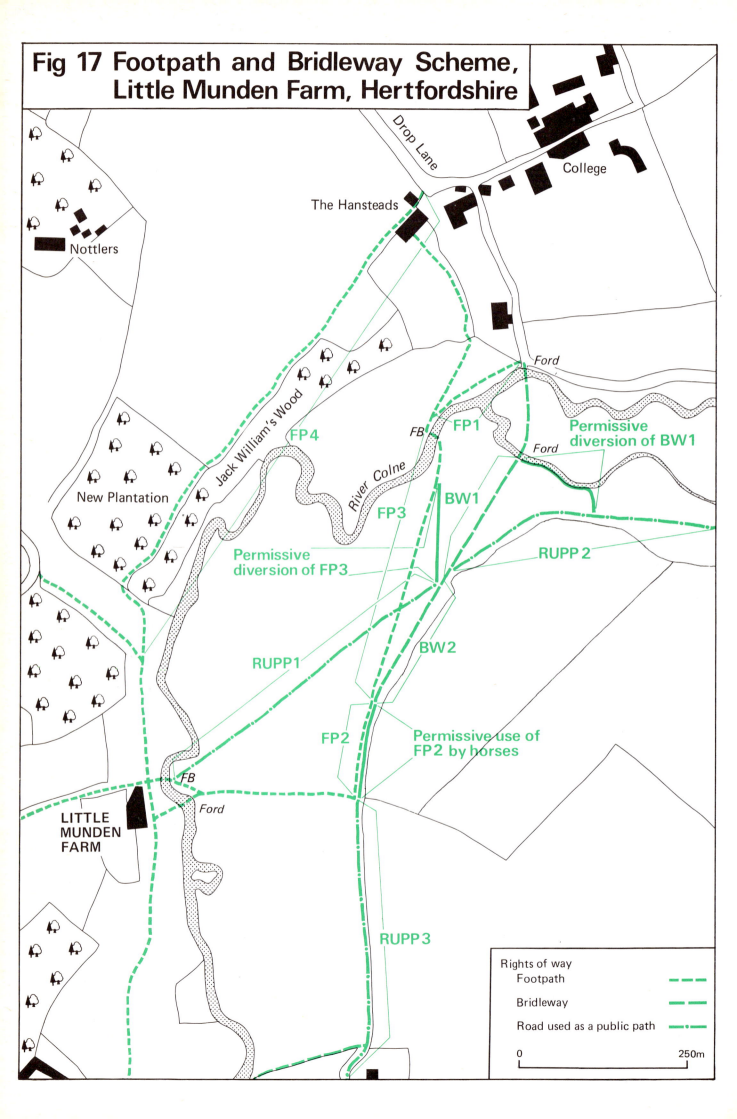

Fig 17 Footpath and Bridleway Scheme, Little Munden Farm, Hertfordshire

Drop Lane

College

The Hansteads

Nottlers

Ford

Jack William's Wood

FP4

FB

FP1

Permissive diversion of BW1

River Colne

FP3

BW1

New Plantation

Ford

Permissive diversion of FP3

RUPP 2

RUPP1

BW2

FP2

Permissive use of FP2 by horses

FB

Ford

LITTLE MUNDEN FARM

RUPP3

Rights of way

Footpath

Bridleway

Road used as a public path

0   250m

Appendix 3: Case Study: Little Munden Farm, Hertfordshire[53]

Introduction

A3.1 Little Munden Farm is a holding of about 50 hectares on a river plain between Watford (3 km.) and St. Albans (5 km.) (Figure 17). It is a mixed farm with a high standard of farming. However, the attractive landscape, the close proximity to two large urban areas and the ease of access resulted in large numbers of visitors and severe problems of trespass and vandalism, with a considerable build-up of friction between the farmer and the public. The severity of the problems was sufficient to enable the project's resources to be used.

The problems

A3.2 Trespass, often resulting in damage, was the main problem. The dense network of public rights of way encouraged legitimate use of the area by the public and the river was a particular attraction. However, visitors left the rights of way, causing extensive crop damage and livestock worrying. The barley crop adjacent to Footpath 1 had been damaged by walkers along the river bank, and, in places, had been completely destroyed. The barley and maize along Bridleway 1 had been severely damaged by irresponsible horse-riders. Part of the farm's ring fence had been destroyed by cars and rough use. Other footpaths passed close to the farm buildings which caused the farmer to worry about their security, as walkers often lingered around them.

A3.3 The farmer had reacted by erecting signs indicating where entry was forbidden; by tightly fencing in Footpath 2 with a double row of barbed wire, so that between that and an overgrown hedgerow passage was virtually impossible, especially as the surface had been ruined by the illegal use of the path by horses in wet conditions; and by cultivating Footpath 3 out of existence and fencing off the fields through which it passed. As a result, bitter feelings had been aroused between the farmer and the general public and the project's task was to attempt to alleviate the problem by a process of negotiation and practical solutions.

The approach

A3.4 Detailed discussions took place with all the parties involved—the farmer, the footpath societies, the local riding stables, the British Horse Society and the local authorities. After hard negotiations, an element of compromise was reached and solutions put forward on an experimental 'permissive' basis which would not be legally binding, but would depend on the good faith of all parties involved. The aim was to improve a rights of way system that was creating problems for the farmer, the riders and the walkers. The solution was designed to benefit the farmer, by reducing trespass and damage to crops; the riders, who would gain an additional quarter-mile of bridleway which would connect with other riding routes, thus creating a circular route; and the walkers, who would be able to pass safely and on a walkable surface.

A3.5 It was agreed that the project staff would carry out fencing work, waymarking, the clearing of rubbish from the river and wardening over the farm. Bridleway 1 would be diverted on a permissive basis so that its route followed the field boundary to join up with RUPP 2 instead of crossing the field. Bridleway 2 and Footpath 2 would both be improved, the latter for its use by walkers and its permissive use by riders, involving segregation of walkers and riders. This provided a more suitable route than RUPP 1 which had ended at the footbridge on the River Colne. Bridleway 1 and RUPP 1 would therefore not be reinstated as long as the horses were allowed to use the permissive routes, thus completing several circular riding routes and linking up with RUPP 3. In addition, the line of Footpath 3 would be changed to link directly across to the footbridge from the junction of Bridleway 2 and RUPP 2. However, if the experiment failed, there was no legal reason why Bridleway 1, RUPP 1 and Footpath 3 across the fields could not be reinstated. Illegal use of Footpath 2 by horse-riders would be difficult to prevent.

A3.6 The improvements to Footpath 2 and Bridleway 2 included widening from 1.5 metres to 4 metres by cutting back the overgrown hedge, and erecting a fence to separate the walkers from the riders, so that both could pass safely and, in winter, the walkers would not find the surface made impassable by horses churning up the mud. In places, the farmer's barbed wire fence had to be moved back into his field, involving the loss of crops to a width of about 1 metre. However, the farmer agreed to this in return for the hedgerow being cut back, thus allowing the headland to be ploughed further out while, at the same time, allowing sufficient room for the horses.

The practical work

A3.7   The cutting back of the hedgerow along a length of 400 metres was a major task and it was decided to use volunteers in order to cut down on the time and cost of the project. Horse-riders were chosen in order to show the farmer that they were more reasonable and considerate than he had previously thought and to demonstrate to the horse-riders the amount of effort required in maintaining and creating facilities for their use and enjoyment. During a period of two weeks, all the local riding establishments were visited and posters advertising the work were placed on posts at either end of the footpath.

A3.8   Meanwhile, the project staff carried out five days work alongside the roadway. A dangerous tree was felled and burned and a waste area of dock and nettle-covered ground between the roadway and the river was cleared to encourage people to use this area instead of wandering onto the farm. The roadside boundary of the area was fenced off to complete the farm's ring fence. It was a post and rail fence with a strand of barbed wire along the top to discourage misuse and the fence was positioned in such a way as to reduce damage by cars. Access to the area remained through a bridlegate and a standard construction stile. In addition, a large amount of rubbish, including concrete posts, wire, bottles, cans and glass, was collected from the area and taken to the local authority waste disposal tip.

A3.9   As the volunteer work on the major task took some time to organise, wardening was carried out on the farm at weekends and Bank Holidays and the staff had to deal with people wandering all over the farm, especially by the river. Damage by horses was also common and, one weekend, was so severe that the farmer decided to fence off RUPP 1 and Bridleway 1 from the fields, with two rows of barbed wire fencing, running parallel to each other at a width that would be dangerous for horses. This put the volunteer work that had been agreed in jeopardy but, after discussion with the project staff, the farmer agreed to put up a fence of plain wire with ample spacing of 4.5 metres between the rows.

A3.10   Visits were again made to the riding establishments to estimate the number of volunteers to be expected so that the type and number of tools required could be assembled. The fire brigade was also asked for advice on the safety precautions necessary for burning hedge trimmings within a restricted space in very dry conditions and were kept informed during the work.

A3.11   The hedgerow trimming began early one morning with four project staff, two children and one independent volunteer, who were joined later by five volunteers from Patchett's Green Stables and one from the pony club. In the afternoon, further hedge trimming and scrub clearance continued and burning of the trimmings proceeded at a slow but steady rate. Another six volunteers arrived, four of whom were from Patchett's Green Stables and two from a local farm where private ponies were kept. In this way, 90 metres of very dense hedgerow were trimmed back and burned, equivalent to 11 man days work. This was a very encouraging start.

A3.12   Further work proposed on succeeding weekends was cancelled because of heavy rain, a Horse Show and extreme fire hazard during the subsequent very dry weather. Apart from spraying the site to inhibit scrub growth,

Volunteers cleared scrub along Footpath 2 to create room for a bridlepath, and a fence was erected to separate horse-riders from walkers

the work programme did not start again for six months when, after considerable negotiations with all concerned, a comprehensive rationalisation plan for the public rights of way across the farm was agreed in order to reduce the level of trespass.

A3.13   Scrub clearance alongside Footpath 2 and Bridleway 2 was undertaken with volunteers on several weekends, amounting to 10 man days and 14 volunteer days. Improvements included the erection of a short length of post and rail fencing incorporating a timber waymark.

A3.14   As part of the original agreement with the local footpath societies, Footpath 4 had to be improved before the major task of separating horses and walkers by means of a fence on Footpath 2 could begin. Accordingly, two stiles were repaired, a third was constructed and a comprehensive waymarking of the path was undertaken.

A3.15   The final improvements to Footpath 2 to accommodate horse-riders on a 'permissive' route alongside the walkers started with the removal of the farmer's barbed wire fence and its re-erection to allow a total width of 4 metres in order to allow 3 metres for horse-riding and 1 metre for walkers. A contractor was hired for two days to bore 150 post holes because the subsoil conditions defeated the project's hand tools. It took project staff, with volunteer help, 18 man days to erect 400 metres of 1 metre high post and rail fencing, using elm wood which had been removed from another work site, for the posts. This was to separate the horse-riders from the walkers (see illustration opposite). Plain steel wire was stapled to the whole length along the top of the rail to reduce the possibility of damage by vandalism. At the entrances to the footpath section, posts were erected to prevent access to horses, and routed signs explained the new experimental rights of way. Further waymarking was undertaken on other parts of the holding.

Conclusions

A3.16   The feelings of outright hostility and suspicion between the British Horse Society and the local footpath group were considerably modified during the negotiations for the rationalisation of rights of way. This scheme, together with wardening throughout the summer, seemed to be managing the situation successfully until one year later, when considerable horse trespass and damage occurred on two other parts of the farm. The project staff helped the farmer by re-erecting a temporary 200-metre length of plain wire fence and a 100-metre new barbed wire fence around a woodland adjoining the farm's distant boundary, these two tasks taking four man days to complete. Since then, the only practical work carried out by the project staff has been the renovation of a sign, a stile and a fence, involving three man days, and so far the scheme is working to the benefit of the farmer, the riders and the walkers.

A3.17   The cost of the work carried out on this farm was as follows (1978 costs):

Materials for 400 metres fencing	£300
Treating and transportation of 200 elm stumps (free from another site)	£145
Wire, stile, 25 metres fencing along river	£116
Hire of contractor and post-hole borer	£75
Total	**£636**

A3.18   This was a very small cost for the results obtained. In the future, there will obviously need to be a long-term commitment to the maintenance of the works carried out, including periodic hedge trimming and the spraying of blackthorn regrowth with brushwood killer. The level of maintenance will depend on the initial workmanship and materials and on the incidence of vandalism.

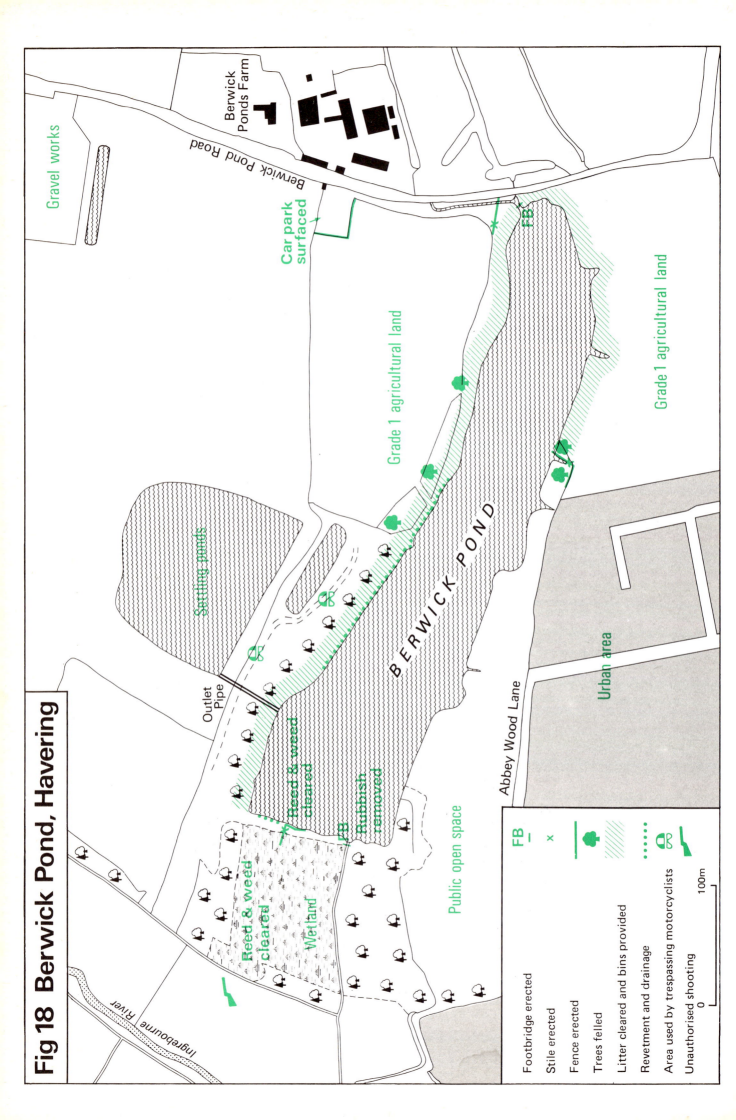

Fig 18 Berwick Pond, Havering

Gravel works

Berwick Ponds Farm

Berwick Pond Road

Car park surfaced

Grade 1 agricultural land

Grade 1 agricultural land

BERWICK POND

Abbey Wood Lane

Urban area

Settling ponds

Outlet Pipe

Reed & weed cleared

Rubbish removed

Public open space

Ingrebourne River

Reed & weed cleared

Wetland

FB

FB   Footbridge erected
×   Stile erected
      Fence erected
      Trees felled
      Litter cleared and bins provided
      Revetment and drainage
      Area used by trespassing motorcyclists
      Unauthorised shooting

0   100m

Appendix 4: Case Study: Berwick Pond, Havering

Introduction

A4.1   This 13.5 hectare site (Figure 18), dominated by a natural lake of 7.6 hectares, provides an illustration, in microcosm, of the nature of the problems which exist in the Havering project area as a whole. It is characterised by competition and conflict between different water and land uses and users.

A4.2   The lake and the surrounding land, except for 3.6 hectares of Public Open Space, are owned by a gravel company and the lake is used by them for washing the gravel produced in their adjacent plant and supplying the ready-mixed concrete plant. The prime objective of the gravel company is to extract gravel in the area and they have been keeping the 50 men at their treatment works employed on a temporary subsidy basis until they receive further planning permissions. They lease both the lake and the agricultural land to a tenant farmer who has an extremely productive horticultural enterprise, employing a workforce of 35 and using the lake for irrigation. These two parties were in open conflict at a recent planning inquiry, when the gravel company appealed against a decision by the Greater London Council not to allow the extraction of gravel from the farm land. The principal objectors were the Ministry of Agriculture, Fisheries and Food, supported by the farmer, who objected to the loss of Grade 1 agricultural land, and local residents, who objected to the destruction of the landscape and the danger caused by heavy traffic. The gravel company lost the appeal.

A4.3   Another problem exists between the farmer and the fishing club over the length of the sub-lease. The farmer sublets the lake, including 2.5 metres of the surrounding bank, to the club on an annual 'word-of-mouth' agreement, for which he receives rent and a percentage of the day ticket money from an average of from 50 to 75 anglers per day. Such a short and informal tenancy means that it is not worthwhile for the club to put money into developing and maintaining the site, in spite of the fact that intensive use by fishermen and, illegally, by members of the general public seeking informal recreation, causes management problems.

A4.4   There is competition for use of the surrounding land by others besides the gravel company and the farmer: a private housing estate, an area of Public Open Space, a woodland and a natural wetland site are all found within 100 metres of the lake.

A4.5   Berwick Pond acts as a magnet for recreation because there are so few alternative sites in the vicinity and it emerged as a site of major importance in the results of the recreation survey[33]. Over-use puts pressure on the natural environment as well as causing conflicts between users. The survey showed that the users were local, except for the fishermen some of whom came from further afield. For the first time, the views of the recreation users became available, although only part of the site was surveyed because the farmer refused to admit that anyone used the site except the anglers and therefore considered a survey on his land unnecessary.

Berwick Pond is used intensively for recreation

121

Problems

A4.6 This intense competition for both land and water results in a number of immediately recognisable problems:

   i.   children riding unlicensed motorcycles round the fields, have destroyed irrigation equipment etc.;

   ii.   there are no rights of way on the land but, apart from the anglers, *de facto* but illegal use, both by pedestrians and children on cycles and motorcycles, has churned up paths;

   iii.   youths from the housing estate regularly use the area for rough shooting and have killed swans and migrating birds;

   iv.   birds are caught in discarded fishing hooks and tangled line;

   v.   litter is a general problem on the banks of the lake;

   vi.   fishermen are disturbed by trespassing noisy children;

   vii.   the banks of the lake are eroded through heavy use;

   viii.   the gravel company has to contend with children swimming in dangerous settling ponds and with straying farm animals, e.g. a cow fell into a lagoon of liquid concrete;

   ix.   pressure on the roads is considerable as farm tractors with implements, lorries servicing the farm and the gravel works and cement tankers and mixer trucks associated with the adjacent ready-mixed plant regularly supplement the normal traffic;

   x.   in a dry summer, the water level drops considerably and the fish stocks are threatened;

   xi.   a large amount of silt from the gravel-washing process has found its way back into the lake, carried with the waste water, which has almost filled up the lake at one end and encouraged reed growth, spoiling fishing and reducing the water storage capacity for irrigation use;

   xii.   lowering of the water table during gravel extraction and Dutch elm disease have resulted in the loss of 42 per cent of the trees in the last few years[54].

A4.7 The problems therefore range from practical ones, e.g. the loss of trees, to those of management, e.g. an unsatisfactory Fishing Club lease, to major planning issues, involving the conflict between gravel and agriculture.

Project work

A4.8 The project officer's involvement began when he was asked by the farmer whether the problems identified at this site came within the remit of the experiment. After an initial analysis, the project officer and the farmer agreed that small-scale works would help to alleviate some of the problems and help to conserve a site that represented an attractive oasis in an area of degraded landscape.

A4.9 The objectives of the work within the overall aim of getting the co-operation of the landowners and tenants in developing a long-term strategy for landscape improvement and land management, were:

   i.   to reconcile the conflicting land uses;

   ii.   to reduce conflict between different recreation activities;

   iii.   to improve the landscape and amenity value of the site;

   iv.   to increase the conservation value of the wetland and promote its educational use;

   v.   to encourage the involvement of the London Borough of Havering in the management of the Public Open Space;

   vi.   to encourage the involvement of the users in the work carried out.

A4.10 The British Trust for Conservation Volunteers, fishing club members, Young Farmers Club members and project staff carried out a number of tasks, including repairing banks with revetments to guard against erosion, building footbridges, erecting vandal-proof fences and stiles to exclude trespassing motorcyclists, carrying out path improvements and drainage works, felling dead trees, installing litter bins and fencing and surfacing a car park for the fishermen to use. In all these small-scale activities, shown on Figure 18, help was forthcoming from the three main interested parties. The fishing club provided money and volunteers; the farmer gave drain pipes and lent a tractor and trailer; and the gravel company provided stone and hoggin to backfill the revetments and to resurface the car park.

Small-scale practical work with the help of volunteers

Banks were repaired with revetments

A car park was resurfaced

A new bridge was built

A4.11   The organisation and costs of one weekend's activities, involving the Trust and members of the fishing club in 27 metres of bank revetment and removal of debris, was as follows (1978 costs):

	Debit	Credit
BTCV supplied punt and sludge pump	£25	
Farmer lent tractor and trailer		
Farmer donated elm logs		
Project officer and contractor felled elms and sawed to convenient lengths	£20	
Project officer and member of fishing club transported logs in member's lorry		
Fishing club paid BTCV expenses		£25
Total cost	**£20**	

A4.12   While the practical work was going on, the project officer contacted local teachers of environmental studies and the Essex Naturalists' Trust, who offered to study the ecology of the wetland, to design a nature trail and to prepare an accompanying leaflet. The project evaluator initiated a recreation site survey[33] and the project officer engaged a landscape architect to prepare a detailed landscape design and management plan for the pond area[55]. The results of these studies indicated the need for different types of management around Berwick Pond:

   i.   intensive recreation management by the London Borough of Havering on the Public Open Space;

   ii.   the protection of the Grade 1 agricultural land to the east;

   iii.   conservation management of the valuable flora and fauna on the wetland site to the west;

   iv.   improved management of the lake for fishing, e.g. silt removal;

   v.   landscape improvement, including tree planting;

   vi.   small-scale improvement works for general access by walkers around the pond;

   vii.   wardening of the pond area by the fishing club's bailiff.

A4.13   It was hoped that the gravel company, the farmer and the fishing club would be able to co-operate in carrying out a programme of development based on the plan which would have attracted substantial grant aid from the Countryside Commission. However, at this point, the underlying conflicts came to the fore when the parties could not agree.

A4.14   Although the fishing club were prepared to co-operate in carrying out the landscape plan, the farmer was reluctant to do so as he felt that even more members of the general public would be attracted to the site. The gravel company were unwilling to co-operate at all unless they obtained planning permission for gravel extraction on a *quid pro quo* basis, when they would be prepared to consider a comprehensive recreational plan over a much larger area in their ownership, involving a substantial investment by their subsidiary leisure company. The project officer proposed that the local authority should purchase the site with Countryside Commission grant-aid and develop and manage it for recreation, landscape, conservation and education purposes and put in a wardening service. At the time of writing the matter rests there, with the landowners being aware of the local planning authority's willingness to seek a joint solution.

Conclusions

A4.15   Several lessons can be learned from this situation. Firstly, given the co-operation of the landowner and tenants, small-scale works involving volunteers, co-ordinated by the project officer, were successful in resolving some of the immediate problems, such as trespass, litter and erosion of banks, and the recreation survey[33] results showed that people had noticed and approved of the improvements carried out. This led to an understanding of the fundamental land use conflicts and their associated long-term financial commitments and here the problems were more intractable and the interested parties less amenable to compromise solutions. Thirdly, in spite of such problems, a considerable opportunity for developing the area exists but it would entail high-level negotiations outside the remit of the project officer. Finally, the case of Berwick Pond illustrates very clearly how countryside management can respond successfully to day-to-day problems and can point the way to the successful solution of large-scale problems outside its own remit. Implementation then depends on political will and the allocation of financial resources.

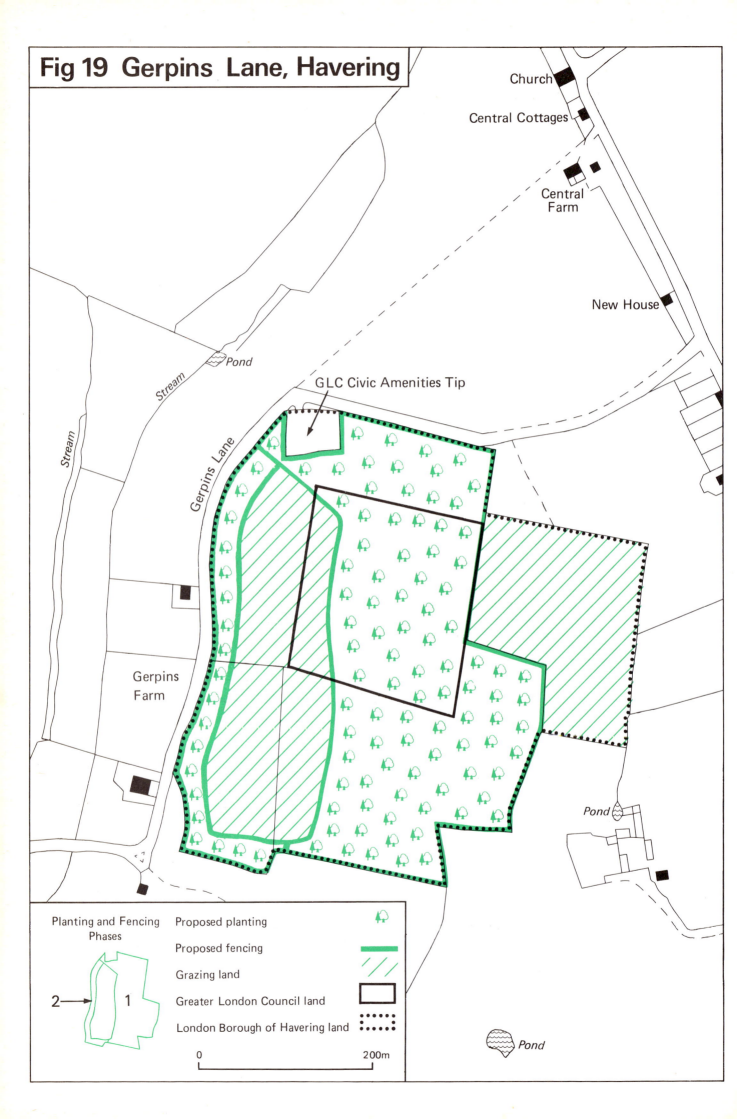

Fig 19 Gerpins Lane, Havering

Church

Central Cottages

Central Farm

New House

Pond

Stream

Stream

Gerpins Lane

GLC Civic Amenities Tip

Gerpins Farm

Pond

Pond

Planting and Fencing Phases

Proposed planting

Proposed fencing

Grazing land

Greater London Council land

London Borough of Havering land

2 → 1

0   200m

Appendix 5: Case Study: Gerpins Lane, Havering

Introduction

A5.1   It was recognised at the beginning of the experiment that one of the most serious problems was the large amount of neglected, semi-derelict land which was a legacy from past gravel extraction and poor-quality restoration. One such area was identified by the project officer as an opportunity to show what could be achieved to improve the environment.

A5.2   The area chosen was 25 hectares of land in Gerpins Lane. It was run down in appearance, devoid of trees and unsuitable for any agricultural use except rough grazing, because poor land restoration had left the site with inadequate top soil and bad drainage. Fortunately, however, the land was in public ownership and provided an opportunity to carry out a grant-aided forestry scheme and the provision of informal recreation facilities.

The run down appearance of land owned by the London Borough of Havering and the Greater London Council

A5.3   The ownership of the land was divided between the Greater London Council, who owned 4 hectares, and the London Borough of Havering, who owned 21 hectares; officers of both councils agreed that a tree planting scheme would be a desirable development. There was an existing tenancy on the land and this would remain, but it seemed reasonably likely that amicable arrangements could be made to reconsider the continuance of that tenancy under the new proposals.

A5.4   The project officer invited the Forestry Commission's technical adviser to inspect the site and he confirmed the feasibility of the idea, and drew up a planting scheme covering 12.6 hectares (Figure 19). The remaining half of the land would be left open for use as grazing by the existing tenant. The objectives of the scheme were:

i.   to improve the landscape which was particularly neglected and run down;

ii.   to take advantage of a long-term opportunity, when the trees are sufficiently established, to introduce some form of low-key recreational use, e.g. amenity woodland with footpaths, bridleways, picnic sites etc;

iii.   to provide an example to adjacent landowners (mostly gravel companies) of how badly-restored land could be put to beneficial use, using simple techniques tailored to the situation;

iv. to improve the soil and drainage through planting and managing trees.

An additional advantage for the local authorities would be a return on investment when the trees were harvested after 25 years.

Proposal

A5.5   It was proposed that a planting scheme covering 12.6 hectares would be established on the Gerpins Lane site, consisting of dense planting some 210 metres wide across the central section of the site which would, when grown, appear as 'horizon' woodland. Tenanted grazing would be retained in the eastern and western sections. The western section would be enclosed by a 6-metre wide belt of roadside planting for landscape purposes.

A5.6   The Forestry Commission agreed that such a scheme would receive their standard grant aid of £100 per hectare for conifers, £225 per hectare for broadleaves, plus an annual management grant of £3 per hectare for 50 years. Forestry transplants approximately 46 cm. high would be planted in the rough proportion of one-third hardwood, two-thirds softwood species. From year 25 onwards the softwood would be progressively harvested and sold, and the land replanted with hardwood so that the eventual result would be a woodland of indigenous hardwood species.

A5.7   In practice, the relatively small size of the scheme and the general situation and intended occupation of the land ruled out the prospect of any commercial undertaking being introduced, but the public ownership of the land gave an opportunity for the local authorities to take the initiative. The Forestry Commission grant would be subject to a suitable woodland dedication scheme to keep the land as woodland, but it appeared possible to reconcile this with the existing tenancy and any eventual recreational use.

Costs

A5.8   The costs were based on Forestry Commission advice on a scheme of 12.6 hectares (1977 figures):

i.   Buying and planting the trees
Estimated cost £2,500, of which £1,700 would be redeemable from the Forestry Commission immediately the scheme had been completed and inspected as satisfactory.

ii.   Maintenance (weeding, replacing dead trees etc. and fences)
Estimated cost £1,250 per annum for the first five years, £250 per annum thereafter. A sum of £37.50 per annum towards maintenance costs would be paid by the Forestry Commission for a period of 50 years.

iii.   Essential fencing of the site against rabbits and stock
Estimated cost £6,000.

iv.   Immediate cosmetic improvement to the site
The improvement of roadside hedges, planting semi-mature trees along the roadside boundaries which were neglected and unattractive—£1,000 approximately.

Financial returns

A5.9   The softwood species planted on approximately 8 hectares would be progressively harvested between year 25 and year 50 and the value of the wood at 1977 prices was estimated to be approximately £5,500 per hectare, i.e. a total of £44,000. This would be a modest return in terms of investment potential, but the main objective was to improve the landscape and the management of the area and the likelihood of some future return on the investment was seen as an added attraction.

Implementation

A5.10   It was intended that the planting scheme would be implemented using contractors recommended by the Forestry Commission and supervised by the project officer. Annual maintenance by contractors would be arranged and supervised initially through the experiment, although the intention in the long term was for the scheme to be run by the local authority's Recreation and Amenities Department.

A5.11   Both the Greater London Council and the London Borough of Havering concluded that, in addition to the physical and functional benefits, the tree planting scheme would be tangible evidence of the practical improvements brought about by the experiment and of their commitment to countryside management work and they approved the allocation of finance for the carrying out of the scheme. However, the matter was held in abeyance, following the non-co-operation of the tenant, who not only objected to some of the proposals but, even after renegotiation, refused to agree to anything until the problems caused by the adjacent Civic Amenities rubbish tip (paragraph 12.29) had been solved. The London Borough of Havering have since approved an amended planting scheme, to be implemented in two phases.

Conclusion

A5.12   This was a good example of how the project officer was able to identify an opportunity presented by the public ownership of land for environmental improvement and recreation provision. However, as in Hertfordshire/Barnet, it was found that dealing with public authorities was always a long drawn-out affair and nothing was effected during the short period of the experiment. A long-term countryside management service would not have this time constraint although, if it was dealing almost wholly with publicly-owned land, its reputation for flexibility and speed of action might suffer. This is something which should be carefully examined.

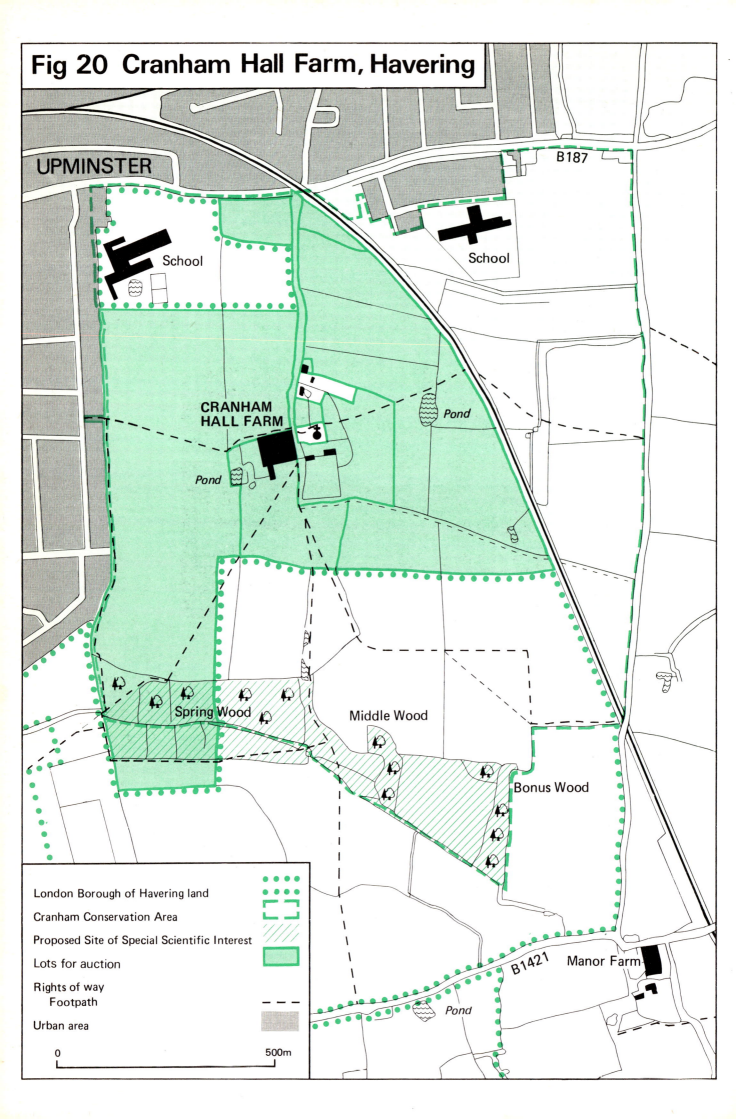

Fig 20 Cranham Hall Farm, Havering

UPMINSTER

B187

School

School

Pond

CRANHAM
HALL FARM

Pond

Pond

Spring Wood

Middle Wood

Bonus Wood

B1421   Manor Farm

Pond

London Borough of Havering land

Cranham Conservation Area

Proposed Site of Special Scientific Interest

Lots for auction

Rights of way
Footpath

Urban area

0   500m

Appendix 6: Case Study: Cranham Hall Farm, Havering

Introduction

A6.1   Cranham Hall Farm is in the north east of the project area (Figure 20), adjoining the edge of Upminster's built-up area. It consists of an open agricultural and woodland area of 150 hectares with a central cluster of nineteenth-century agricultural buildings, which are surrounded by a secluded hamlet with a church, providing a pleasant rural atmosphere rare in an area so close to the urban edge. The hamlet and farmland together form the Cranham Conservation Area, designated as such by the London Borough of Havering. The land is classified as Grade 1 by the Ministry of Agriculture classification and produced vegetables until

Cranham, quiet woodland and a pleasant rural atmosphere

September 1977, when the farmer started growing cereals. The rural landscape is unique in the area and the land is traversed by a footpath network radiating from the hamlet and used intensively for informal recreation by the local urban population. Vehicle access is by Cranham Chase off St. Mary's Lane (B187). The hamlet and approximately 60 hectares of farmland were owned by a property company; the remaining land to the south, including a small wooded area, Spring Wood, and a wetland area known as Cranham Marsh, having been transferred to the borough from the Greater London Council.

Historical background

A6.2   The owners had orginally bought the land as a speculative venture before the existence of a Green Belt policy and had made repeated applications to develop the area for housing, all of which had been refused by the local planning authority. In 1975, the landowners submitted a planning application for the development of a golf course, with Cranham Hall as a clubhouse. The London Borough of Havering were looking for a source of funds to maintain the buildings of architectural interest, which had been allowed to fall into disrepair by the owners, and to put them to a useful purpose within the whole unit. They therefore made a counter-proposal for the development of the land immediately around the hamlet as a farm park, the refurbishment of the buildings as a craft museum and the use of the outlying fields for golf. As part of this deal, the borough would lease their 90 hectares of adjoining land to the company. The company agreed to consider the proposal and made a feasibility study to assess the commercial possibilities of a farm park and golf course.

A6.3   At this point the experiment started. When the project officer first talked to the farmer, complaints were made about trespass from public footpaths and some of these were dealt with immediately by small-scale practical works, e.g. stile and footbridge construction. However, the farmer was much more concerned about

131

the uncertain future of the farm, which was undermining his farming activities and his way of life. He did not want to lose his tenancy nor did he want to see the land go out of agricultural production.

A6.4 The project officer therefore argued against the borough's proposal on the grounds that first-class agricultural land should not be lost to recreation in an area of vacant and derelict land; the unique character of the landscape derived from the fact that the land was farmed and would be substantially altered and diminished by the development of a golf course; the public would be denied the free use of the footpath network, both statutory and *de facto,* and of the woodland; and the farm park, instead of a good farmed landscape, would foster a misleading image of modern agriculture. He made an alternative proposal, where the land would remain in farming, thus conserving the landscape and food production and engendering confidence in the local farming community, but access would be improved without detriment to food production—e.g. waymarking of footpaths, wardening at peak periods—and education and interpretive facilities would be developed, based on a modern, fully-commercial productive farm, thus preserving the farm buildings. He was supported by the Countryside Commission, who expressed concern at the apparent sacrifice of good agricultural land and a rural landscape in order to preserve a complex of agricultural buildings which, although unique in the borough, were not listed, by the GLC and by the Ministry of Agriculture, Fisheries and Food. As a result of this additional advice and information the local planning authority reviewed their policies, refused the application and began negotiations with the owners for alternative proposals more in keeping with the rural nature of the area and aimed at local people. During this period, the farmer, anxious about the uncertain future of his land, and reluctant to make the capital investment necessary for intensive horticulture, had given up growing vegetables and had turned to growing cereals.

A6.5 Meanwhile, the project officer invited the Essex Naturalists' Trust to look at Cranham Marsh. They carried out a botanical survey, which identified it as one of the last surviving examples in Essex of a marshy fen that retains the original peat deposits, together with ancient associated vegetation. In addition to its botanical significance, the site is important as a wildlife habitat and a landscape feature. Essex Naturalists' Trust then applied to the London Borough of Havering for permission to lease the site and to manage it for conservation and informal recreation. At the same time, they approached the Nature Conservancy Council to see whether the marsh could be designated as a Site of Special Scientific Interest and this seems to be a likely prospect.

A6.6 Following the refusal of the application for a golf course, the owners made a sudden and dramatic move. The farm and buildings were put up for sale by auction in eight separate vacant lots (Figure 20), the farmer having received substantial compensation for the termination of his agricultural tenancy. The result of such fragmentation would mean the end of viable farming and the destruction of the integrity and coherence of the farm hamlet and attempts were made to bring the land into public ownership. However, neither the GLC nor the borough could provide the necessary funds in the time available and the lots, which included several houses and the farm buildings, were sold to different owners, but the farmland did not reach the reserve price. The land was divided into parcels of uneconomic size and cannot be farmed properly without agricultural buildings nor without a farmer near at hand to supervise the area and so the land has fallen into disuse. Landscape, nature conservation and public access are other victims. Various non-conforming uses have been set up in the buildings and planning applications are constantly being received for non-agricultural activities, e.g. country club, restaurant, light industry, putting the local authority to a lot of unnecessary work attempting to negotiate less inappropriate schemes and being involved in frequent enforcement action.

Evaluation

A6.7 The roles of the local authority planning department and the project officer have been appraised separately, although they are obviously closely interrelated.

London Borough of Havering

A6.8 The local planning authority is obliged to consider each planning application on its merits. In this part of the Green Belt, most applications are for gravel extraction, for which the local authority makes recommendations, although the GLC are responsible for developments of over 2 hectares. Applications for housing are always refused and in this respect both the GLC and the London Borough of Havering have upheld Green Belt policy effectively. However, recreation is an acceptable Green Belt use and in this case the urban-oriented authority were more concerned to avoid separating the buildings and the land than with the conservation of the landscape. The Ministry of Agriculture objected to the change of use on the grounds of loss of Grade 1 agricultural land when there was other land of lower quality in the area which might be used for a golf course, and the GLC and the Countryside Commission supported this view and added the loss of landscape and informal access as other important factors. The borough then refused the application and their objective became the retention of agriculture.

A6.9 The local authority energetically pursued all possible strategies to prevent fragmentation of the holding and had they been able to purchase the land, it would have been consolidated with the adjacent land in their ownership. However, planning legislation and pressure from the local population failed to allow the local authority to achieve its stated policy of preserving the land for agricultural use.

Project officer

A6.10 The project officer's actions throughout were aimed at maintaining the land in agriculture, thus fulfilling his other objectives of conserving landscape, wildlife and public access for informal recreation. It was also important to gain the farmers' confidence by showing that alternative options were considered and that their interests were being protected, so that they would be willing to co-operate with the experiment. He was instrumental in the application to designate Cranham Marsh as an SSSI, in the pressure for public ownership and in the review of the local planning authority's objectives and policies. In this, he liaised with the planning department, local councillors and residents, the tenant farmer, the Estates Departments of both the London Borough of Havering and the GLC, the Countryside Commission, MAFF, the Essex Naturalists' Trust and the National Farmers Union. The result was that the issues were examined more thoroughly and more detailed information was made available, particularly on agricultural matters. However, the length of these negotiations prolonged the uncertainty over the future of the farm and the farmer adopted a simpler farming system which required less capital investment and eventually succumbed to the financial inducement from the owner to quit.

A6.11 If planning permission for a change of use had been granted, the tenant farmer would have had his tenancy terminated. In the event of the sale, this happened anyway, although the farmer received substantial compensation, and it now seems likely that the land will remain idle. This is an example of how the project officer can identify opportunities but cannot implement them. By becoming involved in practical work on the ground, he is privy to information which the local authorities might not have and he has an important liaison and interpretation function in this respect, but countryside management was never meant to be, nor can it ever hope to be, a substitute for adequate policies on planning and strategic management, such as the acquisition of land in sensitive urban edge situations.

References

1. *East Hampshire, an Area of Outstanding Natural Beauty—a study in countryside conservation.* Hampshire County Council, *et. al,* 1968.
2. *The Sherwood Forest Study.* Nottingham County Council, 1974.
3. *The Lake District Upland Management Experiment* CCP 93. Countryside Commission, 1976.
4. *The Snowdonia Upland Management Experiment* CCP 122. Countryside Commission, 1979.
5. *Glamorgan Heritage Coast—Plan Statement.* South Glamorgan County Council, *et. al,* 1976.
6. *Purbeck Heritage Coast—Report and Proposals.* Dorset County Council, 1977.
7. *Suffolk Heritage Coast Plan.* Suffolk County Council, 1979.
8. *The Bollin Valley—A Study of Land Management in the Urban Fringe* CCP 97. Countryside Commission, 1976.
9. Thomas, D., *London's Green Belt.* Faber and Faber, 1970.
10. Howard, E. (ed. Osborn, F. J.), *Garden Cities of Tomorrow.* Faber and Faber, 1946.
11. Greater London Regional Planning Committee. Second report, 1933.
12. Dalton, Mrs. Hugh, "The green belt around London", *Journal of the London Society,* 1939.
13. Abercrombie, P., *Greater London Plan 1944.* HMSO, 1945.
14. *The improvement of London's Green Belt.* Standing Conference on London and South East Regional Planning (SCLSERP), 1976.
15. South East Joint Planning Team, *Strategic Plan for the South East.* HMSO, 1970.
16. *Greater London Development Plan, approved by Secretary of State for the Environment, 9 July 1976.* Greater London Council, 1976.
17. *Agricultural Land Classification,* Technical Report No. 11. Ministry of Agriculture, Fisheries and Food, Agricultural Land Service, 1966.
18. Davidson, J. and Wibberley, G. P., *Planning and the Rural Environment.* Pergamon Press, 1977.
19. Department of the Environment, *Greater London Development Plan: Report of the Panel of Inquiry.* HMSO, 1973.
20. Travis, A. S. and Veal, A. J. (eds.), *Recreation and the Urban Fringe: 1975 CRRAG Conference Proceedings.* University of Birmingham, 1976.
21. Department of the Environment, *Sport and Recreation* Cmnd 6200. HMSO, 1975.
22. *Regional Recreation Strategy—Issues Report.* Greater London and South East Council for Sport and Recreation, 1978.
23. Advisory Council for Agriculture and Horticulture in England and Wales, *Agriculture and The Countryside.* HMSO, 1978.
24. Countryside Review Committee, *The Countryside—Problems and Policies: A Discussion Paper.* HMSO, 1976.
25. Countryside Review Committee, *Food Production in the Countryside: A Discussion Paper.* HMSO, 1978.
26. Elson, M., "The Urban Fringe: Open Land Policies and Programmes in the Metropolitan Counties", Working Paper 14. Countryside Commission, 1979.
27. Thompson, K., *Farming in the Fringe* CCP 142. Countryside Commission, 1981.
28. University College London, "Land Use Conflicts in the Urban Fringe", Working Paper 11. Countryside Commission, 1979.
29. Phillips, J. C. and Veal, A. J., *Research on the Urban Fringe,* Conference and Seminar Papers No. 6. Centre for Urban and Regional Studies, 1978.
30. Newby, H., "Urban Fringe Management: The Farmers Response", Countryside Commission (unpublished).
31. Countryside Review Committee, *Leisure and the Countryside: A Discussion Paper.* HMSO, 1977.
32. Ferguson, M. J. and Munton, R. J. C., "Land for Informal Recreation: A Geographical Analysis of Provision and Management Priorities", Working Paper No. 2. University College London, 1978.
33. "London Urban Fringe Experiments—Recreation Site Surveys". Countryside Commission (unpublished).
34. Williams, H., "The management of publicly-owned land in the Hertfordshire/Barnet Experiment Area", Working Paper 17. Countryside Commission, 1979.
35. *Local Authority Countryside Management Projects* Advisory Series No. 10. Countryside Commission, 1978.
36. Report of the Bridleways Working Party. Hertfordshire County Council (unpublished).
37. *Grants to Local Authorities for Countryside Management Projects,* CCP 112. Countryside Commission, 1978.

38. *Countryside Rangers and Related Staff* Advisory Series No. 7. Countryside Commission, 1979.
39. Smith, S., "Horticulture Survey". Countryside Commission (unpublished).
40. Cripps, J., *Accommodation for Gypsies*. HMSO, 1977.
41. *Volunteers in the Countryside* Advisory Series No. 11. Countryside Commission, 1980.
42. Culshaw, C., "Fringe Problems—a matter of opinion", dissertation for MSc in Environmental Resources (unpublished).
43. Crafer, M., "Farmability: towards a more comprehensive approach to the classification of agricultural land". Chelmer Institute of Higher Education, Chelmsford (unpublished).
44. *Greater London Recreation Survey, Part 1, Demand Study*. Greater London Council, 1975.
45. *Bridleways and Recreation: policy statement and grants* CCP 133. Countryside Commission, 1980.
46. Worthington, T. and Westacott, R., *New Agricultural Landscapes* CCP 76. Countryside Commission, 1974.
47. *Joint Agricultural Land Restoration Experiments, Progress Report No. 1 1974–1977*. Department of the Environment *et. al,* 1979.
48. Stamp, L. D., *The Land Utilisation Survey of Britain*. Geographical Publications Ltd., 1933.
49. Coleman, A., *Land Use Map 225 East London*. Second Land Utilisation Survey of Britain, 1970.
50. *Food From Our Own Resources* Cmnd. 6020. HMSO, 1975.
51. Verney, R. B., *Aggregates: the Way Ahead*. HMSO, 1976.
52. Mander, R., Project for HND at Seale-Hayne College (unpublished).
53. Goddard, S., Project for HND at Seale-Hayne College (unpublished).
54. Carter, K., "Landscape Evaluation in the Havering Urban Fringe". Countryside Commission (unpublished).
55. Cox, J., "Landscape design and management plan for Berwick Pond". Countryside Commission (unpublished).